BYRON VEN

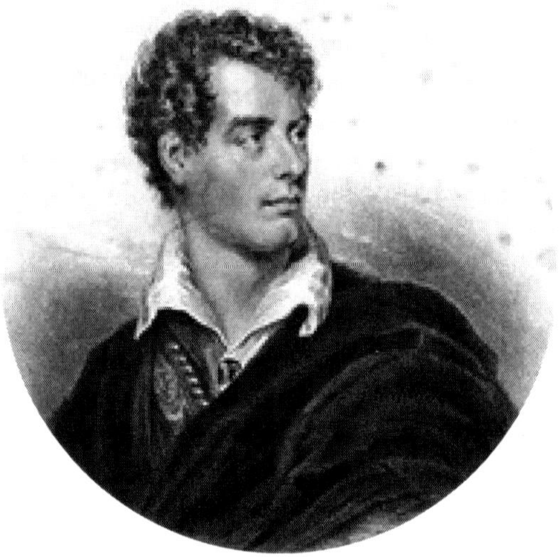

Byron-Venice

An English Milord in Europe & Italy

by
Anne Amison

San Marco Press Ltd
8 Vernon Place, Canterbury, Kent CT1 3HG, UK

San Marco Press Ltd
8 Vernon Place, Canterbury, Kent CT1 3HG, UK
email: sanmarcopress@gmail.com
www.sanmarcopress.com

First printed edition 2014

ISBN 978-0-9567826-4-9

In collaboration with Supernova
www.supernovaedizioni.it

Cover Image
Watercolour by Nicola Tenderini.
www.nicolatenderini.it
email: nicolatenderini@yahoo.it

For Nellie and Bill
with love and thanks

Contents

Byron & Europe: A Brief Chronology

22nd January, George Noel Gordon born in London.	**1788**	
Catherine Gordon Byron moves to Aberdeen with her son. His father settles in France to avoid his debtors, living there until his death in 1791.	**1789**	July 14: Storming of the Bastille. The beginning of the French Revolution.
	1793	Britain and France at war.
George Gordon begins his schooling at Aberdeen Grammar School.	**1794**	Napoleon campaigns in Italy and Austria.
	1797	Venice surrenders to Napoleon. Treaty of Campo Formio: Venice becomes part of the Austrian Empire.
George Gordon becomes 6th Baron Byron of Rochdale.	**1798**	
	1799	Napoleon becomes First Consul.
Byron becomes a pupil at Harrow school.	**1801**	
	1802	Treaty of Amiens. Brief peace between Britain and France.
	1803	The "Napoleonic" wars: conflict in Europe until 1815.
	1804	Napoleon proclaimed Emperor.
Byron enrols at Trinity College, Cambridge, and begins lifelong friendships with John Cam Hobhouse and Scrope Berdmore Davies.	**1805**	Napoleon defeats Austria at Austerlitz. Venice and the remainder of the Italian peninsula are now under French rule. Napoleon is proclaimed king of Italy
Byron's first volume of poetry published.	**1806**	

Byron leaves England to begin a long journey through Europe. He travels across Portugal and Spain (witnessing the effects of the Peninsular War),and on to Gibraltar, Cyprus, Albania and Greece.	**1809**	
Byron in Turkey and Athens.	**1810**	Napoleon divorces Josephine and marries Princess Marie-Louise of Austria.
Byron returns to England. Death of his mother, Catherine Gordon Byron.	**1811**	
Childe Harold's Pilgrimage published. Byron awakes "to find himself famous." Begins his affair with Lady Caroline Lamb.	**1812**	Napoleon's Russian campaign begins, ending in the disastrous Retreat from Moscow.
2nd January: Byron and Annabella Milbanke are married. 10th December: birth of Ada Byron.	**1815**	June 18 Battle of Waterloo: final defeat and exile of Napoleon. Congress of Vienna: Venice, the Veneto and Lombardy under Austrian rule. Holy alliance of Austria, Russia and Prussia formed.
Separation of Byron and Annabella. 24th April: Byron leaves England and travels through Belgium and Germany into Switzerland, spending the summer at Villa Diodati on Lake Geneva. 10th November: Byron arrives in Venice.	**1816**	
Birth of Allegra Byron.	**1817**	
Byron signs a lease on the Palazzo Mocenigo.	**1818**	

Byron's relationship with Teresa Guiccioli begins. In December Byron leaves Venice for Ravenna.	**1819**	Peterloo Massacre, Manchester: troops fire on unarmed protestors.
Byron becomes active in the Ravenna *carbonari*.	**1820**	Neapolitan uprising begins.
Byron moves to Pisa with Teresa and her family.	**1821**	Death of Napoleon on St Helena. Holy Alliance restores the King Ferdinand to Naples. Greek uprising against Ottoman rule begins
Death of Allegra. Death of Shelley.	**1822**	
Byron sets sail for Greece.	**1823**	
19th April. Death of George Gordon, Lord Byron in Missolonghi.	**1824**	

Prologue

I want a hero: an uncommon want

The reader of this book and its hero (or, at least, the protagonist: you will be the judge) will spend a lot of time together. So, you may ask; what is he like?

Well, in 1816 he is 28 years old. Portraits show him as handsome, with a mass of dark curly hair. The poet Coleridge believed that he had never seen a more beautiful face on a man. He is not tall, and is quite slight of build: as a child he was chubby, and his mother ran to fat, so now he takes almost obsessive care of his diet, often living on little more than bread, vegetables and green tea, in order to keep his weight in check. He walks with a limp due to a twisted foot caused by a bungled delivery. His mother spent a deal of money, and put him through a deal of pain, in futile attempts to straighten it. He is at times self-conscious about this, but it depends on his mood. Sometimes he is reluctant to walk across a crowded drawing-room (believing, as he always does, that he is the centre of attention); yet he was happy to go on stage as part of the masquerade at the Drury Lane pantomime of 1815.

He takes great pride in his appearance, dressing in the "dandy" fashion made famous by his friend Beau Brummell; well-cut, well-made clothes, carefully put on and simply worn; no need for unnecessary ruffles and furbelows. He once said: "There are three great men of our age: myself, Napoleon and Brummell. But of we three, the greatest of all is Brummell."

Although no sportsman, he likes to keep himself fit. He spars with other young men of fashion at the boxing studio of "Gentleman" John Jackson; a strong swimmer, he swam the Hellespont on his visit to Istanbul; he is a good shot and a fine horseman.

His looks and fame have brought him celebrity status which he accepts, sometimes reluctantly, sometimes with gusto; and although insistent that he is a poet, not an autobiographer, he is at times content to let the public, and especially young ladies, confuse him with his Romantic heroes *Childe Harold* and *The Corsair*: he has even been painted in rugged Albanian garb.

Although very popular with the ladies and much in demand in society drawing-rooms, his best friends are men. He is good company and very witty. His friends – literary men like the popular poet Tom Moore and his publisher John Murray, embryo politicians such as his closest friend John Cam Hobhouse, the Cambridge don and spendthrift Scrope Davis, Douglas Kinnaird of the Drury Lane Theatre Committee – hold him very dear.

He has travelled widely, having visited Portugal, Spain, Greece, Albania and Turkey. Unusually for a man of his era and social class he has a facility for languages and is fluent in French, speaks and writes Greek and will soon become a confident Italian speaker. In short, he is a European.

He took his seat in the House of Lords in the Whig interest, yet he has flirted with Radical politics; his hero since his schooldays at Harrow has been Napoleon. His maiden speech in the Lords was in support of the frame-breakers, or Luddites, whose centre of operations was near to his ancestral home of Newstead Abbey. He spoke with great feeling against a Bill to make frame-breaking a capital offence and laid the plight of the hand-weavers and their families, brought to penury by the new water-powered weaving shuttles, clearly before Their Lordships; but all to no avail. A similar lack of success greeted his speech in favour of Catholic Emancipation in Ireland and as a result he has given up Parliamentary politics.

He is at times subject to fits of melancholy and these, combined with his Aberdeen Calvinist upbringing and memories of the cruel attentions of his nurse, make him believe at times that he is wicked, probably the most wicked person he knows. Although he flirts at times with free-thinking and Pantheism, his childhood Calvinism remains firmly in control of his moral compass.

This then, is our hero, a complex, contradictory, changeable man: George Gordon, Lord Byron.

Chapter One

1816: *Fare Thee Well!*

Self-Exiled Harold wanders forth again,
With nought of hope left; but with less of gloom.

On 24th April 1816, at 10 o'clock in the morning, George Gordon, sixth Baron Byron of Rochdale, climbed into his newly-built and commodious travelling carriage – designed in imitation of the one which had belonged to his hero Napoleon[1] – and left London for the last time, on his way to Dover and thence to a life abroad. His wife had left him after only a year of marriage, taking their baby daughter. Byron would see neither of them again. He was deeply in debt; his books had been seized and were being offered for sale. He had been publicly snubbed by many of the *bon ton* whose darling he had been for so long. So an extended tour of those parts of Europe which were once again open to English visitors following Napoleon's final defeat at Waterloo seemed an ideal plan. Byron thought that he might end his tour in Rome, perhaps returning to England the following spring.

How had the young man who, only four years earlier, had woken to find himself famous come to this? Largely, it has to be said, because of a well-intentioned, but disastrous, marriage. In September 1814, encouraged by his dear friend, the society hostess Lady Melbourne, Byron proposed to that lady's niece, Annabella Milbanke. Lady Melbourne acted with the best of intentions. She felt that Byron should settle down with a good, steady woman who would provide a calming influence and keep him away from those unsuitable ladies, such as her own daughter-in-law Lady Caroline Lamb, who were constantly pursuing him. However, it should have been clear to anyone who knew both parties that the couple were hopelessly incompatible. Annabella Milbanke, the only child of elderly and doting parents, had been brought up on her father's estate in County Durham, well away from the city life upon which Byron thrived. She had been given an excellent education, which was in itself unusual for a girl at the beginning of the 19th century; Byron called her "the Princess of Parallelograms". Unfortunately, her parents had also encouraged her to believe that her opinion on everything, from mathematics to religion to social reform (later in life she became a pillar of the Co-operative Movement) was the correct one. One of Byron's biographers has described her need "to be right, to be acknowledged to be right, to be unruffled by the faintest breath of criticism," a personality trait she exhibited at nineteen just as strongly as at sixty.

Why on earth did Byron marry a woman he must have realised would not suit him? He always made it very clear that he did not care for clever women. The two women who seem to have made him happiest, his half-sister Augusta and his final mistress Teresa Guiccoli, were warm-hearted and humourous women, neither of whom had any aspirations to be a blue-stocking. Byron's friend and first biographer, Tom Moore, believed that Annabella's reputation for virtue and learning piqued his vanity, "reprobate as he knew he was deemed, to win such a paragon."

The marriage took place on January 2nd 1815 and immediately began to fall apart. On a visit to Augusta and her family, Annabella became jealous of the genuine affection which Byron and his sister showed to each other. She was to persecute poor Augusta for her crime of being loved by Byron until the end of their days. Neither did she make herself popular with Byron's friends; his closest friend John Cam Hobhouse found her selfish and naïve.

Byron had rented a large house in Piccadilly Terrace from the Duchess of Devonshire as his bride's London home; a mistake, as it turned out. It had been a last-minute decision, taken by Lady Melbourne whilst the newly-weds were on honeymoon, and the rent was very high: £700 a year. This was the last straw for Byron's unhappy financial situation, hence the bailiffs in his living-room in the early spring of 1816.

Annabella brought with her to Piccadilly Terrace her old nurse, now in the combined role of lady's maid and companion: Mrs Clermont, a woman whom Byron rapidly came to detest. He believed that her tale-telling and passing on of servants' gossip were a prime cause of the failure of his marriage.

Annabella was soon pregnant, and Byron found a refuge from her humourlessness and his ever-increasing financial worries at the Theatre Royal, Drury Lane[2], where he became a member of the Management Sub-Committee. His close friend Douglas Kinnaird (who held his Power of Attorney after he left England) was also a committee member. Byron was amused and irritated in equal measure by committee work: amused when the committee commissioned a play from the popular playwright William Sotheby only to discover that he had lifted an entire scene from Byron's poem *The Corsair*; irritated by arguments about lighting the theatre – would gas poison the audience? - and by constant worries about the sobriety or otherwise of their leading actor, Edmund Kean.

Byron, who suffered throughout his life from melancholy, went through a particularly severe bout of that malady in the winter following his marriage. He told his friend Tom Moore that "my health has been a good deal disordered and my mind ill at ease for a considerable period," indeed he seems to have suffered from a brief but severe mental breakdown around the time of his daughter's birth. His wife proving to be neither sympathetic nor useful – it would appear that Mrs Clermont frightened her with tales that Byron was going to commit suicide or resort to domestic violence – Augusta moved into Piccadilly Terrace to care for her brother, and to try to mediate between him and his wife. Byron later stated categorically that his wife knew Mrs Clermont's tittle-tattle to be untrue.

By the time his daughter Ada was born on 10th December 1815 Byron was deeply in debt. The hoped-for sale of his estates near Rochdale, which would have put him financially in the clear, seemed fated never to happen. His publisher, John Murray, tried to help by making an offer of £ 1,050 – well above the going rate – for the copyrights of two new poems, *Parisina* and *The Siege of Corinth*, but Byron gratefully declined. He considered closing his London house and going abroad alone for a while, but permanent separation from his wife was far from his mind.

Then, a bombshell: Annabella took Ada for a short visit to her parents in January 1816. A letter came from her father saying that she would not be coming back. Byron's marriage was effectively over. He continued to write loving letters, begging her to return, but to no avail. He would never see his daughter Ada again.

Entire books have been written about the Byron marriage and even today, people take sides. Yet no-one has ever reached a satisfactory answer as to why it failed so spectacularly and so quickly. Tom Moore, who had read them, stated that Byron's *Memoirs* (burned in John Murray's fireplace shortly after their author's death) dealt mainly with the events of his marriage. Whatever happened, Byron emerged from the brief experiment in marriage a changed man. The purgatorial fire of a year with Annabella made him sadder and wiser; more world-weary, it is true, but perhaps also more tolerant. The arch and cynical youth of the popular imagination, the Byron described by Lady Caroline Lamb as "mad, bad and dangerous to know," who had written to Lady Melbourne of his conquests and planned seductions, was gone forever. The twenty-eight year-old who left England in April 1816 can perhaps best be described as the adult Byron. Although he still did not suffer fools gladly, those who knew him in Italy and in Greece remembered him with great fondness.

However, Byron still had one adventure ahead of him before he set out from England. Ever since the publication of the first two cantos of *Childe Harold's Pilgrimage* in 1812, he had received countless letters from young ladies of sensibility, asking for portraits or locks of hair. Usually he ignored them, but something about a letter from "E. Trefusis" which arrived in March 1816 must have piqued his curiosity. Perhaps he simply wanted a diversion from the way his life was collapsing around him.

E. Trefusis' letter, in rather purple prose, makes the writer's intentions pretty clear:

"I place my happiness in your hands… If a woman, whose reputation has yet remained unstained, if without either guardian or husband to control she should throw herself on your mercy, if with a beating heart she should confess the love she has borne you many years, if she should secure you to secresy and safety… could you betray her, or would you be silent as the grave?... Either you will or you will not."

This was soon followed by a second letter, this time signed "C. G. B." The tone is more businesslike, but the anticipated result is in little doubt:

"Lord Byron is requested to state whether seven o'clock this Evening will be convenient to him to receive a lady to communicate with him on business of peculiar importance. She desires to be admitted alone and with the utmost privacy."

This time Byron replied:

"Ld. B is not aware of any "importance" which can be attached by any person to an interview with him – & more particularly by one with whom it does not appear that he has the honour of being acquainted – he will however be at home at the hour mentioned."

The lady who wished to be admitted alone and with the utmost privacy was Claire Clairmont. Only eighteen years old, she already had quite an interesting history of her own. She was born in France in 1798 and named Clara Mary Jane Clairmont (she began to call herself Claire at about the same time as her relationship with Byron began). Her father was certainly French but was probably not married to her mother, although that lady called herself "Mrs Clairmont" and was passing herself off as a widow by the time she married the well-known Radical author and journalist William Godwin in 1801. Claire was thus the step-sister of Mary Godwin and, as a fluent French speaker, had accompanied Mary and Percy Bysshe Shelley when they had eloped to France in 1815. Claire and Shelley got on extremely well, although her constant presence, attention-seeking and frequent hysterics ("Jane's horrors" Mary called them) were an irritant to Mary, who wanted Shelley all to herself.

Shelley was at this time a great believer in free love. He had already invited Harriet, the wife he had married in 1811 and by whom he had two children, to join his and Mary's union (he was somewhat puzzled by her refusal to do so), and it is very likely that by 1815 he had also slept with Claire. She spent much of 1815 living alone in Devon, and it has been suggested that this was because she was carrying Shelley's child. "E. Trefusis", a West Country name, may well be one that she came across during her stay, possibly even the alias she used at the time.

By the beginning of 1816 Claire was back in London and, unusually for a middle-class eighteen year-old girl at that time, was living alone. Thus she had the opportunity to catch a Romantic poet of her own, one rather more famous than Shelley – whose work was at that time known only to a very small circle – and one whose verse she and Mary had been reading since the impressionable age of fourteen. She may have been getting her own back on Mary, whom she held responsible for separating her from Shelley. She may have been an immature girl dazzled by celebrity. Whatever her reasons, she laid her plans to capture Byron with an almost military precision.

Claire first told Byron that she wanted to be an actress and hoped he would help her into Drury Lane. So Byron wrote a letter of introduction to Douglas Kinnaird. In order to keep his interest Claire changed tack: perhaps a literary career would suit her better: would Byron give an opinion on her half-written novel?

All of Claire's manoeuvring led to the end result she craved; she and Byron slept together. However, he soon wearied of her. His plans for leaving England were now finalized. It was already April and he intended to be off before the end of the month. The last thing he needed at present was another long-term relationship and, always a deeply moral man at heart despite his public image, he had a profound dislike for her ideas about free love, picked up from Shelley. Claire wrote to him that she knew he "found my opinions detestable, my theories depraved."

Desperate to keep the relationship alive, and still obviously believing that Byron was a candidate for Shelley's commune of free love, Claire engineered a meeting between Byron and Mary. She then wrote to him, apparently on Mary's behalf, saying, "Mary… entreats me in private to obtain your address abroad that we may, if possible, have again the pleasure of seeing you," so she was already forming a plan to follow Byron. By the time he left London, she was pregnant.

The scandals that this would create were still in the future. For now, Byron was about to send one more frisson of pleasurable disgust through the society which had previously lauded him with the publication of his two "Separation Poems", *Fare Thee Well* (to Annabella) and *A Sketch* (about the malign Mrs Clermont). To read *Fare Thee Well* is to look at the disconnected thoughts of a man who simply cannot comprehend why his wife has left him. He worries about his child, growing up without knowing him: how will she be taught to think of him? He feels hurt, betrayed, and asks:

Could no other arm be found,
Than the one which once embraced me,
To inflict a cureless wound?

Byron continued to hold this view until at least the end of 1816. In September he wrote to Augusta that: "the separation – has broken my heart – I feel as if an Elephant had trodden on it." In November he wrote to his estranged wife hoping that they could still be reconciled. *A Sketch* shows the profound dislike Byron felt for his wife's servant:

Quick with the tale and ready with the lie –
The genial confidante, and general spy"

The verses are harsh; especially since they were addressed to someone who could not answer back; but Byron was clearly writing in the white heat of anger and held Mrs Clermont responsible for "the ruin thou hast wrought," ie: the separation. Who has not said or written things in the heat of the moment that they later regret? Luckily for most people, their follies are not laid out in print after almost two hundred years.

Byron had only fifty copies printed, intending them to be distributed only to close friends; but the poems inevitably found their way into the newspapers. This was misinterpreted as a deliberate act of cruelty on Byron's part, and gave a number of former friends the opportunity to snub him in public at his last appearance before setting out; at a party given in his honour by the Prince Regent's current mistress, Lady Jersey.

When Byron rode out of London, with him in his Napoleonic carriage were his friends Hobhouse and Scrope Davies, accompanying him to say farewell at Dover; his page Robert Rushton and his valet William Fletcher. Both Rushton and Fletcher had travelled with Byron before, on his Mediterranean journey of 1809. Fletcher was newly-married – ironically, to Lady Byron's maid – and had not liked abroad the last time he had been there but, ever since his engagement as groom when My Lord was sixteen, where Byron went, he went. Also with the party were a Swiss servant called Berger (Byron's medium-term plan was to travel to Geneva), and Byron's newly-engaged personal physician, Doctor John Polidori.

Travelling with his own physician was not a case of aristocratic mollycoddling; Byron was genuinely concerned about his health, both mental and physical, at the time of the separation. He made frequent references to his mental state in letters to his friends in England, and when Hobhouse was planning a visit sent him a list of various medicaments, including potash and sulphuric acid which he probably combined to self medicate for palpitations, a symptom of anxiety. He was also following the "light vegetable diet" recommended by physicians of the time to clear the liver of too much black bile, the cause of melancholy.

By late April, Byron had doubtless also noticed that the weather was not helping his mood. 1816 was set to be notably cold, unseasonable heavy frosts were killing the new shoots of the crops, and the temperature in London was struggling to reach 4°C. That this was caused by a volcanic eruption in the Indian Ocean, Byron would neither know nor care. What he would notice was that the dark and gloomy weather, caused by the cloud of volcanic dust drifting across the upper atmosphere, had a negative effect on his mood.

It is unclear how Byron came to engage Polidori. Twenty years old and something of a prodigy, he had qualified as a doctor at Edinburgh University at the remarkably early age of 19. Polidori's father, Gaetano, had been secretary to the Italian writer Alfieri, whom Byron greatly admired and perhaps this is what initially interested him in the young man. On the other hand, it is possible that Polidori wanted to work for Byron simply because he was Byron: he had some literary pretensions himself and was just the right age to have been, like Claire Clairmont, a hero-worshipping adolescent at the time of the publication of *Childe Harold* in 1812. His later attitude to Byron bears all the hallmarks of disillusionment. "There is no-one so likely to become embittered as a fan whose idol refuses to live up to the preconceived idea of him."[3]

Byron said his farewells at Dover and on the evening of April 25th his party set sail for Ostend, arriving at their hotel at 2am the following morning. Polidori, who was keeping a journal with an eye to publication, recorded two interesting facts: first (and clearly, to him most interesting), like a typical Englishman abroad he didn't like the tea, which was perfumed; second, "Lord Byron fell like a thunderbolt upon the chambermaid."

The Byron party travelled at a stately pace through the Low Countries, stopping off at important towns to see the sights. Polidori obviously took his role as diarist very seriously: day by day he recorded places of interest, local customs, the exact number of steps up to the steeple of Ghent cathedral and important works of art. At Antwerp, where the party arrived on 29th April, he and Byron viewed a number of paintings by Rubens. Polidori gave them careful attention, his diary account covering numerous paragraphs. He records titles, characters, use of colour, his opinion of their artistic merit. Byron sums the whole thing up in a few lines to Augusta:

"I think Rubens a very great dauber – and prefer Vandyke a hundred times over – (but then I know nothing about the matter)… it may all be very fine – and I suppose it must be Art – for – I'll swear – 'tis not Nature."

Little wonder it soon became clear that Lord Byron and his doctor did not see eye to eye.

Meanwhile, the Napoleonic carriage was proving to be a liability. It broke down on the way from Ghent to Antwerp, and again on the journey to Brussels. Byron then decided that it (complete with bed, travelling library, plate-chest and dining set) was not large enough to accommodate five people plus coachman, so he bought another coach to transport the servants. This in turn broke down on the way to view the battle-field at Waterloo, so Byron asked for his money back. The seller not only refused, but put a notice in the local paper stating that Byron had absconded without paying for the coach. Perhaps news of his money troubles had come before him, perhaps the man simply saw his opportunity to add to, and be connected with, the Byron legend.

The Napoleonic carriage continued to prove troublesome, forever breaking down on lonely roads so that Polidori was afraid of bandits and infected the servants with his fears. Byron drily observed that Fletcher, at least, should have known better, having been with him in Turkey.

He roundly abused the coachmaker, Baxter, in a letter to Hobhouse, calling him a pickpocket for charging ?500 for such shoddy workmanship: Hobhouse should inform him that Byron expected a reduction. In fact, Byron never paid a single penny of

Baxter's bill. Perhaps the coach was extracting a rough poetic justice.
The visit to Waterloo took place on 4th May and, as usual, Polidori gave a detailed and pedestrian account of all they saw. Byron, who had already noted Napoleonic engineering works in Antwerp with the comment "poor dear Bonaparte", confined himself to writing to Hobhouse that he had bought some helmets and sabres from the battlefield, and that he detested the victors (he held the opinion that the disastrous weather of the Moscow Campaign of 1812, rather than any superiority on the part of the allied forces, was ultimately responsible for Napoleon's defeat.) He did however write about Waterloo in his newly-begun continuation of *Childe Harold's Pilgrimage*:

And Harold stands upon this place of skulls,
The grave of France, the deadly Waterloo

Descriptions of the battlefield rapidly give way to a meditation on death, "conqueror and captive" Napoleon, and the loss of power.

Lord Byron and party soon moved into Germany, Byron planning to follow the course of the Rhine through Cologne, Koblentz, Mains and Karlsruhe. At Cologne Byron had another adventure with a chambermaid "whose red cheeks and white teeth had made me venture upon her carnally", and was much amused when the innkeeper, convinced that his own wife was the partner in the carnal activity, swore at him "like a Squadron of Cavalry" until he saw his wife walking out of her own room "& the girl out of mine."
Meanwhile, it was becoming apparent that Doctor Polidori needed a great deal of looking after on his own account. His diary for 4th May records "Got up very bad," while Byron complained to Hobhouse "Polidori is devilish ill – I do not know with what – nor does he," and added that Polidori had only treated two patients on the journey so far, "one of them himself". Imagine, then, Byron's relief on arriving in Geneva on 25th May, knowing that he need no longer be in such close daily proximity with the good doctor. Hours at a stretch in a carriage with Polidori must have been hard work. No wonder Byron put his age as "one hundred" in the hotel register.
Byron's plans in Geneva were simple; to avoid the English and to enjoy European literary society by way of the literary salon of his friend, Madame de Staël, whose house across the Lake at Coppet was a magnet for poets, writers and philosophers.

However, before he could visit Coppet, Byron's hopes of quiet literary salons were interrupted. He had been pursued across Europe by increasingly overwrought letters from Claire Clairmont, threatening to follow him to Geneva. She had somehow persuaded Shelley that a trip to Switzerland was an excellent idea: perhaps holding out the carrot of a meeting with her lover, Lord Byron, whom she knew Shelley greatly admired (he had read *Lara* aloud to her and Mary in 1814); she may even have hinted that Byron was just the man to join Shelley's free-love commune. This was certainly the picture she presented in letters to Byron as she, Mary and Shelley, who had left England just a week after him, drew inexorably closer. She wrote of the approach of the Otaheite [Tahitian] philosophers – Tahiti was regarded at the time as kind of free-love Utopia – and suggested that Byron would fall in love with Mary and enjoy an "attachment," thus showing how deeply she misunderstood Byron's character. An affair, or a liaison with a lady married to an understanding husband who would be conducting a similar discreet arrangement of his own, was one thing. It was quite another to abandon the accepted mores of society and be part of some free-thinking, free-loving commune: he may have flirted with Radicalism, but was not ready for anything so radical as that. He would have no intention of allowing any child of his to be brought up in such a set-up either, as Claire was soon to learn.

Immediately on his arrival at Lake Geneva, Byron began a daily exercise regime of rowing out into the lake and then swimming. On 27th May, returning from a visit to the Villa Diodati (on the opposite shore to the town of Geneva, which Byron had found to be crawling with English) which he was hoping to rent for the summer, he and Polidori met the Shelley party, who just happened to be walking along the shore. The whole thing had no doubt been carefully contrived by Claire, who now knew to her cost that Byron would not reply to her letters. Polidori sums up Shelley's domestic set-up thus:
"PS, the author of *Queen Mab*, came; bashful, shy consumptive, twenty-six; separated from his wife; he keeps the two daughters of Godwin, who practice his theories, one LB's."
Shelley was a hypochondriac. Believing that he had consumption, on meeting a doctor the opportunity for a free consultation had been too good to miss. The rest of Polidori's information must have come from Byron; the Shelleys did not broadcast their domestic arrangements and Mary travelled as "Mrs Shelley" (which is how Polidori afterwards refers to her in his diary). Byron had also told Polidori about his relationship with Claire,

and his belief that she was also sleeping with Shelley. He had taxed Claire with this as early as April: she had offered to let him see Shelley's letters to her in order to show that their relationship was purely fraternal; however, letters that Byron wrote after the birth of his and Claire's child show that he continued to believe that she had a sexual relationship with Shelley.

Byron and the Shelleys fell into the habit of meeting daily, either for breakfast or dinner. The two poets were a little wary of each other at first, but were soon on friendly terms. When Byron took a short lease on the Villa Diodati, moving in on 10th June, the Shelleys rented the Maison Chapuis, a short distance down the hill. Across the lake, an enterprising hotelier installed a telescope so that his English guests could spy on the two disreputable ménages and be shocked, convincing themselves that sheets and pillowcases left out on the balcony to dry by Byron's laundress were in fact young ladies' petticoats.

Once settled into the Villa, Byron resumed his relationship with Claire. He was quite honest: "I never loved nor pretended to love her – but a man is a man – & if a girl of eighteen comes prancing to you at all hours – there is but one way." However, her silly behaviour soon began to outweigh her physical attractions, and he preferred to spend his evenings with Polidori so that Claire did not find him alone. Eventually she asked Byron to send Polidori out "to write a dictionary" and nursed a grudge against the doctor ever afterwards. Byron finally made it clear that Claire was not to come to the Villa without Shelley and Mary; by the end of the summer he would not let her in at all.

He soon began to develop a real and lasting friendship with Mary, however. Mary Godwin, still only nineteen, had eloped with Shelley because she genuinely loved him, not because she was persuaded by his theories of free love. She had not had a happy childhood. Her mother Mary Wollstonecraft had passed through a succession of unconventional relationships and had attempted suicide before finding brief contentment with Mary's father William Godwin. She died two days after giving birth to Mary. Mary grew into a serious girl who adored her father, although she always had a difficult relationship with her stepmother, Mary Jane Clairmont. In the two years since her relationship with Shelley began, Mary had already lost one baby and was taking great care with the health of little William, then just a few months old: Polidori took the child to be vaccinated against smallpox whilst they were in Geneva.

If Claire at eighteen was childish and silly, Mary was in some ways older than her years: the death of her child, and the perpetual money worries of living with Shelley, who often took out loans to help his friends (including Mary's ever-penniless father) and then spent days walking about London, not daring to stay in his lodgings lest the bailiffs call, had made her grow up quickly. Byron found her quiet, serious disposition a source of great calm after his troublesome year.

Byron was not the only person to be drawn to Mary: Polidori's diary makes it clear that the Doctor fell in love with her. "Went into a boat with Mrs S"; "Read Tasso with Mrs Shelley"; "Walked to Mrs Shelley"; "In the evening to Mrs S" is an almost daily refrain in the diary. Standing on the balcony at the Villa Diodati one evening, he saw Mary walking up the hill. He was in such a hurry to go down and offer her his arm that he jumped off the balcony, slipped and sprained his ankle. The Doctor had to be helped inside and doctored by Byron, who teased Polidori about his feelings and threatened to tell Mary all about it, causing Polidori to go into a terrible sulk. Polidori's love for Mary may have provoked him into the jealousy of Shelley which he now began to show, and which reached its peak one day when the group of friends were sailing on the Lake. Shelley beat the Doctor in a race and Polidori took it to heart, offering Shelley out in a duel. Shelley told him not to be so silly, but Polidori persisted with his challenge until Byron told the young man that, if he didn't shut up, he would take Shelley's place in the duel – and he knew how to use a pistol.

Polidori, a Roman Catholic, also seems to have been uncomfortable with some of the conversations Byron and Shelley had in the evenings at Diodati. Shelley at this time veered between describing himself as an atheist and a deist. Byron, as the verses he was writing about Lake Geneva show, was flirting with pantheism:

Are not the mountains, waves, and skies, a part
Of me, and of my soul, and I of them?

The two of them, and no doubt Mary, discussed Good and Evil, the immortal soul, the possibility of the existence of God. It was too much for Polidori. Tom Moore, who obtained most of his information about events at the Villa Diodati from Mary Shelley, writes in his biography of Byron that the doctor put their "more elevated subjects of conversation" to flight with flippant remarks and odd jokes. Polidori wrote about these conversations, and his anxieties concerning them, in a short story, *Ernestus Berchtold,* published in 1819. In this the Byronic character, Olivieri, "made it a point to bewilder everyone", describing Catholicism as a religion for the poor and sick at heart while speaking of the "absurdity and falsehood" of its teachings, while Byron's childhood Scottish Calvinism was "cold as [its] native rocks."

The group of young people (Byron, at twenty-eight, was the oldest, ten years older than both Mary and Claire) had to spend a good deal of their time indoors, because the weather had not improved; indeed, 1816 was to be called "The Year Without a Summer". The temperature in Geneva during June and July was the lowest recorded for sixty years. Mary's journal relates that it took ten men to literally hold the carriage in which the Shelley party travelled to Geneva on the track as they crossed the mountains, due to strong winds and snow. Byron, like many before and since, decided that the bad weather was all the fault of the Tory Government, blaming the widely-loathed Foreign Secretary:
"...we have had such stupid mists - fogs – rains - and perpetual density – that one would think that Castlereagh had the foreign affairs of the kingdom of Heaven also – upon his hands."
Perhaps inspired by the metaphysical conversations he was having with the Shelleys, and certainly affected by the weather, which was not having a positive impact on his mental health (he later told Tom Moore that he had been "half mad" during his time at Geneva) Byron wrote the poem *Darkness*. The gloomy weather as the clouds of volcanic ash blocked out the sun is apparent in the first few lines:

I had a dream, which was not all a dream.
The bright sun was extinguish'd, and the stars
Did wander darkling in the eternal space,
Rayless, and pathless, and the icy earth
Swung blind and blackening in the moonless air;
Morn came and went--and came, and brought no day.

His own mood is reflected as he speaks of "dread", "desolation" and "a selfish prayer for light", but then the poem turns Apocalyptic. People set their own homes on fire in their desperation for light and warmth. Famine follows (this was a reality as Byron wrote; Swiss farmers were slaughtering their livestock due to a shortage of fodder, there were to be food shortages and high prices across Europe and North America for several years), then war comes; the two last surviving men die and the earth becomes "a lump of death." The poem ends on a nihilistic note:

And the clouds perish'd; Darkness had no need
Of aid from them – She was the Universe.

So it no doubt came as a tremendous relief to Byron when he was able to drive away these gloomy thoughts with an evening of ghostly tales. On 16th June the whole party gathered at the Villa for an evening of being pleasantly scared, reading aloud from a French translation of German ghost stories. One was about a corpse's head being brought back to life. Doctor Polidori would be able to tell them about the dissections he had attended during his medical training at Edinburgh, and the electrical storms raging across the Lake – more widespread than ever in that catastrophic summer – turned their thoughts to the new science of galvanism, whereby the limbs of dissected animals had been made to move when given electric shocks.[4]

Next day, every member of the group began to write their own ghost story, except Polidori, who was searching for inspiration. Mary's tale drew on their conversations about the corpse, the electric storms and so much more besides as she wrote *Frankenstein*. Byron wrote a fragment of a tale about a vampire, but he had no facility for fiction and, after reading it aloud one evening soon put it aside. Polidori began his own "ghost" story shortly afterwards, but soon abandoned it. Instead, he took what he remembered of Byron's story and wrote *The Vampyre*. If Mary gave one staple character to British horror, Polidori, inspired by Byron, created the other one. Vampires had appeared in fiction before this, but usually as the goblin-like creatures seen in Germanic versions of the story. Polidori, by including his own, by now somewhat jaundiced, view of Byron in his tale, created the suave vampire which has become a staple of everyone from Bram Stoker to Christopher Lee. Polidori's tale would cause Byron a great deal of annoyance when it was published in 1819.

At midnight on June 18th there were more ghost stories, and Byron decided to entertain the company with a disturbing recitation. A favourite poem of his at this time was Coleridge's *Christabel*, in which the beautiful heroine is haunted by a Lamia; half woman, half serpent. Byron had sponsored the poem's publication by Murray, together with his own *Corsair*. He now chose the passage where the snake-woman disrobes:

Like one that shuddered, she unbound
The cincture from beneath her breast:
Her silken robe, and inner vest,
Dropt to her feet, and full in view,
Behold! her bosom and half her side—
A sight to dream of, not to tell!
O shield her! shield sweet Christabel!

It was all too much for Shelley; the late hour, other-worldly atmosphere they had jointly created, the recitation. He had an attack of sensibility, thought of a woman who had eyes instead of nipples, took one look at Mary and ran screaming from the room.

The company wisely decided to leave ghost stories alone for a while after this. Perhaps Mary and Byron jointly decided that what Shelley needed was some fresh air, since a few days later, on 23rd June, Byron and Shelley set out on an eight-day tour of the Lake by boat. Using his sprained ankle as an excuse, Polidori was left behind. It seems that Polidori resented this and high words were exchanged. Polidori went to his room, convinced that he had finally gone too far and Byron would dismiss him. Over-reacting, he decided that he was on the verge of ruin. He prepared a dose of poison from his medicine-chest and was about to write a suicide note when Byron knocked on the door to shake his hand. Polidori, to Byron's surprise, burst into tears and confessed all.

Byron was no doubt relieved to escape from this overheated atmosphere for a few days. He and Shelley planned an excursion around the Lake, stopping off at points of interest. It may have been on the first evening, as they sat on a wall watching the local children play, that Shelley broke the news that Claire was pregnant. After a man-to-man talk it was agreed that Byron would acknowledge the child. At this stage he was content for the child to spend its early years with Claire, although from now on he was adamant that he would not see her again.

Next day, as the boat approached Evian, they witnessed an electrical storm which heralded a change in the weather. The following day was one of strong wind and high waves which by the afternoon had grown into a storm so violent that the boatmen expected that they would sink. Byron took off his coat and prepared to swim for it, encouraging Shelley to do the same; luckily the boatmen were able to take them into a sheltered harbour. Shelley later wrote that he had looked death in the face on this occasion, and felt "a mixture of sensations, among which terror entered, though but subordinately… I knew that my companion would have attempted to save me, and I was overcome with humiliation when I thought that his life might have been risked to preserve mine."

Maurice, one of the boatman, was still entertaining English visitors with a much-embellished account of this story ten years later. In his version, "had they been out five minutes more, the boat must be wrecked." It all added to the Byron legend.

The tour now continued without further incident. Next day they explored the mouth of the Rhone, and after breakfast on the following day sailed to Chillon, where they had a guided tour of the castle. Shelley listened carefully to the guide. He was able to tell his friend Thomas Love Peacock that the roof of the main dungeon was supported by seven columns, that the lake here was 800 feet deep, that heretics were imprisoned at Chillon during the Reformation. Byron did no more than half listen while he carved his name on a pillar. Yet the story of François de Bonivard, a patriot of Geneva imprisoned here by the Duke of Savoy in the sixteenth century, struck a chord. A few days later he wrote *The Prisoner of Chillon*, in which Bonivard soliloquises about his imprisonment along with his two brothers, each chained to a column so that they two died, separated from him by the darkness, while he became accustomed to the prison by long use until

My very chains and I grew friends
Finally the prisoner
Regain'd my freedom with a sigh

as Byron asks the reader to consider the nature of freedom: is it a physical state, or a state of mind?
Byron wrote his poem almost immediately after visiting Chillon, when his and Shelley's journey was delayed by rain and they were staying at an inn in a small village called Ouchy. They ended their tour with a couple of literary visits: to Rousseau's former home in Clarens and the house where Gibbon had stayed in Lausanne while completing *Decline and Fall of the Roman Empire*.

Perhaps mindful of the need to keep Claire well out of Byron's way for the time being, Shelley, Mary and Claire set out again almost immediately on an Alpine tour. This gave Byron the opportunity to make his long-delayed visit to Mademe de Staël at Coppet. This famous woman of letters was now approaching the end of an incident-packed life. She was born in 1766, the daughter of Louis XVI's finance minister Jacques Necker, and in 1786 she married Erik Magnus Staël von Holstein, the Swedish ambassador. This meant that she was able to stay in Paris safely during the early years of the Revolution despite her royal connections, although she took the precaution of moving to her Swiss estate at Coppet, on Lake Geneva, before the worst excesses of the Terror. She made regular visits to England from the 1790s onwards where she was a popular guest with those society hostesses who had literary leanings, especially after the publication of her Romantic novel *Corinne* in 1805. When Byron had first met her, in London early in 1815, he had not been impressed. He always claimed not to like clever women, and Madame de Staël, then approaching 50, seemed to him "a very plain woman forcing one to listen & look at her with her mouth full of ink." However, Madame de Staël was a great defender of Byron on both literary and personal fronts and he knew that he would meet interesting people at Coppet. Ambassador de Staël having died in 1802, she now lived there with her lover (they were actually married, but this was not widely known until after her death) Monsieur de Rocca.

Byron found Madame de Staël to be a different and calmer woman in her own surroundings. "In her own house," he wrote, "she was amiable," and "she was a good woman at heart." However, she surprised him by frankly discussing the Separation with him and advising him to go back to his wife. He must have felt that he reacted badly in his initial shock when she introduced the subject, as he felt the need to write to her and explain his behaviour. None of the friends who wrote to him from England, he told her, were allowed to mention his wife or the events of the separation in any way, except to give him news of his daughter Ada. However, he still loved his wife.

Madame de Staël advised him to write a letter declaring that he was willing to be reconciled with Lady Byron, and a note from him the next day, telling her that "my letter is at your disposal" indicates that he took her advice. If he did write the letter it has not survived, although he wrote to his wife from Milan in November, telling her he had been through mental torture since the separation and "if there were a means of becoming reunited with you I would embrace it."

Madame de Staël also had news of another figure risen from the past to haunt him in a real-life version of the ghost stories from the Villa Diodati. She gave him a novel to read, newly-arrived from England where it was creating a *success de scandal*: Lady Caroline Lamb's *Glenarvon*. Madame de Staël, who had been a guest of Lady Melbourne at Brocket Hall in 1813, and had quarrelled with Lady Caroline over her persistent abuse of Byron, was fully aware of the history of the relationship. Whether she warned Byron what to expect when he began to read the novel is not known.

All the complexities and irritations left behind with his English life suddenly caught up with Byron. His affair with Lady Caroline had lasted, on his part, for a few months in 1812, although she had continued to follow him, and even broke into his rooms more than once, before he left his apartment at Albany when he married.

Lady Caroline Lamb was a member, by birth or marriage, of several of the leading Whig families of the day. Born Lady Caroline Ponsonby in 1785, her aunt was the famous Georgiana, Duchess of Devonshire. She had been an hysterical child and a doctor had advised that she should not be disciplined because of her "nerves". Thus she grew up to expect her own way. In 1807 she married William Lamb, younger son of Lord Melbourne. At the ceremony she had a fit of rage when the officiating bishop did something to annoy her, tore her wedding-gown and had to be carried from the room. Her self-centredness was such that she believed William, then making a name for himself in Parliament, did not show her enough attention and so when, in 1812, she was introduced to Byron, then being fêted in society, she was convinced that she had at last found the love of her life. She followed him everywhere, often dressing as a page. Byron's interest soon waned as his friendship with her mother-in-law Lady Melbourne grew, and as he tried to cool their affair she began to bombard him with theatrical letters, turned up at his rooms (to the consternation of Fletcher, who could never work out how she got in) saying that she and Byron were going to elope, and had hysterical fits.

A trip to Ireland – it was hoped that a change of scene would calm Lady Caroline down – had no effect. She offered to sleep with any man who would challenge Byron to a duel. She choreographed an elaborate ceremony at the Melbourne's country home, Brocket Hall; apparently burning Byron's letters on a bonfire whilst girls dressed in white danced round the flames and a page-boy read verses that she had written specially for the occasion. Meeting Byron at a ball in July 1813, high words were exchanged; she smashed a glass and cut her arms. William Lamb was put under pressure to announce a formal separation, but he stuck by his wife despite her continued aberrant behaviour: one day Byron came home to find that she had been there and written "Remember Me" in a book he had been reading and had left open. All the pent-up emotion caused by being the target of such a persistent stalker burst forth. He wrote:

Remember thee! Remember thee!
Till Lethe quench life's burning stream
Remorse and shame shall cling to thee,
And haunt thee like a feverish dream.
Remember thee! Ay doubt it not,
Thy husband too shall think of thee!
By neither shalt thou be forgot,
Thou false *to him, thou* fiend *to me!*

Much of this, only very thinly disguised, appeared within the pages of *Glenarvon*, which Lady Caroline wrote in the spring of 1816; sitting up into the early hours while dressed – inevitably -

as a page. Its publication finally put her outside the bounds of polite society, who considered her crime to be not in doing something so commonplace as having an affair, but in conducting it so publicly. William was devastated, but still stood by his wife.

Lady Caroline was not a gifted writer, and the events of *Glenarvon* are conducted at the same breathless pace at which she appears to have lived her life. She barely bothers with characterization, relying on her readers to fill in any gaps from knowledge or gossip. The protagonists are Calantha, Lady Avondale (a very-thinly disguised Lady Caroline Lamb), her loving and placid husband (William Lamb) and Clarence Ruthven, Lord Glenarvon (Byron), who balances the multiple roles of serial seducer, society gentleman, Irish rebel leader and commander of a British naval frigate. The plot combines the struggle for Irish independence, mysterious Italians, missing heirs, and murder. Lady Caroline also throws in pen portraits (mostly satirical) of leading society hostesses and Byron's mistresses, as well as incidents from her own affair with Byron. A letter he wrote to her at the end of their relationship is carefully transcribed in the text.

The book ends when Ruthven, far out at sea in his frigate, sees a vision of a ship with black sails. On deck are a ghostly friar and Ruthven's first, and only true, love. The friar throws her into the sea. Attempting to save her, Ruthven dives in and is lost beneath the waves. It brought forth this response from Byron:

> *I read* "Glenarvon" *too by Caro. Lamb,*
> *God* damn!
> *The author, he said, was "an infamous Bedlamite."*

In London, meanwhile, the infamous bedlamite was carrying out her final act of revenge. She wrote a series of letters to Lady Byron, who was her cousin by marriage. They had been close acquaintances during Annabella's London seasons in 1811 and 1812. The letters contained dark hints of secrets about Byron and Augusta which, Lady Caroline suggested, only she knew. Lady Byron, in many ways quite unworldly but also retaining a prurient interest in anything to do with her husband and jealous of his obvious affection for Augusta, finally agreed to meet her. Lady Caroline then "revealed" Byron's "dark secret", that he had committed incest with Augusta, and that her daughter Medora Leigh was his child. She also told Annabella that Byron had slept with boys at Harrow. It is hard to tell which of these two pieces of information shocked the unworldly Annabella the most. The information about Harrow is hardly surprising, being the normal experience for most boys of the period educated at public school. However,

the widely-repeated incest allegation, although it has provided grist for a great deal of speculation among Byron scholars over the years and is now firmly installed as part of the Bryon legend, can be traced no closer to Byron than Lady Caroline, who claimed that Byron confided in her during their brief affair. Lady Caroline Lamb, a noisy self-publicist, seems an unlikely confidante for an intimate secret. Augusta's husband, George Leigh, gave no credence to the idea: they continued to be a devoted couple and Augusta eventually bore him eight children. Nor did it make any impact on Augusta's position as Lady of the Bedchamber to George III's wife, Queen Charlotte. Byron was clearly not burdened with any great guilt, as he did not share "the secret" with anyone else, not even his closest friend Hobhouse, "from whom I have no secrets." And Lady Caroline certainly chose her moment to reveal it, perhaps motivated by a determination that Byron and his wife should not be reconciled. Lady Byron, another woman who was unable to keep anything to herself, soon began to whisper this tale among her closest friends in order to justify, in retrospect, leaving Byron. She also began a none-too-subtle cross-examination of Augusta, conducted entirely by letter. Augusta in turn wrote worriedly to Byron, for at the end of August he wrote to reassure her that Lady Caroline knew no secrets:
"Who can care for such a wretch as C[arolin]e, or believe such a seventy times convicted liar? and in the next place, whatever she may suppose or assert – I never "committed" any one to her but *myself*."
However, his wife and his former mistress obviously continued their speculations and (in Lady Byron's case) to climb onto a moral high horse, as the following year Byron said that he was "sick of being the theme of their mutual inventions."

No wonder Byron hoped to find the calming influence of European literary society at Coppet. He certainly seems to have enjoyed his visits there, and even took Polidori with him on two or three occasions, but he mostly only found the family at home: Madame, the handsome and good-natured Rocca, her newly-married daughter Albertine and her husband: Byron noted with some sadness how affectionate the young couple were to each other. For literary company he had the Abbï de Breme, a well-known figure on the Milanese literary scene whom he met only briefly – they would make closer acquaintance in Milan, where they exchanged much de Staël-related gossip – and Auguste Wilhelm von Schlegel, who had been tutor to Madame's children and was now a semi-permanent houseguest at Coppet, although after Madame de Staël's death in 1817 he became a professor at Bonn university. Schlegel, well-known in

German literary circles, had spent thirteen years translating Shakespeare into German. He was no doubt keen to engage an English poet in discussion on the subject of literature. Byron loved the theatre. His letters are peppered with quotations from plays, ranging from less well-known dramatists such as Thomas Otway to Shakespeare. His time on the Drury Lane Committee had given him hands-on knowledge of the mechanics of theatrical production. He had been a friend of Sheridan, and had just sent Douglas Kinnaird a dramatic poem on Sheridan's death, to be declaimed on the Drury Lane stage. So he must have had high expectations of his conversations with Schlegel. However, he was soon brought back to reality. Schlegel contradicted everything that was said to him, and Byron soon decided that he was a fool. He summed him up in verse as a man who would try the patience of a saint:

– the fellow Schlegel
Was very likely to inveigle
A dying person in compunction
To try the extremity of Unction.

At the end of July the Shelleys returned from their Alpine tour and the visits to Coppet were suspended as Shelley and Mary resumed the pattern of spending their evenings3 at the Villa Diodati. There was even a brief resumption of ghostly talk with a visit from Byron's friend "Monk" Lewis in the middle of August. Matthew Lewis was known as "Monk" because he was the author of a hugely popular Gothic sensation novel, *Ambrosio, or the Monk*. He had published it in 1794 and followed it with several other works in a similar vein, combining his literary career with stints as a diplomat and MP. He had recently returned from a tour of the estates in the West Indies which he had inherited on his father's death in 1815, and discussed with Byron, Shelley and Mary his concerns about the condition of the slaves there and his plans to improve their lives. While Lewis was at the Villa Byron and Shelley witnessed his will, which made provision for fairer treatment and better conditions for the slaves.

Inevitably, given their earlier discussions and the presence of a man who made a living writing about the supernatural, the conversation turned to ghosts. Shelley was surprised to find that neither Byron nor Lewis believed in ghosts; indeed both men were agreed "that none could believe in ghosts without also believing in God." Shelley no doubt argued vigorously against this view since, though he professed atheism, he was a great one for metaphysical speculation and was quite willing to believe in manifestations from the spirit world.

Polidori, no more comfortable with such conversations in August than he had been in June, again seems to have tried to turn the conversation to other topics. One ploy that he used was to persuade the party to listen to a tragic drama he had written (Probably *Ximenes, or the Modern Abraham*, which he asked John Murray to consider for publication in 1817). His self-delusion that two talented poets and, if Lewis was present, a successful author, would be interested in his play is breathtaking, but as Tom Moore says, "his ambition of distinction far outwent both his powers and opportunities of obtaining it." He was, says Moore, "in a constant hectic of vanity." The company must have known what to expect, since Byron "to lighten the infliction" volunteered to read it aloud. Moore, in what is probably an eye-witness account from Mary, says that they all did their best not to laugh, especially as Polidori was keeping a "jealous watch" on them, while Byron, making an effort to find something positive to say to the Doctor, could only come up with "I assure you, when I was on the Drury Lane Committee, worse things were offered to us." Faint praise indeed, given that Byron had found about five hundred manuscripts on the shelves at Drury Lane, not one of which he judged to be fit for production.

By now, the summer at the Villa Diodati was drawing to a close. Byron's friends Hobhouse and Scrope Davis were expected to arrive on 26th August, and the Shelleys were due to set out on their journey back to England on 29th. Byron gave Shelley a manuscript to deliver to John Murray: his new canto of *Childe Harold* and *The Prisoner of Chillon*. He repeated his promise to care for Claire's child, but refused to see Claire before she left. Indeed, in the brief overlap between Hobhouse's arrival and the Shelleys departure it was decided that, given the scandalous tales that had been reaching England from the hotels of Geneva, it would be best if no-one except Shelley visited the Villa. Thus the prim and proper Hobhouse was able to write to Lady Melbourne reassuring her that all was well with Byron:
"I am happy to be able to assure you that, in spite of all ridiculous rumours, none of its apartments receive any more disreputable guests than Mr M Lewis and myself. It is true that a neighbouring farm house did, until lately, give shelter to an establishment rather of a singular description, between whom and my friend malicious report assigned some small intimacy, but as I never saw either of the inmates… except a good-natured strange being, the son of one Sir Timothy Shelley, I really have no evidence to bring upon this scandalous topic.

First Venetian Interlude

I loved her from my boyhood ...

As he began his new life outside England, how much did Byron already know about the city where he was soon to make his home? Long years of war, and the sheer practical difficulties of travel, meant that few English visitors had experienced the reality of Venice. However, the English reading public had a clear, if not always accurate, picture of the Venetian lagoon, the city and its government thanks to popular literature.
In Canto IV of Childe Harold's *Pilgrimage Byron tells his readers that he, like them, has been reading about Venice since childhood, and names the authors whose works had created his personal mental map of beautiful, wealthy, decadent Venice:*

> I loved her from my boyhood; she to me
> Was as a fairy city of the heart,
> Rising like water columns from the sea,
> Of joy the sojourn, and of wealth the mart;
> And Otway, Radcliffe, Schiller, Shakespeare's art,
> Had stamped her image in me…

Five works of fiction – two novels, three works by two playwrights – had stamped an image of Venice in Byron's mind: Thomas Otway's play Venice Preserv'd, *Mrs Ann Radcliffe's novel* The Mysteries of Udolpho, *Schiller's* The Ghost Seer *and of course* Othello *and* The Merchant of Venice.

Mrs Radcliffe's hugely popular Gothic page-turner, The Mysteries of Udolpho, *was published in 1794 when Byron was eight years old and already a voracious reader (he later claimed to have read "above four thousand novels" by the time he reached nineteen). He was unlikely to find much to interest him in the endless romance between the one-dimensional hero, Valancourt and the tedious heroine, Emily, who spends so much time in tears that the reader suspects her of being permanently damp. However, the magnificent red-blooded villain, Count Montoni, would capture any boy's imagination. He rushes headlong through the novel's pages, at one moment planning to force Emily into marriage with a Venetian nobleman, at the next imprisoning his wife until she gives up her fortune to him, then leading a robber-band in the Apennines and finally coming to a bad end in the Venetian state prisons.*

Mrs Radcliffe never visited Venice and happily admitted that all her information about the city came from Mrs Hester Piozzi's account of life there in the mid-1780s. However, the novel's descriptions of the magnificent yet gloomy palazzi *lining the Grand Canal, gondola parties on the lagoon, the* passeggiata *in Piazza San Marco which began at midnight and continued until the small hours, clearly made a lasting impression on the young Byron. Indeed, his reflections upon the city more than twenty years after first reading the novel includes a close paraphrase of the novel. Mrs Radcliffe has Count Montoni and his party arrive in Venice during* carnevale, *and as Emily's gondola drifts past groups of masked dancers, accompanied by music "made sweeter by the waves over which it floated," the scene seems "almost to realise the romance of fairyland." Little wonder that the image fixed in Byron's mind was of "a fairy city of the heart."*

The poet pays the novelist the compliment of an even closer quotation. The first glimpse of Venice in The Mysteries of Udolpho *comes as the Count's party cross the lagoon at sunset. "As they glided on," Mrs Radcliffe writes, "the grander features of this city appeared more distinctly: its terraces, crowned with airy yet majestic fabrics, touched, as they now were, with the splendour of the setting sun, appeared as if they had been called up from the ocean by the wand of an enchanter, rather than reared by mortal hands." Byron opens* Childe Harold *Canto IV with this vision of the city:*

> I saw from out the wave her structures rise
> As from the stroke of the enchanter's wand.

Mrs Radcliffe no longer commands a wide readership, but not many authors are paid the double compliment of being praised by Byron and satirised by Jane Austen.

If The Mysteries of Udolpho *left young Byron wanting more Venetian Gothic, help was soon at hand in the form of Schiller's novel. It was first written in 1798 and published in instalments in a periodical magazine that Schiller was editing. An English translation entitled* The Ghost Seer *appeared almost immediately, with a second, more popular translation called* The Armenian *in 1800.*

Schiller claimed that he wrote The Ghost Seer *in order to explore the contrasting ideas and theories of Kant and Swedenborg. If that is the case, readers are left wondering what on earth he would have written had he set out with the intention of writing a breathless Gothic novel. The first part of the novel centres around the mysterious figure of the Armenian, first glimpsed in Piazza San Marco by a German Prince* and the nameless narrator who is a member of his retinue. Before disappearing he whispers a cryptic message to the Prince, which turns out to be a prophecy. A man of many guises, he reappears as a Russian officer at a séance and as the companion of a beautiful lady with whom the Prince believes himself to be in love. His true identity and purpose remain unknown. The second part of the novel is an epistolatory exploration of the Prince's Venetian "dissipations" – hinted at in a tantalising manner that would have held great appeal to schoolboy readers like Byron – and his search for a mysterious lady whom he has seen at prayer in the church of San Giorgio Maggiore. The book is purposely incomplete – Schiller had grown weary of it – and breaks off on a cliff-hanger as the Prince becomes a Roman Catholic, the Armenian once again at his side.

Byron told his publisher John Murray that The Ghost Seer "took a great hold of me when a boy," and the mysterious Venice of Schiller's imagination[5] stayed in his mind. The large community of Armenian merchants in Venice were no invention of Schiller, and it can be no coincidence that one of the first places Byron and Hobhouse visited whilst still playing the tourist in the first days after their arrival in the city was the island of San Lazzaro degli Armeni, where about seventy Armenian monks lived and worked. Byron even remembered the book as he was enjoying the delights of the passeggiata, the late evening stroll around Piazza San Marco. It is here that Schiller's Prince first meets the mysterious Armenian who gives him a cryptic message, "He died at nine o'clock" before disappearing into the crowds. Later, the Prince receives a message informing him that a relative who stood before him in the line of succession died at nine o'clock that night. Byron told Murray that "I never walked down St Mark's by moonlight without thinking of it & – "at nine o'clock he died!"

However, if Byron had hoped to emulate another episode from the novel, he would soon have found that this was no longer possible, thanks to his hero, Napoleon. One of the key episodes of The Ghost Seer finds the Prince and his entourage crossing by gondola to the island of San Giorgio Maggiore in order to see Paolo Veronese's magnificent Wedding At Cana, which imagines Jesus and his mother as guests at a wedding feast which bustles with Venetian life including Moors, Turks, dwarves and musicians, all of them almost life-size in a huge canvas which covers an entire wall of the monks' refectory. It is on this occasion that the Prince sees and falls in love with the mysterious lady. Byron could, of course, be rowed across to the island of San Giorgio, but he would find monks and painting gone, both by order of Napoleon. Veronese's masterpiece was now on display in the Louvre, having been sliced into portable segments so that the French could transport it more easily.[6]

"Shakespeare one gets acquainted with without knowing how. It is part of an Englishman's constitution," says Henry Crawford in Mansfield Park, published in 1814. Byron, who had an encyclopædic knowledge of the plays, would no doubt agree. The plays made up the core repertoire of city and provincial theatres, families read them aloud together, "we all talk Shakespeare, use his similes and describe with his descriptions." This was most certainly true of Byron, whose letters are peppered with quotations from and allusions to the plays.

Byron's Shakespearean education seems to have begun when, aged eight, he was taken to see The Taming of the Shrew in Aberdeen. The boy showed early evidence of his later passion for the theatre, joining in with the performance. In London in his early twenties he was a regular theatre-goer and made a point of seeing the plays of Shakespeare whenever they were performed. The future Drury Lane committee-man commented critically on what he saw, finding The Merry Wives of Windsor dull but enjoying the full-blooded acting of Edmund Kean. He saw Kean's Richard III three times, finding it "Life – nature – truth without exaggeration or diminution... Richard is a man; and Kean is Richard."

Of Shakespeare's two Venetian plays, Othello (which, despite being subtitled The Moor of Venice, is set mainly in Cyprus) seems to have made the strongest impression, if the number of allusions to the plays in Byron's letters are any guide. And from Shakespeare he would gain a rather more true-to-life image of Venice than from his other reading, since it is within the realms of possibility that Shakespeare visited Venice some time between 1585 and 1592. Shakespeare worked for noble patrons including the Earls of Southampton and Essex, so he may well have been given the opportunity to become a member of the entourage of an Elizabethan diplomatic mission to the city.

The Merchant of Venice focuses on the merchants, traders and moneylenders with businesses based in the bustling Rialto district, the rumours of lost cargoes and lost fortunes that swept the city daily as news and gossip were exchanged. Shakespeare has enough local knowledge to give two of the play's characters the name Gobbo, the Venetian term for a hunchback (and the popular name for the bent figure which supports the column in the square facing the church of San Giacomo di Rialto). He writes of the position of the Jews in Venice, confined to the island of the Ghetto, locked in at night behind gates patrolled by guards whose wages they had to pay.[7] He understands the government of Venice, and even has the Doge (whom he calls the Duke) preside over Shylock's trial, to which Portia comes disguised as a lawyer from Padua, where the university, then as now, was famed for its law degree.

The hero of Othello is a condottiere, a skilled mercenary of the kind often employed to command the armies of the Republic.[8] The siege and capture of Cyprus, which had been part of the Venetian Empire, by the

Turks took place in 1570, a mere thirty years before Shakespeare wrote his play. In choosing an outsider as his protagonist Shakespeare was reflecting the cosmopolitan nature of a city built on trade. Traders from every part of Europe and the counties of the Mediterranean were an everyday sight in Venice's streets. The Greeks had built their own Orthodox church, sailors from the Dalmatian coast were so commonplace that the embankment where their ships docked was known as Riva degli Schiavoni [Slavs]. The German trading-centre, the Fondaco dei Tedeschi, was decorated with frescoes by Titian and, despite the siege and loss of Cyprus, Turkish merchants were allowed to build their own fondaco *in 1621.*

Arriving in Venice, Byron visited the Rialto "for the sake of Shylock," and his letters show a constant awareness that he was living in a city peopled with Shakespearean character and incident. Shakespearean allusions always tripped effortlessly from his pen, but at this time Othello *and* The Merchant of Venice *were clearly uppermost in his thoughts. For example, he was approached by a man who had rented property to an Englishman who had since died, owing him money. Would Milord (who, being English, was clearly assumed to be acquainted with all other Englishmen) help him recover his money? Byron put this matter into Murray's hands with a witty reference to Shylock. "If you are acquainted with any dead man of the like name a good deal in debt – pray dig him up – and tell him that 'a pound of his fair flesh' or the ducats are required." Shakespearean references came so thick and fast that his friends tried to play him at his own game: to no avail. Writing to Douglas Kinnaird, who had obviously misused a quotation from* Othello, *Byron adopts the tone of a grumpy schoolmaster, "Your quotation from Shakespeare – humph – I believe that it was applied by* Othello to his *wife* – who by the way was *innocent – the Moor made a mistake – & so have you."*

When Byron wrote to John Murray in the spring of 1817 describing the literary sights of Venice, he claimed to "hate things all fiction & therefore the Merchant & Othello *– have no great associations to me – but Pierre has…" Pierre was the hero of Thomas Otway's 1682 play,* Venice Preserv'd, *based on a failed conspiracy of 1618 which aimed to overthrow the Doge and Senate and make Venice a province of Spain. Otway makes Pierre, whose historical counterpart was a French mercenary in the Venetian navy, into a witty, cynical fighter for liberty and individual freedom, exactly the sort of character Byron would find appealing.*

Otway's play struck a chord with the theatre-going public from its first performance, and it remained a popular repertory piece until the 1830s, its place as secure as a work by Shakespeare. Byron's interest in it probably sprang from his friendship with the playwright Richard Brinsley

Sheridan, who was also an MP with Radical sympathies between1780 and 1812. In October 1795 Sheridan staged Venice Preserv'd *at Drury Lane as a comment on his own times. Afraid that the ideals of the Revolutionary French Government, with which Britain was at war, would spread across the Channel, Pitt's Government had introduced a series of repressive laws intended to crush Radical opposition. Newspapers loyal to the Government accused Sheridan of inciting rebellion. Otway's play, which deals with a plot against a corrupt state and ends with a treason trial and execution, was simply too close to home.*[9]
At the first Drury Lane performance of Venice Preserv'd, *Pierre's speech condemning the Venetian Senate:*

> … to see our Senators
> Cheat the deluded people with a show
> Of liberty, which yet they ne'er must taste of.
> They say, by them our hands are free from fetters,
> Yet whom they please they lay in basest bonds;
> Bring whom they please to infamy and sorrow.

was greeted with prolonged applause. On the day of the production's third performance, a mob attacked George III's carriage when the King was on his way to open Parliament. The blame was laid at Sheridan's door, and Venice Preserv'd *was banned for seven years. Meanwhile Pitt's government took the opportunity to pass yet more repressive legislation.*
Byron, only seven years old in 1795 and living in Aberdeen, would have been unaware of all of this. However, when the young poet and the elderly playwright became friends in the years just before Byron's marriage, Sheridan would often reminisce. Byron's company "seemed to bring back his own youth and wit," and the two men shared not only Radical politics but also common interest in the Drury Lane Theatre. Sheridan, especially after a drink or two, enjoyed nothing more than gossiping and "quizzing" the famous, so what more natural than to tell his young friend of the time when he almost got one over on William Pitt?
*As he explored Venice and recalled his evenings with Sheridan – whose death was still fresh in his memory –*Venice Preserv'd *brought other, more unhappy memories to mind. The heroine of Otway's play is Belvidera, a noble lady disowned by her family for marrying a poor man. Her husband, Jaffeir, joins and later – at Belvidera's insistence – denounces Pierre's conspiracy. As Pierre is led to the scaffold Jaffeir stabs his friend, to spare him an ignoble death, and then himself. Belvidera goes mad and dies. Whatever his opinion of Pierre, Byron most certainly did not care for Belvidera, telling Murray, "I am aware of what you say of Otway – and am a very great admirer of his – all except that maudlin bitch of chaste lewdness & blubbering curiosity Belvidera – whom I utterly despise, abhor and detest."*

Belvidera is widely regarded as one of the first great female roles written for the stage. In Byron's own day Mrs Siddons played her to great acclaim. However, she obviously reminded Byron only too clearly of his wife. The thought of a rich man's daughter who suddenly finds herself short of money, who bewails her woes loudly and is always only too happy to tell her husband the right thing to do, was simply too close to the bone to be tolerated.

So what was Byron's mental map of Venice in 1816? He knew a great deal about how the Serenissima was governed: the Doge, powerless figurehead of a powerful state, the workings of the Senate and Great Council. However, like a modern reader whose knowledge of Italy comes mainly from novels about the mafia, he probably had a rather skewed picture of how power in the Serene Republic operated, since most of his reading-matter concerned itself with conspiracy, summary justice, poisoning and torture. He knew of the Venetian Empire which had once spread across the Mediterranean, of the mercenaries and condottieri *who had helped her keep hold of that power and of the huge wealth and influence which trade had given to the city until both Empire and Trade began to slip from Venice's grasp in the sixteenth and seventeenth centuries. He was aware of how she had re-created herself as pleasure capital of Europe with* carnevale*, courtesans and gambling, those oh-so-tempting dissipations at which Mrs Radcliffe and Schiller had hinted. In short, he had an image of Venice very similar to that of most of his contemporaries, that it was a glittering city of corruption and easy virtue. As he would soon discover, the reality of post-Napoleonic Venice was somewhat different.*

Chapter Two

1816: Thus Far on my Way to Venice

It did not become foreigners ignorant of the language to judge everybody in Italy.

On their arrival at the Villa Diodati, Hobhouse and Scrope Davis were greeted by a slender,[10] melancholy Byron. No doubt the arriv-al of friends from England, full of English news, brought back the full implications of his separation, which he had been able to push to the back of his mind during the Shelleys' time in Geneva. Scrope Davis wrote to Augusta that "they *found* him very gloomy." However, his spirits improved during his friends' stay. This was largely due to Hobhouse, who took one look at his friend and decided that what he clearly needed was taking out of himself with a few days in the fresh air. So on September 17th Byron and Hobhouse set out on a ten-day Alpine tour.

Byron had decided that he did not want to find Doctor Polidori at the Villa when he came back from his trip, as the Doctor's behaviour had clearly not improved since the Shelleys' departure, and Byron was weary of his constant tantrums. Boating on Lake Geneva, Polidori had managed to hit Byron's knee very hard with his oar and, rather than apologise, had remarked "I am glad to see that you can suffer pain." Enough was enough. Perhaps Byron had waited for Hobhouse to arrive out of concern that dismissing the Doctor would lead to a repeat of his earlier suicidal hysterics. However, on being told that it was time to part and given £ 70, Polidori took the news calmly – it can't have come as a surprise – and set off to walk across the Alps into Italy.

Byron kept a journal of his Alpine tour with Hobhouse which he later sent to Augusta. He was clearly in no mood to have his Romantic sensibilities overwhelmed by the beauties of nature. His comments include: "Arrived at the Grindelwald… very fine glacier;" "Got to Interlachen in three hours – pretty lake." Indeed, he told Augusta that he was unable to escape from his thoughts, "the recollections of bitterness… have preyed upon me here" so that he was never able "to lose my own wretched identity in the majesty and the power and the Glory – around –

above – & beneath me." Some images from the tour lodged in his mind, however, as he was to use them when he came to write *Manfred* early the following year.

Typically of Byron, the journal comes to life when he writes not about scenery, but about people. So he gives Augusta comic accounts of Hobhouse hitting his head against a door and blaming the door, and of the two of them falling down a steep slope and laughing like a pair of schoolboys. He is also much diverted by an English lady at Chamonix, sitting in the shadow of Mont Blanc and exclaiming " 'did you ever see anything more rural' – as if it were Highgate or Hampstead." There are gentle descriptions of ordinary people: several pretty girls, crossing a lake in a boat rowed by women – one of them also very pretty, and the villagers of Brientz enjoying a dance in the inn where he is spending the night.

During the tour Byron also bought a dog. The amazing thing was that he, a great animal-lover, had lasted so long without one since leaving England. He described the dog, Mutz ("Short-tail") as very ugly and very badly-behaved, but he planned that Mutz should be a guard-dog on the crossing into Italy, as there were rumours of bandits in the Simplon Pass. The badly-behaved Mutz accompanied Byron to Venice, where he learned to shut the door with his nose but, clearly finding the city a demi-paradise after his outdoor Swiss life, could never be persuaded to abandon his habit of stealing the kitchen joint.

Arriving back at the Villa Diodati by the end of September, it was time for more partings. Byron and Hobhouse were off into Italy, planning a brief stay at Milan and then on to Venice for the winter. At this stage, Byron still intended that his stay in Italy should be short-term, writing to Augusta and to his wife that he planned to be in England in the spring of 1817.

With the new term at Cambridge – and more importantly the racing season at Newmarket – about to begin, Scrope Davis set out for England, taking Robert Rushton with him. Like Fletcher, Rushton had been in Byron's service for a number of years, and had accompanied him and Hobhouse on the first part of their journey in 1809. He was always referred to as a "page", and this seems to trap him in perpetual adolescence. However, he was by now twenty years old and a married man. On his return to England he took up a post with Byron's friend James Wedderburn Webster.

Before leaving the Villa for the last time, Byron, family matters clearly on his mind, sent several letters to Augusta, and received one back. He had a great deal to tell her. First of all, he wanted her to know that he had sent various geological specimens with Scrope Davis as gifts for her daughters, especially his favourite niece, Georgiana, and for his own daughter Ada: geology was much in vogue in the late eighteenth and early nineteenth centuries and, since its use as a weapon by both sides in the Evolution debate was still some years in the future, collecting and organising geological samples was regarded as a suitable interest for young ladies.

Second, the manuscript he had sent with Shelley for delivery to John Murray had contained a poem dedicated to Augusta, with the proviso that she should read it and could, if she wished, veto its publication. Augusta now wrote to say that she did not wish the poem to be published. She had somehow been persuaded by Lady Byron to forward all the letters she received from her brother and (after making copies to bolster her personal conviction that the two of them had once indulged in "improper" behaviour, and even passing them around her own close friends so that they could enjoy a frisson of pleasurable disapproval over the intimate and affectionate terms in which Byron addressed his sister), that lady offered reams of good advice about how she should word her replies. Lady Byron felt that it would be wrong for Augusta to allow the poem to be published, as it would only encourage readers to believe the rumours (spread by Lady Byron's own associates) that their relationship had been more than fraternal.

So, as a result of his wife's jealousy and meddling, Byron's beautiful poem To Augusta was not published in his lifetime. In it he gives thanks for her love and devotion. She had remained constant when others (and Lady Byron would have known where this barb was directed: Augusta had stayed at Piccadilly Terrace during Byron's mental breakdown while his wife hurriedly left) did not. The poem ends:

For thee, my own sweet sister, in thy heart
I know myself secure, as thou in mine;
We were and are – I am, even as thou art –
Beings who ne'er each other can resign;
It is the same, together or apart,
From life's commencement to its slow decline
We are entwined – let death come slow or fast,
The tie which bound the first endures the last!

Byron was well aware where the responsibility for Augusta's decision regarding the poem lay; and he now made his own retaliatory move in the ongoing game of chess, conducted by intermediary and letter, that was to be his relationship with his wife for the remainder of his life. He had heard, he told Augusta, that Lady Byron, who had been ill, was planning to winter abroad. Augusta was to convey in the strongest terms that Ada was not to be taken out of England. (He was probably aware that his wife would not need to be told but would read the letter herself). The implied threat to Lady Byron was that Byron (who had every right to do so under English law at that time) would claim custody of his daughter. Byron's own reasoning was that he did not wish his daughter's health or safety to be put at risk on a continent just beginning to recover from almost 30 years of war and already in the grip of food shortages: she was after all still less than a year old. It has been suggested, however, that he did not want Ada's mother to seek refuge in a country, France for example, whose legal system gave greater maternal rights of custody than could be claimed in England. In response, Lady Byron had Ada made a Ward in Chancery: now she could not be taken out of England without the Lord Chancellor's permission – by either parent.

Byron and Hobhouse left the Villa Diodati on 6th October. The bandits in the Simplon Pass proved to be a damp squib – although their driver had been most careful to stop and solemnly point out the spot where a party of English travellers had been robbed. Crossing the Alps had long been regarded as a risky business. Eighteenth century travellers had often preferred a complicated land and sea voyage to the expense and trouble of dismantling their carriages to be packed onto sleds or carts for the journey from Switzerland to Italy. Napoleon, however, refused to allow the Alps to stand in the way of the rapid troop movements upon which he depended. In 1801 he commanded that a road suitable for heavy artillery should be built across the Simplon. Four years later it was completed. Byron and Hobhouse were among the first post-war travellers to make the journey in the comfort of a private carriage. They arrived safely in Milan a mere six days after leaving the villa.

Hobhouse clearly regarded their Milanese hotel as very second-rate, and was still complaining when he went to bed, his temper not improved by the quality of his dinner. Byron, still in the grip of his lowering diet, took only tea.

Next morning, at breakfast, a visitor was announced: Doctor Polidori. So thick-skinned that he found nothing awkward in meeting his ex-employer again so soon, and so self-important that he listed the cream of Milanese literary society, whom he met solely through Byron's good offices, as "friends and acquaintances' in his diary, Polidori at least proved useful over the next few days as Byron and Hobhouse, not yet fluent in Italian, explored the city, although he would soon display his usual knack of getting himself into trouble.

Milan was Byron's first experience of an Italian city, and he loved it. Under Napoleon it had been the capital of the Kingdom of Italy and the Viceroy, Napoleon's stepson Eugene Beauharnais, had held court here. The Milanese had greatly enjoyed the glitter and self-importance. Now, lumped with the rest of northern Italy into a mere province and cash-cow of the Austrian Empire, they felt betrayed. As Byron and Hobhouse met members of Milanese society, they found that their own political views were widely admired. They were able to expound at length upon their dislike of the way Europe had been divided among the victors at the Congress of Vienna, and their hatred of the present English Tory Government. In return, Hobhouse learned that, had Napoleon entered Italy as an Italian[11] and a liberator, he would have been welcomed with open arms. As it was, the Milanese had no desire to be a mere province of France, and even less to be a province of the hated Austrian Empire: Hobhouse heard numerous anecdotes of thuggish and rude Austrian officials. A Count who applied for a passport to travel to Rome (the Austrians were notoriously reluctant to allow their subjects to travel lest they discover revolutionary ideas) was granted one by the Governor only if he promised not to visit any foreign embassies. On being told that this gave the impression that the rulers were afraid of their subjects, the Governor replied "we have got you now and we will keep you under."

It was probably in Milan that Byron first heard of the Carbonari, the secret society mostly made up of ordinary working men (the name means "Charcoal Burners") working for Italian freedom. During his stay in Milan, discussions about the Carbonari focussed on rumours of a revolt fermenting in the town of Macerata in the Papal States. The revolt eventually broke out in June 1817 but was crushed by papal troops. If whispers of the Carbonari were not enough to get Byron's radical juices and sympathies for the underdog flowing, in Milan he also met two Greeks, one a student at Padua University, the other at Pisa, who talked of their plans to return to Greece and work for its liberation from the Ottoman Empire. This cause was close to the hearts of both Byron and Hobhouse ever since their travels there in 1809. So the seeds of the future lives of both these young men were already sown as they spent a pleasant autumn in Milan: John Cam Hobhouse, MP, would one day be a leading member of the Greek Committee, based in London, which raised funds for the liberation of Greece. Byron, when living in Ravenna in 1820, gave a list of the gentlemen's clubs to which he belonged including: Watier's (the dandy's club, presided over by Brummell), the Cambridge Whig Club, the Harrow Club, "and to the Italian Carbonari... though last, not least." His sacrifice in the Greek cause is too well-known to require any description here.

But all that was far in the future, and now it was time to play the tourist. Byron rarely suffered from melancholy when Hobhouse was with him, probably because he never had the time. The coming days were filled with visits to "Churches, Theatres, libraries and picture galleries" Byron admired the cathedral, and was much taken with the remains of an incomplete triumphal arch intended to honour Napoleon, which he found positively Roman in its glorious ruin. He much preferred the works of art in the Brera gallery to the "daubs" he had seen in Antwerp, and remarked that the gallery had "some fine pictures". Had he known that a number of these fine pictures had been looted from Venice by the French specifically to beautify Eugene's viceregal court, he might have reacted differently.

On a visit to the Ambrosian Library, a treasure-house of medieval manuscripts, Byron fell a little in love. While Hobhouse was engaged in a political discussion with the librarian, who told him it was a good thing the manuscripts were not catalogued, as then the French would have known what to take,[12] Byron happened upon a collection of letters between Lucrezia Borgia and the poet and churchman Pietro Bembo. Byron found the letters delightful and, although at the time of writing Lucrezia was the wife of the Duke of Ferrara and Bembo was a Cardinal, he was convinced that they were love-letters. He tried to have copies made, but this wasn't allowed, so he made a number of visits until he had learned several of them by heart. He also saw a lock of Lucrezia's hair which, he decided, was so beautiful that he had to have some. Whether by charm, good luck or sleight of hand, he was able to boast to Tom Moore that he had taken a single hair as a memento, "I stick to the Pope's daughter, and wish myself a cardinal."

Byron and Hobhouse also made a number of visits to La Scala. They found the theatre magnificent, but soon discovered that it was a place one visited in order to be seen rather than to see. It was fashionable to move from box to box exchanging gossip, usually about the occupants of other boxes, some of which kept their curtains closed all evening – it was commonplace elsewhere in Europe to open them at least for the ballet and the important arias – and Hobhouse remarked that, because the Mila-

nese went to the theatre and opera merely to socialise, the same piece was frequently given nightly for months on end and no-one noticed.
Indeed, it was at La Scala that Byron and Hobhouse's introduction into the world of Milanese literature began, since on their first evening the Abbé di Breme, to whom Byron had been introduced by Madame de Stäel, came into their box. They enjoyed a long conversation and a few days later di Breme invited them to dinner where they met several leading figures of the Milanese literary world. They were welcomed with enthusiasm; Byron as one of Europe's leading poets, Hobhouse as the author of an eye-witness account of events in Paris between Napoleon's escape from Elba and the battle of Waterloo.[13] However, any expectations of breathing a more refined air and enjoying serious discussions about the great figures of Italian literature were, as at Coppet, soon disappointed: everyone they met could not wait to be alone with their English guests in order to gossip and dish the dirt about each other. Byron would find nothing unusual about this. In his youthful satire English Bards & Scotch Reviewers, published in 1809, he had been quite vituperative about almost all of his contemporaries, even some who later became close friends, like Tom Moore. He later regretted the poem and wished he had only said what he thought, not published it. However, his contempt for the Poet Laureate, Robert Southey, was soon to reach fever-pitch – Southey was spreading malicious gossip in London about the alleged goings – on at the Villa Diodati. The savagely witty dedication to Southey of Canto I of *Don Juan* would be Byron's revenge.
However, in Milan, a typical encounter ran thus: on 16th October di Breme introduced Byron and Hobhouse to the poet and translator Vincenzo Monti, whom Hobhouse in particular greatly admired, regarding him as the premier Italian poet of his day. Monti took the opportunity to harangue his English guests about the poor state of Italian verse, and when he was gone di Breme felt the urge to tell them that the poor old soul (he was 72) was a shadow of his former self and would turn his coat for a gold snuff-box (having spoken out against the French Revolution, he had later supported Napoleon and now praised the Austrians). On another occasion, Monti proclaimed his hatred of Ugo Foscolo. Foscolo, after living in Venice for many years, had burst upon the Italian literary scene in 1802 at the age of twenty-four with the publication of his epistolatory novel *The Last Letters of Jacopo Ortis,* featuring a fashionably suicidal hero. After serving in the army of his hero Napoleon in both Italy and France Foscolo had written an open letter to the Emperor urging

him to establish a free and united Italy. He had left Milan when it became an Austrian possession and was living as an exile in London.

Foscolo and Hobhouse were to meet in London in 1818 where Foscolo, widely regarded in the capital as "another Byron, come from Italy in exchange" was making an impact in Society. Byron had asked Hobhouse to produce a companion volume of Notes to Canto IV of *Childe Harold's Pilgrimage*. At Hobhouse's request, Foscolo wrote a chapter about modern Italian literature in which he took the opportunity to write a glowing biography of himself while settling a few old scores in print with his erstwhile Italian colleagues. Foscolo, probably wisely, insisted on anonymity, and the chapter was published under Hobhouse's name.[14] As a result Byron, living in Venice and completely oblivious to what Hobhouse and Foscolo were up to, received several rude letters from Milan.

It was in di Breme's opera box that Byron and Hobhouse met an as-yet unknown literary figure who interested the two of them far more than the Milanese literary set. This was Marie-Henri de Beyle, better-known by his pen-name of Stendhal. De Beyle, still a literary unknown, had a far greater claim to fame in the eyes of Byron and Hobhouse: he had been secretary to Napoleon and with him on the Moscow Campaign. They listened avidly to his stories of Napoleon; how in his depression during the retreat from Moscow he had signed decrees in the name of the Roman general Pompey the Great; of the army, decimated by dysentery and extreme cold. Despite his unprepossessing appearance: Hobhouse called him "a little fat whiskered man," while to Polidori he was "a fat lascivious man," they were predisposed to like him due to his personal knowledge of their hero.

De Beyle, however, proved to be a false friend to Byron. Although originally complimentary, describing Byron as a "handsome and charming young man… [with] the sweetest manner," he deliberately misinterpreted Byron's relationship with Polidori, a mere travelling companion by the time of the meeting with de Beyle, yet described by him as "an excellent pimp, an Italian doctor." No doubt de Beyle intended to lead his friends to believe that he was associating with the womanising roué of Byronic legend. In his later writings, de Beyle managed to imply that Byron regarded him as a literary equal, rather than simply being interested in his memories of Napoleon. On the slender basis of a handful of meetings in Milan he kept up a long-term yet two-faced correspondence with Byron, so that as late as 1823 he could write "When I first read *Parisina* my soul was stirred for a week", whilst telling another correspondent that "verses bore me," and making bitchy remarks about Teresa Guiccoli, whom he never met. Byron was lucky to escape with a short acquaintance.

Doctor Polidori remained a frequent companion of Byron and Hobhouse for much of their stay in Milan. Hobhouse, who had spent little time in close proximity to him before now, soon got the measure of the good doctor. One day Polidori turned up full of a scheme to become personal physician to Caroline, Princess of Wales, the estranged wife of the Prince Regent, who was living in Italy at that time. He asked Hobhouse to write him a letter of recommendation to the Princess. Hobhouse, like many of his contemporaries, was a supporter of that Lady. The general feeling was that she had been badly treated and humiliated by her husband, who had paraded his mistresses before her. Now Hobhouse recorded in his sympathy for the princess as a prospective employer of Doctor Polidori with the pithy comment in his diary, "poor thing, she must be mad."

It is possible that Polidori, present at a number of literary dinners and soirées, had again behaved as badly as at the Villa Diodati, when he had interrupted Byron and Shelley's metaphysical discussions with attention-seeking behaviour. There is certainly evidence that he found some of Byron's conversations, especially with the Abbé di Breme, just as disturbing as those at Diodati. Hobhouse's diary records one such evening, when di Breme, a Roman Catholic priest, spoke of his doubts about the reality of miracles, and Byron remarked that, personally, he could commit to neither Christianity nor atheism. In *Ernestus Berchtold,* his jolly tale of incest and sorcery, much of which is set in Milan, Polidori describes his hero Ernestus listening to similar conversations, "I heard the deist and the atheist contend," and undergoing a crisis of faith (Polidori, like Ernestus, was a Roman Catholic); "Night after night upon my sleepless couch, I called upon the God, whose existence I doubted, to visit me."

Certainly Polidori's behaviour was about to provoke a genuine crisis. One evening at La Scala, he was sitting in the pit when a party of Austrian soldiers came and sat down in the row in front, their tall caps blocking his view of the stage. Being Polidori he was patently oblivious to their swagger and either forgot or chose to ignore the fact that soldiers always behaved as they liked – and carried arms. So, after making loud remarks in Italian about people who wore hats indoors, Polidori asked the soldier to take his cap off. Asked to go outside, he thought he was being offered out in a duel, but instead was taken to the guardroom, arrested and abused "in Billingsgate German."

Byron, who was in di Breme's box, was sent for and gave his name and card. This enabled Polidori to be released on bail (and probably spared a beating). Next day however, despite Byron making a personal visit to the Governor, Polidori was given twenty-four hours to leave Milan, which he did "with rage and grief so struggling in my breast… and all I could think of was revenge against Swarrow [the Governor, Count Saurau] and the officer in particular." Hobhouse sums up the affair with the laconic "I could not help thinking Polidori must have been talking foolishly in public somewhere." Byron prophetically remarked "someone or other will probably transfer his adventures to me," which is precisely what happened the next time Doctor Polidori appeared on the scene: in print, rather than in person.

Three days later Byron and Hobhouse also set out from Milan, but in the opposite direction: Polidori was heading to Florence, while Byron was "thus far on my way to Venice." Neither of the friends was in a hurry. The pleasant autumn weather was a welcome antidote to the cold wet summer, so they meandered across the northern Italian plain taking in the sights. As they approached Lake Garda they suffered the inevitable hold-up of any journey with Byron, carriage trouble, which prevented them from seeing as much of the lake as they had hoped. However, as they crossed Austrian territory the after-effects of the war and the current impact of Austrian taxation were plain to see in the wretched and starving peasantry; that evening the owner of the inn where they stayed told them of the high taxes levied by the Austrians and the number of working people trying to emigrate as a result. They would find more evidence of the impact the Austrians were having on their newly-acquired "Province of Lombardy-Venetia" when they reached Venice itself.

Before that, however, it was time for a Shakespearian interlude: Two Gentlemen in Verona. Luckily, this time Hobhouse was happy with the hotel and with the quality of his dinner, so once again they gave themselves up to sightseeing in a town which seems to have presented itself to visitors two hundred years ago much as it does today. The Roman Arena in the centre of the town was even then used as an open-air theatre in the summer months, although the winter entertainments were earthier: forty years earlier a bullfight had been put on in honour of the Austrian Emperor Joseph II, while Byron and Hobhouse narrowly missed the chance to see trained dogs besieging a castle.[15]

Although Byron enjoyed seeing the Arena, describing it as "superb – and in high preservation" he was most interested in the town's links with Shakespeare. The original story of Giulietta and Romeo takes place in Siena; however Matteo Bandello's novel of 1554, which was Shakespeare's main source, lays the scene in Verona. By the late eighteenth century, Shakespeare's Europe-wide popularity led to attempts to anchor the story in history: medieval political factions, the Montecchi and Capelletti, were claimed as the original Montagues and Capulets. Add to this the visits of generations of grand tourists on the look-out for Shakespearian locations and the result was that the townspeople of Verona were more than happy to show Juliet's tomb to visitors. Byron was intrigued that "Of the *truth* of the story they seem very tenacious." He visited Juliet's tomb, and was pleased to find it in a lonely and neglected spot, not scrubbed up for the visitor, which he found appropriate for so sad a story. The man who had written his name in the dungeon at Chillon could not resist removing a few loose pieces from the tomb, which he sent as souvenirs for Augusta's daughters and Ada. It is interesting to note that the popular modern tourist attraction "Juliet's balcony," is a much later addition, dating back only to 1936. Perhaps visitors to the city in the early nineteenth century, under the influence of the Romantic Movement, preferred to visit the tomb to muse upon love and death. The balcony, hinting at a night of passion, was more problematic at a time when morals were being tightened and texts bowdlerised.[16]

Next day Byron and Hobhouse set out for Vicenza, famed as the prosperous centre of the Italian silk-trade. However, the cold, wet spring and summer had destroyed the mulberry crop, leaving 10,000 people out of work, many of them begging on the streets. Once again, Hobhouse heard stories of the Austrian neglect of their new province; in a few days he and Byron would see for themselves the full impact of that neglect on Venice.

Vicenza's European fame was as the home and workshop of the celebrated 16th century architect, Andrea Palladio. Palladio's classical style was widely-admired in England, although English architects and returning grand tourists were clearly unaware that the marble rotundas, wide salons and pillared loggias, ideal for sunny Italy, would be so ill-suited to the damp English landscape. Society gentlemen like Byron and Hobhouse had endured many chilly house-parties in "Palladian" mansions, and so they were keen to experience the real thing in its natural surroundings. In common with many modern visitors, the friends were disappointed at how difficult it was to admire Palladio's architecture in Palladio's own city. One thing which did not disappoint, however, was the Teatro Olimpico. This magnificent auditorium, designed by Palladio in deliberately "antique" style, still has in situ the marble proscenium and perspective stage-sets installed for the opening performance of Sophocles' Oedipus Rex on March 3rd 1585. The wooden banks of seats, curving sharply up in a semi-circle, give the building an excellent acoustic, which Byron tested from the stage. He spoke two pieces from memory, both no doubt brought to his mind by his antique surroundings. One was from Euripides' Phoenician Women, a kind of sequel to Sophocles' Oedipus and featuring a number of the same characters. The speech Byron recited is by Creon, the uncle of Oedipus, who has just learned that the only way to save the city of Thebes from attack and annihilation is to make a sacrifice of his son. He refuses, saying:

> *Why, what could one say? 'Tis clear what my words must be. For I will never plunge myself so deeply into misfortune as to devote my son to death for the city; for love of children binds all men to life, and none would resign his own son to die. Let no man praise me into slaying my children. I am ready to die myself – for I am ripe in years – to set my country free.*

Having received a classical education at Harrow, where the masters taught almost exclusively in Latin and Ancient Greek, Byron (a fluent speaker of Modern Greek) probably recited this speech in the original language. He undoubtedly spoke his second piece in Latin, because he knew it by heart from his time at Harrow. It is a speech from Virgil's *Æneid*, involving Turnus, a prince who has just learned that Latinus, who had promised his daughter in marriage to Turnus, has broken his word and betrothed her to Æneas instead. On Speech Day at Harrow in 1804, a fellow-pupil, Robert Peel (the future Prime Minister) had spoken the part of Turnus with the 16 year-old Byron as Latinus.

> *But let the potent orator declaim,*
> *And with the brand of coward blot my name;*
> *Free leave is giv'n him, when his fatal hand*
> *Has cover'd with more corps the sanguine strand,*
> *And high as mine his tow'ring trophies stand.*

Speaking extempore and with only Hobhouse as an audience, Byron recited two pieces about sacrifice and freedom.

Second Venetian Interlude

In Venice Tasso's echoes are no more ...

In 1807 a nineteen year-old student at Trinity College, Cambridge, compiled a Reading List*, running to several pages, of works of poetry, history and the liberal arts which he claimed to "have perused in the original, or Translations," along with "above four thousand novels." He added that he had read most of them before he left Harrow, as since arriving at university he had largely given himself up to poetry and women. The student was, of course, Byron. If he had truly read everything on the list he would indeed be a prodigy, many of the authors he mentions are barely known to the modern educated reader, among them an Italian poet whose work struck a chord with Byron, Torquato Tasso. When Byron compiled his* Reading List *Tasso had enjoyed huge popularity across Europe for more than two hundred years. He was born in Sorrento in 1544, travelled widely around both Italy and France, and for a number of years was poet at the court of the Duke of Ferrara. His most popular work, in his lifetime and afterwards, was* Gerusalemme Liberata*, or Jerusalem Delivered, completed when he was thirty-one.* Gerusalemme *is a sprawling epic, ostensibly an historical work set in the crusades, but packed with witchcraft, romance and fantasy. Together with its near-contemporary, Ariosto's* Orlando Furioso*, it was* The Lord of the Rings *of the age.*

The poem inspired a number of composers: by Byron's time Salieri, Gluck, Haydn and – Byron's favourite – Rossini were just some of those who had used it as a source, usually focussing on the sub-plot of the witch Armida and her conversion to Christianity through the love of a good man.[17] *Love poems and ballads from* Gerusalemme *were the popular songs of the time and, when they reached Venice, proved an instant hit with the gondoliers. The verses were soon adapted into the local dialect of Venexiano and fitted to the traditional barcarole, which the gondoliers sang to help them keep a steady rhythm when rowing. To non-Italians the barcarole sounded "an odd sort of tune," but everyone who wrote about Venetian life in the eighteenth century referred to gondoliers singing Tasso. It became almost a shorthand for Venice, whether to Venetians such as Goldoni, who knows he is back home after a theatrical tour of the* terraferma *when the gondolier rowing him across the lagoon sings a ballad from* Gerusalemme*, or to authors creating an atmosphere. In* The Ghost Seer *Schiller soon establishes a Venetian* *ambience simply by describing gondoliers singing Tasso.*

A cultured visitor arrived in Venice with the expectation of hearing Tasso. The absence of song, the eerie silence of an oppressed people, was a shock to Byron when he arrived and found that "Tasso's echoes are no more." Tasso's absence made an impact on Byron during his first Venetian winter, and in the spring of 1817, passing through Ferrara on his way to meet Hobhouse in Rome, he decided to seek Tasso out. In the Library at Ferrara he read Tasso's letters, but what moved him most was a visit to Tasso's cell in the Hospital of Santa Anna. Tasso was confined here for six years from 1579 following a severe mental breakdown which had led him to insult the Duke of Ferrara and, even worse, he may have publicly declared his love for the Duke's sister, Leonora.

Across the centuries, Byron recognised a fellow-sufferer. His own mental state had been fragile ever since his breakdown in 1815, which had helped to bring about the Separation. He had recently told Tom Moore that, despite the benefits of his lowering diet, there had been many times when he "would have blown my brains out, but for the recollection that it would have given pleasure to my mother-in-law." He had experienced his first damp and gloomy Venetian winter, guaranteed to lower the spirits,[18] *and had suffered what he described as a "low fever", which kept him awake at night for several weeks. Within days of visiting Tasso's cell he created his own response to the poet's plight,* The Lament of Tasso.

The Lament *is written in the first person. Languishing in his cell*

> Which nothing through its bars admits, save day,

Tasso speaks of his sadness in finishing Gerusalemme. *Writing it had helped him escape from his despair. The epic had become like a child to its creator, but*

> Thou too art ended - what is left me now?
> For I have anguish left to bear – and how?

He also recalls his love for Leonora, which brought him to the cell,

> That thou wert beautiful, and I not blind,
> Hath been the sin which shuts me from mankind.

As the poem progresses, Tasso seems more and more to speak with Byron's own voice, as he recalls the solitary boy, like Byron at Harrow, who escaped from taunts and blows (in his early years at Harrow Byron suffered a great deal of bullying due to his lameness and his Scots accent) and "dream'd uncounted hours." Byron and Tasso are both aware of "sickness of heart" and Tasso, like Byron, contemplates dashing out his brains. The poem ends with Tasso prophesying that his cell will be remembered when the Duke's feasts and revels are long forgotten.

Gerusalemme, *published while Tasso was in his cell, was an instant success, yet the author never earned a penny from it. Released in 1586, he wandered through Italy, restless, melancholy and poverty-stricken, until in 1594 Pope Clement VIII invited him to come to Rome and be cared for. He died in the monastery of S. Onofrio, on the Janiculum Hill, the following year. The withered trunk of Tasso's Oak, under which he is supposed to have sat musing upon the past, is still visible today, as is his tomb in the peaceful church nearby. Byron, riding around the hills of Rome during a brief visit in the spring of 1817, was inspired to return to the subject of Tasso in Canto IV of* Childe Harold's Pilgrimage. *This time, however, he focussed on the Duke of Ferrara, Alfonso D'Este. Byron laid the blame for Tasso's confinement at the Duke's door, picking up the theme which threads its way through the entire canto: tyranny:*

> Alfonso! How thy ducal pageants shrink
> From thee! If in another station born,
> Scarce fit to be the slave of him thou mad'st to mourn.
>
> Thou! form'd to eat, and be despised, and die,
> Even as the beasts that perish, save that thou
> Had'st a more splendid trough and wider sty.

Chapter Three

The most oppressed people in Europe

"The Suabian sued, and now an Austrian reigns –
An Emperor tramples where an Emperor knelt."[19]

On 10th November 1816, Byron and Hobhouse reached the port of Mestre. As darkness fell, they climbed into a gondola and were rowed three miles across the lagoon to Venice. Coming down the Grand Canal, they knew they had truly arrived when they passed under a bridge and heard the cry "Rialto". Within minutes they had disembarked and were taking tea with their English-speaking host at the Hotel Gran Bretagna.[20]

Next day, as they began to explore the city, what would they find? A place very different to the city experienced by pleasure-seeking Grand Tourists before the French Wars put a stop to European travel, and also very different to the Venice of today. It is time for a brief explanation of how the events of the past twenty years had affected the city.

On 1st May 1797, the reign of the Most Serene Republic of Venice, *La Serenissima*, the queen of the Adriatic for over 1,300 years, came to an inglorious end. The rulers of the city, the Doge and Council, surrendered the city to a French army, commanded by Napoleon, which already occupied Venice's mainland provinces, the *Terraferma*. Although a servant of Republican France might well be expected to respect and honour such a long-lived Republic as Venice, Napoleon reportedly loathed all that Venice stood for, regarding the Doge and Council as oppressors of the Venetian people. Since at this time he came no nearer to the city than the villa of the final Doge, Ludovico Manin, in Fruili, he did not have the opportunity to learn the error of his ways by hearing the ordinary citizens of Venice protest about the end of their Republic, chanting "Viva San Marco" even as their French "liberators" erected a "Tree of Liberty" in the Piazza. Ugo Foscolo, then eighteen years old and filled with Revolutionary zeal, was one of those who danced around the tree. When the French established a governing council, Foscolo became a secretary. His speeches were reportedly models of Revolutionary ardour.

Venice did not remain long under French control on this occasion. In October 1797 Napoleon, in a hurry to return to Paris where his political rivals were jockeying for position, handed it and the *Terraferma* provinces over to Austria at the Treaty of Campoformio. Venice, now a prize in the game of Napoleonic "pass the parcel" which was gripping Europe, was set to change hands on two further occasions over the next eighteen years.

However, before handing Venice to the Austrians, French troops did all they could to ensure that their allies did not acquire too great a prize. Ships under construction in the Arsenale dockyards were destroyed and the dockyards themselves were damaged. The Rev. John Eustace, who visited Venice in 1801 as tutor to three young English gentlemen, reported that:

"The arsenal, occupying an entire island, and fortified not only by its ramparts, but by the surrounding sea, is spacious, commodious and even magnificent... In short, nothing is wanting to make this celebrated arsenal perhaps the first in Europe; excepting that for which all arsenals are built, *stores* and *shipping*; and these the French in their late invasion either plundered or destroyed."

There was, no doubt, a strategic reason for the destruction of the Arsenale. There was no reason apart from greed and petty vandalism for the other French actions: paintings by artists such as Bellini, Tiziano and Tintoretto were looted and carried off to France, so that the French people could be rewarded for their sacrifices not only by military victories but with the charm of art and statuary. The Doge's ceremonial barge, the Bucintoro, in which he had been rowed annually into the lagoon to conduct the Republic's marriage to the sea was, in a symbol of Venice's new subject status, taken to the Arsenale and stripped of all its gilding and finery. The hull was put into immediate use as a prison-ship. When Byron arrived in the city almost twenty years later he noted that it was still in the Arsenale, *rotting, unrestored*. Meanwhile, the French used the main body of the boat in a pyrotechnic display intended to show the disheartened populace who was now master in Venice: it was towed into the *bacino* where it was set alight and burned for three days.

Troops used cornices and frescoes for target-practice. As a final insult, the four horses of San Marco, which had looked proudly over the Piazza since the 13th century, were taken to Paris and installed on Napoleon's new Arc de Triomphe, "where they remain a monument to the treachery of French friendship," the Rev Eustace noted, adding:

"It is difficult to conceive any motive, except an innate propensity for mischief, which could have prompted them [the French] to disfigure the buildings and statues, to break the marble stairs by rolling cannon-balls down them, and to dismantle the *Bucentaur*, the famous state galley of the republic. Highwaymen have been known to spare or restore a seal, a ring, a trinket, to indulge the whim or the feelings of the owner; and robbers and housebreakers refrain from damaging furniture which they cannot carry away… Yet such is the peculiar cast of this people, whose armies at Venice, in every town in Italy, and indeed in every country they have over-run, have uniformly added insult to rapacity, and have wounded the feelings, while they plundered the property, of the miserable inhabitants."

Venice now "enjoyed" a brief period as part of the Austrian Empire until 1806. The arrival of General von Wallis in February 1798 must have brought home to any remaining doubters that the Republic was truly a thing of the past: Venice was simply another province of the Austrian Empire, and all citizens were required to give an oath of allegiance to the Emperor at Mass on 25th February. The Austrians insisted that all Venetians convert their cash and savings into the Imperial currency. This caused a run on the banks and the price of basic foods (which were already scarce because of the war) rose. This in turn caused a great deal of sickness. Things did not begin to improve until 1799.

A conclave of Cardinals which met in Venice in the winter of 1799-1800 to choose a new Pope may have helped briefly divert Venetian minds from their subject status and poverty. Pius VI died in France in October 1799, a prisoner after refusing to give up his role as ruler of the Papal States to the French, who were occupying Rome. Opinion among the cardinals was that the French would interfere in any election held in Rome, so they chose Venice, where the Emperor had promised both freedom and safety. Thus the election of Pius VII was announced from San Giorgio Maggiore on 14th March 1800.

The remaining years of Austrian rule were marked by the constant crossing and re-crossing of the *Terraferma* provinces by Austrian armies on their way to fight Napoleon who, after inflicting a massive defeat on a combined Austrian and Russian army at Austerlitz in 1805, claimed all of Italy as part of his Empire. Thus in January 1806 the French returned to Venice. This time they would remain until 1814.

Napoleon, Emperor since 1804,[21] appointed Josephine's son, Eugene Beauharnais, Viceroy of Italy. Eugene made Milan his capital and the administrative centre of Italy, Napoleon having made it perfectly clear that top jobs were always to be given to Frenchmen, never to Italians. Venice was reduced to the status of a mere provincial centre. Insult was added to injury when Eugene decorated his court with many looted art treasures, the same ones that Byron was to see in the Brera Gallery in Milan in 1816.[22]

The French administrators now had time to make serious decisions which would have a long-term impact on Venice. Some were made with the best intentions. Having, as they believed, dragged Venice into the nineteenth century politically, they now took the opportunity to try to do the same thing architecturally. For example, plans were drawn up to further beautify Piazza San Marco, described by Napoleon as "the finest drawing-room in Europe." The Procuratie Nuove, on the south side of the Piazza, which had been the administrative offices of the Venetian Republic, was converted into a Royal Palace in preparation for the Emperor's visit in 1807. It was felt that the Emperor might like a view of the *bacino,* so a fourteenth century granary was demolished and the small Giardini Reale was created. No-one is gifted with foresight: in the years of food-shortage that lay ahead, a granary would have been of far more benefit to the people of Venice than a small and dusty garden. The palace lacked a ballroom, so a new wing was planned, the Ala Napoleonica at the west end of the Piazza which today houses the Correr Museum. This involved the demolition of a sixteenth century church by Jacopo Sansovino, the architect of the lovely *loggetta* at the foot of the *Campanile* of San Marco and also of both the Marciana Library opposite the Palazzo Ducale and the Procuratorie Vecchie on the north side of the Piazza. Sansovino had designed both buildings in a restrained classical style which the more overblown Ala Napoleonica, with its pediment of Roman Emperors (there is a gap in the centre which was to be filled by their modern heir) is unfortunately unable to imitate. Hobhouse, looking at the Ala Napoleonica in 1816 not long after its completion, commented:

"The palace of government built at the other end of the square by Napoleon, who pulled down the church of San Germiano [sic] to find a place for it, looks too new for the rest of the buildings."

Plans for the Ala Napoleonica were well underway when the Emperor finally made a brief visit to Venice in November 1807. The bad weather throughout his stay reportedly matched Napoleon's mood.

Sansovino's church of San Geminiano was by no means the only religious building which the French viewed as ripe for redevelopment. Between 1805 and 1814 a wholesale closure and demolition of religious houses was implemented and their property seized: this produced another bumper crop of high quality art which could be shipped to Paris or Milan. Monasteries and nunneries were converted into warehouses, mills, a factory, even a prison. Churches were demolished.

Worse was to come. Unemployment was already high due to the closure of the dockyards, and in 1810 almost 2,000 people were cast onto the streets when a decree commanded the immediate closure of sixty religious houses. Over 500 monks and friars, and more than 1,000 nuns were made homeless, forbidden to wear religious dress or to re-establish any kind of community. The men were expected to find work, the women to return to their families.
The closure of monasteries and nunneries could be viewed in a positive light. For Venetian women, in particular, the decision to enter a religious life was often not made freely. The figures above show that far more Venetian women than men lived in a religious house: often because they came from noble, yet impoverished, families who could not afford to give dowries to all their daughters. Many young girls with no vocation became nuns, and by the last years of the Republic convents were a byword for loose living: nuns held parties and dressed in fashionable clothes, some even had lovers; for example Casanova claimed to have had two mistresses who were nuns.
Yet even if the French decree was intended to end abuses of the religious life, it created far more problems than it solved: with unemployment already at chronic levels the poor were now deprived of a major source of charity, including those religious houses, such as the Piéta, which took in the illegitimate children of prostitutes, of which Venice had enough and to spare. And the Venetian patrician families were suffering the effects of the economic downturn brought about by the end of the Republic just as much as the rest of society. An ex-nun was expected to return to her family: but what was she to do if they were unwilling to take her in? Doubtless, for many of the women made homeless in this way, there was little alternative except to join the ranks of Venice's prostitutes.
For the poor who relied on charity, even worse than the closure of the religious houses was the closure of the *scuole*. These were groups of lay people who banded together with the aim of helping others. By the time of the second French occupation there were 385 *scuole*. They were part professional guild, part charitable organization. Each *scuola* was democratically run by its members. The *scuole* provided pensions for the widows of their members, took care of the elderly and orphans, gave help to poor and disabled Venetians. A number of *scuole* had built fine meeting-houses decorated with works by artists such as Tintoretto and Veronese.
It is not clear why Napoleon was so determined to close the *scuole*: many of the art treasures looted from them were sold cheaply on the open market, so he may simply have needed ready cash. It may have been a determination to break yet anoth-

er symbol of Venetian independence: Napoleon seems to have held a particular animus against the former Republic, partly as a result of Venetian refusal to join an anti-Austrian alliance he had been putting together in 1796, partly because of attacks on his soldiery and anti-French riots in the *Terraferma* in 1797.

Only in the famine years that lay ahead would it become apparent just how much the Venetian poor had depended on the assistance of the *scuole*. Many *scuole* were demolished. Today only the major *scuole* buildings survive, their charitable *raison d'être* destroyed. Hobhouse visited perhaps the most beautiful of the remaining *scuole*, the Scuola Grande di San Rocco, in 1816. He commented in his diary that:

"…the revenues were formerly 64,000 ducats. These were seized at the fall of the Republic… their charities were immense. At present very little donation takes place, or perhaps nothing."

The space created by the demolition of so many churches and *scuole* inspired Giannantonio Selva to draw up a scheme to convert Venice into a neo-classical city of wide boulevards on the Parisian model. Selva had been considered one of the bright young architects of the last years of the Republic. Born in 1751, he studied in Rome and travelled widely in Europe before returning to Venice where his first big commission was the new La Fenice Theatre, which opened in1792. Byron, a great theatregoer, described it as:

"… the finest, by the way, that I have ever seen – it beats our theatres hollow in beauty and scenery – and those of Milan and Brescia bow before it."

Despite the various fires to which La Fenice has fallen victim over the years, the exterior of the theatre still follows Selva's austere classical design. Whatever Selva's personal opinion of the French, he did not let it stand in his way when he was offered the opportunity to re-create Venice as the classical city of his dreams. Today, when Venice is viewed as an architectural jewel to be treasured, this seems like heresy. However, Selva's views were far from unusual for much of the nineteenth century. After returning from his tour with his three young charges, the Rev. Eustace wrote a guidebook, *Classical Italy: From Venice to Rome*. Originally published in 1812, it was a widely-read work which influenced the tastes and views of generations of travellers. Dickens refers to it in *Little Dorrit*. Here is the reverend gentleman's opinion of the Piazza:

"The famous *Piazza de San Marco*, surrounded with arcades, is more remarkable for being the well-known scene of Venetian mirth, conversation and intrigue, than for its size or its symmetry. It is inferior in both respects, to many squares in many great cities."

The Basilica of San Marco comes in for severe condemnation from the learned pen:
"The church of St Mark, the great patron of the city and of the republic, occupies one end of the square, and terminates it with a sort of gloomy barbaric magnificence. In fact, the five domes which swell from its roof, and the paltry decorations which cover and encumber its porticoes, give it externally the appearance of an eastern pagoda... and adorned with clumsy mosaics...
"Its architects, it is related... took Santa Sophia for their model, and seem to have imitated its form, its domes and its bad taste."[23]
The French and Giannantonio Selva, therefore, were simply reflecting popular tastes and prejudices when they began to lay out their plans for a modern city in the Castello district, beyond the Arsenale. First a waterway, the Rio Santa Anna, was filled in to create a wide, straight boulevard running towards the church of San Pietro di Castello: until 1807 this church was the cathedral of Venice. Formal gardens on either side of the boulevard were planned in space created by the demolition of redundant convents; the modern visitor can still stroll in them and admire the various monuments to virtuous Venetians and famous visitors: Richard Wagner in particular stares belligerently over the lagoon next to a rather more pacific Verdi. The boulevard was originally called Via Eugenia, in honour of Eugene Beauharnais. For a student of Italian history the current name is far more satisfying: Via Garibaldi.

In April 1810 Venice's once and future rulers became dynastically linked when the Emperor Napoleon, aged 41, married 19 year-old Marie-Louise, daughter of the Emperor Francis. Napoleon, with a view to founding a dynasty, had divorced Josephine: not only had she not produced an heir, her non-royal heritage did not fit with his growing Imperial ambitions. The marriage, which soon produced the longed-for heir, drew the Emperor Francis into the Napoleonic web of alliances. The Austrian Empire was only able to disentangle itself after the disastrous Russian campaign when, sensing that Napoleon was fatally weakened and with an eye to the main chance, they invaded northern Italy in 1813. With the Austrians on the *terraferma* and a British naval blockade out at sea, the Venetians found themselves "without food, without water, without money, without any valid reason to press them to join the Napoleonic cause."
The fall of Napoleon and his imprisonment on Elba led to the Congress of Vienna of 1814. After a slight interruption caused by Napoleon's escape and the Battle of Waterloo, the allies saw him permanently incarcerated on St Helena before settling down once more to allocate the spoils of war.

Although they restored the Pope to his former secular role as ruler of the Papal Sates north of Rome, it seems never to have crossed the minds of the chief negotiators at the Congress – Byron's *bête noire* Viscount Castlereagh, the Austrian Chancellor Prince Clemens Metternich and Tsar Alexander I of Russia – to restore Venice to her pre-1797 status as a free and independent Republic. *La Serenissima* was merely another prize for the victors to share out amongst themselves. Austria's reward was most of northern Italy: Lombardy, the Veneto and Tuscany. Parts of the area became semi-independent city-states ruled by relatives of the Austrian Emperor Francis I: his younger brother Ferdinand became Grand Duke of Tuscany, his daughter Marie Louise (disentangled from her unfortunate dynastic alliance to the former Emperor Napoleon) was rewarded with the title of Duchess of Parma. Venice and her *terraferma* provinces, now named Venetia, were to be ruled directly from Vienna. Along with Lombardy, they were the direct responsibility of the Viceroy (the first Viceroy was Rainer, one of the Emperor's many brothers). Unlike Eugene Beauharnais, who had exercised his viceregal powers almost exclusively from Milan, the Austrian Viceroy was instructed to spend half the year in Lombardy and the other half in the Veneto.

The returning rulers believed that they would be welcomed as the saviours of Venice from French rule. Hobhouse was shown a speech made by the Emperor:

"... when the Venetian deputies complimented him on the cession of their city to him, he promised to make Venice recover all her splendour."

Indeed, the Austrians showed early signs of putting this into practice. Many of the artistic treasures which the French had taken to Paris were returned, including (after a personal appeal from the sculptor Canova) the four horses of San Marco. These were returned to their original position overlooking the Piazza, with a new inscription recording their removal by hostile cupidity (ie: French greed) and their return as a sign of peace.[24]

The Emperor Francis also allowed the religious orders driven from Venice by the French closure of their convents and monasteries to return to the city, and encouraged the *scuole* to re-form and recommence their charitable work.

So, when Byron arrived in Venice in 1816, her citizens, still traumatized by the end of their Republic almost twenty years previously, were having to digest the fact that they had finally been reduced to the status of a mere Austrian province; a situation which would have to be endured for a further 50 years. As Rev. Eustace put it:

"That bold independence which filled a few lonely islands, the abode of sea-mews and of cormorants, with population and with commerce, is bowed into slavery; and the republic of Venice, with all its bright scenes of triumphs, is now an empty name… it is now a petty province of the Austrian Empire."

This had a considerable impact on the daily life of the average Venetian. They were heavily taxed and their young men conscripted for the benefit of a foreign power, their reading material was closely monitored and censored, Imperial polices only exacerbated Venice's economic decline. However, as Byron pointed out, the situation in which the Venetians found themselves, although deeply unpleasant, was being repeated across Europe. The French Revolution and the Terror were less than a generation in the past. Every politician in Europe was constantly listening out for the rumble of the tumbril and the swish of the guillotine. Even Byron's countrymen were not immune from repressive legislation, as he pointed out in the dedication to Canto IV of *Childe Harold's Pilgrimage*:

"What Italy has gained by the late transfer of nations, it were useless for Englishmen to inquire, till it becomes ascertained that England has acquired something more than a permanent army and a suspended Habeas Corpus…"

All classes of Venetian society were affected by Austrian policies. The end of the war, although extremely welcome, went hand-in-hand with a serious food shortage. This was caused largely by the effect on agriculture of the appalling weather conditions experienced across Europe in 1816, although the return of many former soldiers to their communities no doubt also had an impact: men who had been away for years suddenly had to be re-integrated, fed and (hopefully) employed. For the Venetians, the Europe-wide problems were exacerbated locally by further decline of local industries. The Emperor Francis decided that, since Austria had no ambitions as a naval power, he had no use for the sad remains of the once-powerful Venetian navy, and the last few ships were sold to Denmark in 1815, another reminder to the people of Venice of their subject status.

Venice's long history as a trading centre, which many Venetians no doubt hoped to regain with the end of the war and the end of the British naval blockade of European ports, was dealt a severe blow when the Austrians continued to favour the port of Trieste, just 120 kilometres across the Gulf of Venezia. Trieste had been part of the Hapsburg Empire since 1382 and the Hapsburgs had developed it as a rival port to Venice from the beginning of the 18th century. It had direct road links to Vienna and was granted 'free port' status, meaning that all goods imported into Trieste could be traded freely within the town without additional taxes, an encouragement to commerce. Many Venetians hoped that Venice would also become a free port. After all, Napoleon had granted limited free port status to the island of San Giorgio in the Venetian lagoon (the harbour wall and little lighthouse can still be seen, to the side of the church of San Giorgio Maggiore). Why not spread the benefits and give an economic boost to a city and region which so badly needed it?

Here another negative aspect of Austrian rule comes into play: slow Imperial decision-making. This was partly due to the creaking Imperial bureaucracy, relying heavily on committees. Reports were commissioned, their eventual completion was awaited and then, with rival factions taking up opposing points of view, their contents were discussed. A report on the poll tax in the Veneto, for example, commissioned in 1817 in response to the famine caused by the disastrous harvests across Europe in 1816, had not been implemented by the time of Manin's revolution over thirty years later. The slow pace was also partly due to the Emperor Francis' complete inability to reach a decision. The Emperor prided himself on the fact that he would listen to advice from any of his subjects, and even set aside two mornings a week to meet ordinary people, by appointment. However, this gentle, pedestrian soul, whose hobbies were making sealing-wax, collecting interesting seals and, more alarmingly, painting eyes on the bottoms of chamber-pots which he presented to ladies of the court, usually agreed with the opinion of the last person to whom he had spoken. Throw in slow communications in the early 19th century – the journey from Vienna to Venice took at least a week – and the fact that no-one on the ground in Venice had decision-making powers. A Venetian doctor, Dr Sartori, had to compile a report on deaths caused by the famine. He told Hobhouse that many people:

"… have died of hunger and of [eating] grass, and other crude substances found in their intestines. Such misery was never known in his memory in Italy."

The doctor explained to Hobhouse the various and complex stages of Austrian bureaucracy, which Hobhouse in turn noted in his diary:

"The course of municipal power in the state comes from the Emperor – the *camera aulica*,[25] the Governor of Venice, the counsellor of the government, the *centrale congregazion* comprised of noble Venetians – the *provincial congregazion* composed of nobles and citizens at Venice in greater numbers than the central, provincial delegation composed of a delegate named by the Emperor in each province, a Chancellor of the census residing in every district of each province…"

And so on, through another four stages of committee and influence! No wonder it was impossible to respond with any immediacy to events which required a rapid solution such as the famine. Both the physical distance between Vienna and Venice, and the complete failure to grasp the seriousness of the famine, can be seen in a conversation between Hobhouse and Colonel Finch, an Englishman living in Italy:

"Finch told me that the physicians of Venice had sent a memoir to Vienna relative to the diseases arising from the extreme poverty of the people here – the Aulic Council [Imperial Committee] sat on the question, and has sent particular orders to the preachers here to recommend from the pulpit wine and meat, in preference to a poorer diet."

The Austrian failure to understand what was going on in their new province is breathtaking, particularly as they had recently imposed new taxes on foodstuffs including wine and meat. Byron tells a more light-hearted anecdote about the installation of the new Patriarch of Venice, which underlines the Imperial ignorance. In a letter of 1817, he reports:

"The Patriarch of Venice was installed the other Sunday – the court of Vienna decreed in an edict - that he should proceed to St Mark's in a "Coach and four" – but (as Incledon says in "The Son and Heir of Sir William Meadows") "thaut's impossible"; the Venetians grinned, as you may suppose, at the knowledge of topography displayed in this Cesarean decree – which was truly 'German to the matter.' "

So, whilst the Imperial bureaucracy slowly ground into gear on the matter of Free Port status for Venice, unemployment worsened. Trade stagnated in the city: an Austrian tax on goods entering and leaving the Veneto – even if only to or from the neighbouring province of Lombardy – led to the development of Genoa as an alternative port on the west coast. The continued decline of Venice as a port had a knock-on effect at the Arsenale, as no new trading-vessels were commissioned. In 1817 a thousand men were employed there (declining from over 16,000 in its heyday.) By 1825 this was down to a mere 250 employees. The British Consul in Venice, Byron's friend Richard Hoppner, reported in 1818:

"It has been the firm policy of the Austrian government, ever since it was confirmed in possession of these provinces, to advance trade at Trieste at the expense of Venice, a measure which has so far succeeded as to leave scarcely a trace behind of that commerce to which the latter owed its past splendour."

Despite the appalling economic situation in the Veneto, the Austrian rulers still viewed it as an as-yet unexploited region of their Empire, ripe for a little milking of taxes. As has already been mentioned, a poll-tax was introduced in 1815 and met, as such a tax always does, with violent opposition: tax collectors in the *terraferma* were attacked. It was Austrian policy that anyone unable or unwilling to pay the tax should have their goods seized. In reality this meant that any farm-worker or craftsman who was unable to pay would lose the tools of his trade. Although Hobhouse speaks of the "Chancellor of the census residing in every district" there had been no full census of Venice and the *terraferma* for many years, therefore it was not possible to collect the tax effectively. A census was announced in 1817. Another Austrian bureaucratic exercise; it reported in 1849.

As well as the poll tax, a Venetian lawyer, teacher, professor, artist or businessman had to pay an additional tax. There were taxes on essentials such as salt, flour and basic foodstuffs including vegetables and meat, as well as (to a Venetian) the everyday necessities of wine and tobacco. Hobhouse, writing in November 1816, stated:

"… the sum sent from the Venetian territory alone [to Austria]… is said to be fourteen millions of francs quarterly. The articles of consumption from the mainland are all highly taxed – we could find no white wine but Malaga at our great inn – the Paduan wines pay eighteen francs a barrel duty. Wood is very dear…"

In many ways Hobhouse was a typical English traveller. On the one hand he held up his hands in horror at Venice's economic decline and Austrian rapaciousness. On the other hand he was more than happy to take advantage of low prices. His diary records a number of bargains. For example, when Byron left the Hotel Gran Bretagna to move to lodgings Hobhouse decided to take rooms too, choosing an apartment in the Calle dei Avvocati, which runs from the Campo Sant'Angelo to the Grand Canal and the Teatro Sant'Angelo. Whereas Byron was paying twenty francs a day for his lodging, Hobhouse paid only eight francs, including "fire, candles, linen and lodging." He proudly records the cheapness of his meals, and the good value of his new boots, but is shocked to learn from a conversation with a Venetian shop-keeper that, "the present English in Italy are thought saving and to travel for economy"!

Byron's lodgings were with an ordinary Venetian, Pietro Segati, a draper (Byron calls him "a Merchant of Venice") with a business in the Frezzeria, one of the main shopping streets of Venice between the Piazza and the Rialto. How would someone like Signor Segati be affected by Austrian rule? In a conversation with Hobhouse, he said that: "...the Austrians had diminished the imports by two thirds", which would obviously be hard upon a businessman relying on raw materials such as linen, velvet and silk, which once arrived daily and plentifully on the Venetian dockside. Prices of everyday goods had rocketed: "Under the French the abundance of corn was so great that the poor got their bread for twenty lire the sack of flour… last winter corn was sixty." No wonder that Signor Segati "averred that not an Italian in Venice lived as a friend with an Austrian." He and his wife, Marianna (Byron's first Venetian mistress) would be hit hard by the city's economic decline which led to merchants like themselves making economies. Many families cut back on domestic servants, whose numbers declined by as much as 90% in the first decades of the nineteenth century, adding to the growing numbers of unemployed in the city. Indeed, there was an exodus from the city, partly in search of work. Hobhouse had heard various statistics, but they all told the same story: "The population diminishes daily – some say that from '97 it has fallen from 130 to 110,000, others from 110 to 95,000." (Hobhouse's informants were not far out in their reckoning: the population declined from around 136,000 in 1799 to 100,000 in 1822.) Another reason for the declining population, not only in the city of Venice but also in the *terraferma,* was that young men were slipping across the border into the neighbouring Papal States in order to avoid conscription into the Imperial army and navy. There was no tradition of compulsory military service in the Veneto: serving the state in the navy or on a merchant vessel had always been regarded both as an honour and a chance to make some money. Conscription had been introduced by Napoleon, always in need of soldiers for his endless military campaigns, and was retained by the Austrians who expected all able-bodied young men to register for an annual levy. Those who were selected would be expected to serve for a minimum of eight years. Common ways of evading the draft were crossing the border, self-mutilation (cutting off a finger and self-inflicted hernias were not unknown), entering a seminary, even getting married. Once in the forces, desertion rates were high. It was not simply the prospect of eight years away from home, serving in appalling conditions and with little chance of promotion (all officers in the Imperial army were German-speakers) that made the army so unpopular: the Austrians were so hated that young men from Venice and the lagoon islands, sailors from their earliest years and part of a long maritime tradition, did all they could to avoid service in the Imperial navy. The aristocracy took the easy option: they bought their way out of service.

There is little wonder that the army was so hugely unpopular:

although Lombardy and the Veneto were provinces of the Austrian Empire, acquired by treaty at the Congress of Vienna and not through battle, the army seems to have acted like an occupying power, lording it over a subject people. Shelley, staying with his family at Este on the *terraferma*, noted that the Austrians "impose free quarters on the inhabitants," in other words any household could be expected to give free board and lodgings to an Imperial soldier. The army also appears to have been in the habit of taking whatever it wanted from the locals. Tom Moore, Byron's first biographer, relates an incident when the Austrians were requisitioning private citizens' horses for use by the army. When Byron, who was at his summer villa on the Brenta Canal at the time, and who kept horses for his daily exercise, received a requisition to hand the animals over:

"... this he positively refused to do, adding, that if an attempt were made to take them by force, he would shoot them through the head in the middle of the road, rather than submit to such an act of tyranny upon a foreigner, who was merely a temporary resident in the country."

Byron was allowed to keep his horses. Ordinary citizens, however, did not have his advantages of a diplomatic passport, a foreign title and the friendship of the Governor.

The Mocenigo were an ancient and respected Venetian family with a history of over 500 years service to the Republic: they had provided Venice with seven doges. Yet in 1818 the family finances were in a dire situation: a poor harvest on the Mocenigo *terraferma* estates proved to be the straw that broke the financial camel's back. Many Venetian nobles had found it difficult to make ends meet even before the fall of the Republic; indeed there had been a special fund to assist aristocrats fallen on hard times. A poverty-stricken nobleman was housed and given an allowance just as long as he didn't marry and bring more young aristocrats into the world. The French, although they had imposed high taxes throughout Italy, had, with post-revolutionary zeal, taxed aristocratic families particularly heavily. In 1797 such families had had to pay a forced loan of 300 million lire to Napoleon, and high taxes were again imposed during the second French occupation. Along with all Venetians, the nobles were further impoverished by the British blockade of European ports during the War and the economic collapse attendant upon Austrian rule. No wonder Lucia, the recently-widowed Countess Mocenigo, jumped at the opportunity to lease the family apartment in Palazzo Mocenigo on the Grand Canal to a British poet, whilst she moved into smaller rooms.

In many ways, Lucia Mocenigo was lucky: many *palazzi* were demolished because their owners could no longer afford their upkeep. The Commissione all'Ornato, a body originally established during French rule to improve the appearance of the city, drew the attention of the Austrian authorities to the decay of many beautiful buildings but, like all Imperial committees, it had little, if any, power to try to put things right. On the day after their arrival in Venice in 1816, Byron and Hobhouse, on a gondola tour of the Grand Canal like so many tourists since, were shown: "deserted palaces" and told that:
"... many of the patricians had pulled down their houses to satisfy their creditors with the precious materials, and those who were not left to beg had retired to the mainland."
Hobhouse later saw that this was true when he stayed with Byron at his summer villa on the Brenta and met:
"... the shattered remains of Venetian nobility, now spread and mixed and lost amidst the Jews and merchants who have purchased the better villas of this once patrician retreat."[26]
This asset-stripping was not a short-lived phenomenon: in 1837 Benjamin Disraeli wrote of Venetian noble houses being broken up "like old ships" and the furniture turning up in Bond Street sale rooms, so that "Many a fine lady now sits in a doge's chair." However, Lucia Mocenigo obtained a pretty good financial arrangement from Byron: a rent of 200 louis d'or a year, which was a high rent for Venice at that time. (Some idea of how high can be seen by the fact that, more than 20 years later, Claire Clairmont's salary as a governess was only 48 louis per year.)

Venice had always been a place where the printed word was freely available. It was known throughout Europe as a centre for printing and book-making, and had often attracted the ire of the Inquisition for the fact that dangerous books were there for all to read. The Marciana Library, opposite the Basilica of San Marco, had been (until rifled by the French) a world-famous repository of rare books and manuscripts, freely available to all scholars. So the heavy censorship of all books, newspapers and even images imposed by the Austrians was yet another severe shock to the Venetian psyche. The censors were expected to look out for all works "against the interests of the sovereign, the state, the dominant religion and public morality," whether these were novels, text-books (scientific and medical texts could easily be banned on grounds of obscenity, the Emperor "considered the cultivation of the arts and sciences as having a revolutionary tendency"), even religious works. *Du Pape*, a book about the papacy, was banned because, in writing that the Pope's authority came directly from God, the author was seen as denigrating the powers of the Emperor. It was illegal to display a picture of Napoleon or any member of his family, leading to the bizarre situation where the people of Parma were breaking the law if they showed a portrait of their own Duchess, the Emperor's daughter Marie Louise, since she had been married to Napoleon.

Newspapers were closely monitored and were expected as top priority to relate court news, and then to state the facts of current issues without any editorial comment or the possibility of offending a foreign power. All residents of Venice, including foreign visitors and consular staff, had to apply to the censor if they wanted to subscribe to a newspaper or journal from abroad. Byron commented on this in 1818 in a letter to his friend Tom Moore:

"An English newspaper here would be a prodigy, and an opposition one a monster; and, except some extracts from extracts in the vile, garbled Paris gazettes, nothing of the kind reaches the Veneto-Lombard public, who are, perhaps, the most oppressed in Europe."

However, on one occasion Byron found himself the subject of a news story with an anti-Napoleon bias:

".. a review of C[hilde] H[arold], in which it proclaims me the most rebellious and contumacious Admirer of Buonaparte – now surviving in Europe."

Byron goes on to add that the article was a translation from a German newspaper. Such criticism of him in Venice must have been unusual (perhaps this is why he mentioned it) since Byron was acquainted with the Venetian censor, Signor Petrotini who, despite the anti-Austrian sentiments Byron displays at the beginning of Canto IV of Child Harold's Pilgrimage, (the epigraph to this chapter is just one example) recommended that an Italian translation of the poem be published with only a few cuts, adding: "it is not only England that applauds the living genius of Lord Byron, but also Italy."

On another occasion, Signor Petrotini made a more personal intervention in order to look after Byron's interests. In 1817 a translation of Lady Caroline Lamb's *Glenarvon* came into the censor's office. Signor Petrotini refused to allow the novel to be published until he had seen Byron personally and discussed the matter with him. Byron took the opportunity to make his views on censorship clear:

"I told him I did not recognize the slightest relation between that book and myself – but that whatever opinions might be on that subject – I would never prevent or oppose the publication of *any* book, in *any* language – on my own private account."

The issue of Imperial surveillance of individuals is linked to censorship. Byron's letters make it clear that his mail was being opened, read and, on occasion, retained for some time before it was delivered. Indeed, since political comments of the kind he made to Moore are very rare in his letters from Venice, it seems that he was self-censoring his letters since he was aware that they were being read. Byron constantly complains that letters are slow to arrive, telling both Tom Moore and his publisher John Murray that he has sent several letters to them yet has had no reply for months. Proofs of his poems, sent by Murray for correction, never arrive: perhaps, being completely incomprehensible to the censors and therefore considered likely to be seditious, they were simply thrown away. He believed that, as a well-known opponent of the Tory Government, there was no point in him trying to send or receive anything via the diplomatic bag, telling Murray:

"It is useless to send to the *Foreign Office* nothing arrives to me by that conveyance – I suppose some zealous Clerk thinks it his Tory duty to prevent it."

Byron sent important items: corrected proofs, gifts for his sister Augusta or his daughter Ada, with travellers who were returning to England, asking them to make sure they were delivered to Murray's offices. This was probably his way of making sure that they reached their destination and were not lost during typically slow Imperial searches.

Of course Byron, a high-profile foreigner, would expect to be kept under surveillance. However, all inhabitants of the Veneto, however humble, received similar close observation.

It would be naªve to suppose that any country in Europe, in the repressive years that followed the fall of Napoleon, did not spy on its people. In England, spies and agents of the Crown kept Radicals and agitators under close observation. Indeed, during the year 1817 alone, the chief Government spy, Oliver, acting as *agent provocateur*, was single-handedly responsible for the arrest of 35 unemployed Derbyshire frame-knitters. Even in this climate, however, the Austrian Empire had a reputation for keeping a particularly close eye on its subjects, and it was generally recognized even at the time that the population of Veneto, from students at the University of Padua to gondoliers and prostitutes, were targets of special police observation. The purpose of all this surveillance was simple: to prevent sedition, unrest and crime. However, the heavy-handed nature of police activity in the province of Lombardy-Veneto was so blatant that even foreign travellers, as always greatly concerned about issues relating to crime and personal safety, remarked upon the intrusive police presence there compared to what they saw in other parts of Italy. The authorities made it difficult for Venetians to travel abroad, whether for pleasure or study: who knew what radical and subversive ideas they might bring back with them to infect the rest of the populace? They were also extremely suspicious of any foreigners who wished to visit, or worse still, live in Venice or the *terraferma*: Byron, like all other foreigners (including consular officials) had to officially register his passport and address. Given his public support in England for radical groups such as the Luddites and causes like Catholic Emancipation, he was lucky to be allowed into Lombardy-Veneto at all: "politically dangerous" foreigners were kept out.

Ironically, the lack of foreign, and particularly English, visitors to Venice made the city particularly attractive to Byron. The public interest generated by his separation and departure from England had made him the centre of attention, much of it negative, whenever he had met with English people as he crossed Europe. Understandably, this both wearied and annoyed him. He wrote with great relief to John Murray in 1817 that " 'English gentlemen' are very rare – at least in Venice," adding:"Venice is not a place where the English are gregarious – their pigeon-houses are Florence – Naples – Rome &c – & to tell you the truth, this was one reason why I staid here."

Byron had only one notable run-in with the police – and it was the crime-fighting branch, not the secret police – during his time in Venice. It happened when he was staying at his *terraferma* villa at La Mira. When he was out riding, a man in a hired carriage shouted abuse at him. Byron caught up with the coach and was further abused, so he leaned in and delivered a slap to the face before opening the carriage door and asking his abuser to come out and settle the issue like a man. After more abuse, Byron was then threatened with a charge of battery without provocation, so he gave his name and address and challenged his abuser to a duel. The man went to the police, but since all the witnesses spoke in Byron's favour Byron was told that, had he not struck his abuser, the man could have been imprisoned. This seems a harsh penalty for verbal abuse of a man more than able to take care of himself, but bears out the heavy-handed reputation of the Venetian police.

Later, when he was living in Ravenna, the Byron legend would prove useful in his dealings with the secret police. By then, his reputation was such that any gossip, however far-fetched, was accepted as a fact and recorded in police files.[27] But that would not happen until 1821.

Third Venetian Interlude

… and silent rows the songless gondolier

Byron was fascinated by gondolas and gondoliers. In one of his very first letters after his arrival in Venice, he proudly informed Tom Moore that "My gondola is, at this present, waiting for me on the canal." Reflecting both his own Romantic reputation and that of the city, he wrote to Augusta "I am going out this evening – in my cloak & Gondola – there are two nice Mrs. Radcliffe words for you."

Had he known the likely origin of the name, he would have been greatly diverted. Many writers derive the name gondola from either the Greek word kontylion, *meaning a vaginally-shaped drinking-cup, or* cuntelas, *a small ship. Being conveyed round Venice in a vessel of such a name and shape would have been most entertaining to the man who, he said, wrote better verse "When a C – t is tied close to my* Inkstand*"*

By the time Byron arrived in Venice, gondolas had already acquired much of their reputation as places for intrigue and dalliance. Yet their original purpose was purely practical: a boat with a shallow draft suitable for rowing around the myriad waterways of Venice – many of which are only a few feet deep – without risk of running aground. Building a gondola is the work of a skilled craftsman, expertly fitting together a jigsaw of 280 pieces of wood to create a boat which must have an asymmetric shape so that one man can row a straight course with a single oar: a symmetrical gondola would go round in circles.

Gondolas were essential in enabling Venetians of all classes to move freely about their city: after all, until 1854 the Rialto was the only bridge across the Grand Canal. The gondola is almost as old as the city it serves: Doge Vitale Falier refers to it by name in a document of 1094. It was a regular feature of Venetian life by the 15th century: Carpaccio's paintings show elegantly dressed gondoliers with typical Venetian passengers such as a lady and her lapdog who sit under a canopy to protect them from the sun and rain.

This canopy, or felze, *was originally a light, moveable open structure, but it evolved into the closed cabin, "like a coffin clapt in a canoe" which intrigued Byron. The* felze *had a front door, windows with blinds and a comfortable couch.*[28] *Its original purpose was to allow Venetians to travel in some degree of privacy from their famously nosy fellow-citizens, but the opportunities for dalliance the* felze *offered soon became apparent: a 17th century law went so far as to forbid the city's many courtesans to so much as travel in a gondola with a* felze. *The Countess Marina Benzoni, who in Byron's day was a society lady famous for her* conversazioni, *even had a song written in honour of her alleged carryings-on under the* felze. *In her youth before the fall of the Republic, her behaviour with the Venetian poet Antonio Lamberti inspired him to compose a song – suitably enough, it was a barcarole, a Venetian boating-song whose rhythm reflects the rocking of a gondola on the water.* La Biondina in Gondoleta *(The Blonde in the Gondola) recounts how Antonio took Marina out in the gondola by moonlight. As she lay in his arms, the kindly breezes lifted her clothes to reveal more and more to her lover's eyes:*

What wonderful things I said,
What lovely things I did!
Never again was I to be so happy in all my life!

No wonder Byron felt that the felze *could*

contain a deal of fun,
Like mourning coaches when the funeral's done!

In 1816 gondolas were as ubiquitous as the cabs and carriages Byron had left behind in London. And, like those London carriages, gondolas came in two varieties, public and private. Public gondolas were either ferries, plying back and forth at a set point, just like the traghetti which cross the Grand Canal today, or taxis for hire. Visitors to Venice paid for the exclusive use of a gondola and gondolier for the duration of their stay, indeed Byron and Hobhouse did so as soon as they arrived in the city. Wealthy Venetian families usually had several gondolas at their constant beck and call. In the equivalent of competing with the neighbours by way of a top-of-the-range coupé or a greener-than-thou hybrid car, rich families of the Serenissima vied to outdo each other with the amount of gilding, heraldic decoration, putti *and luxurious fabrics covering their gondolas. Sumptuary laws had to be passed in 1562 and 1633 forbidding richly-decorated craft, and by 1709 it was decreed that all gondoliers, even those employed by a wealthy household, could wear only simple attire, except – as today – for weddings. So Byron, like the modern visitor, found plainly uniform gondolas, which glide "along the water looking blackly".*

Gondoliers were central figures in Venetian society: experts in navigating to or from any point in the intersecting maze of waterways, they quite literally kept the city moving. They also operated their own code of honour: no gondolier would ever gossip about the goings-on under his felze, *or betray any of the locations to which he had rowed a client. In a city which thrived on intrigue – personal, political and mercantile – this gave gondoliers considerable status. It also brought certain perks. For example, a gondolier who rowed someone to the theatre to watch a play was given a free seat in the pit. No doubt keen to impress those able to pass on a recommendation (or otherwise) to other customers, the eighteenth-century Venetian playwright Goldoni liked to make sure that gondoliers were regularly and kindly represented in his works.*

A gondoliere de casada, *or household gondolier, had higher status than the gondolier for hire. As an employee he was housed and well-fed, as were his family and, very often, his friends. John and Effie Ruskin rented an apartment in what is now part of the Gritti Palace Hotel in the winter of 1851. Effie was surprised to find that, should she wish to speak to her cook, the kitchen seemed to contain "the whole parish", including the household gondolier (called, inevitably,* Beppo*) "and stray Gondoliers and women whom I never saw before."*

When Byron moved into Palazzo Mocenigo, the twenty-one year-old gondoliere de casada, *Tita, came as part of the package. He soon became a trusted servant, and Byron paid 1200 livres (the equivalent of a year's wages) to buy him out of Austrian military conscription in 1820. In common with so many of his servants, Tita was devoted to Byron, and gave up both his home and his gondolier's calling to continue in his service after he left Venice. He was with Byron in Missolonghi.*

In order to maintain the steady rhythm of the oar, gondoliers often sang as they worked – not the hackneyed sole mios *and opera tunes of the modern tourist serenade, but the traditional barcarole which helped them keep time with the oar and the water. Just as a folk-singer takes traditional tunes and adds new – often topical – words, so Venetian gondoliers adapted popular verses of the day to fit the barcarole. It was a commonplace by Byron's day that gondoliers invariably sang parts of Tasso's epic poem* Gerusalemme Liberata, *and almost every visitor to Venice, from Goethe to Doctor Johnson's friend Mrs Thrale, felt the need to mention this. In 1786 Goethe was lucky enough to hear a gondoliers' singing "duel." One gondolier positioned himself near the canal side, whilst the other was some distance away. The two singers duetted, extemporised recitatives and threw the song back and forth between them for hours. "Each," wrote Goethe "is the echo of the other." He felt that "The sound of their voices far away was extraordinary, a lament without sadness, and I was moved to tears."*

However, thirty years later war and occupation had taken their toll, and gondoliers had little to sing about. Byron soon found that "the Chaunt of Tasso" was only rarely heard. The gondolier had become songless.

Chapter Four

Marianna

With all its sinful doings, I must say,
That Italy's a pleasant place to me

A few days after arriving in Venice, Byron, accompanied as ever by his valet Fletcher, moved from the Hotel Gran Bretagna into lodgings above a draper's shop in the Piscina de Frezzeria.[29] Most English travellers who planned a stay of more than a week moved into lodgings: they were cheaper, more commodious and tended to be "all found" – bed linen, light, heat and meals were provided, and no doubt Byron found it easier to follow his lowering diet when he did not have to dine at the *table de hôte* or in the *trattorie* which Hobhouse continued to frequent.

The Frezzeria, named for the arrow-makers who originally occupied this part of the city, is just beyond the west end of Piazza San Marco, running parallel to the back of the Ala Napoleonica. Today, the narrow *calle* is thronged with visitors heading for either the Piazza or the Rialto, but Byron's rooms did not overlook anything like such crowded bustle. Venice was at her nadir. Few people had money to spend in a draper's shop. Hence, no doubt, the Segati family's need for a paying guest. Byron, chronically short of money, was quite content with his Frezzeria rooms: he had, after all, spent most of his childhood in lodgings in Aberdeen.

Whether his landlady was part of the initial attraction that the rooms held for Byron is unclear, but Marianna Segati seems to have set her sights on Byron very quickly, and lost no time in explaining the ground rules of a liaison in Venice "that nearly every woman has an established lover, that jealousy is very rare." So, having moved into the Segati household on 14th November, three days later Byron wrote to tell Tom Moore that he had fallen in love and, since the somewhat strait-laced Moore reproduced most of the letter as a series of asterisks in his Life, Byron also appears to have confided that the relationship became sexual almost at once.

Marianna was twenty-two years old, the mother of a little girl. She had a beautiful voice: Byron said that she was sweetly and softly spoken, while Hobhouse noted that she was invited to sing at *conversazioni*. According to Byron, she was "pretty as an Antelope", by which he meant that she had large dark eyes, dark curly hair and small, regular features. She clearly adored Byron, and her calm affection was just what he needed after his turbulent year. Marianna saw Byron as a – by her standards – wealthy English Milord, but she had no idea that he was a celebrated poet, so she was no fame-hungry Claire Clairmont. Nor did she have Lady Byron's overwhelming need to be right. She simply loved him, cosseted him and listened to him. A month into their relationship, he told Augusta: "I have been very tranquil – very loving – & have not so much embarrassed myself with the tortures of the last two years – and that virtuous monster Miss Milbanke, who has nearly driven me out of my senses."

To his English friends, Byron always dismissed Marianna's husband Pietro as a comedy cuckold, busy elsewhere and unaware of what was going on under his nose. In reality, Byron had now become part of the complex Venetian code governing the *cavaliere servente*. The custom of a lady being attended by her *cavaliere servente* was an old one which, by the early eighteenth century, had become such an accepted part of Venetian life that a lady's right to a *cavaliere servente* was often written into marriage contracts. The *cavaliere servente*, also called a *cicisbeo* (from an old Italian word meaning "whisper", as one of his duties was to pass on gossip) was chosen at the end of the first year of marriage and had to be of the same rank as the lady he served. Many women did not even like their *cicisbeo*, but would have brought shame on their family by not having one. His duties were largely menial: he was expected to hand the lady into her gondola, sit beside her at dinner, escort her to the opera. Constant attendance was expected. Meanwhile, the lady's own husband was acting as *cavaliere servente* elsewhere, while yet another gentleman danced attendance on that *cavaliere servente*'s wife. Byron summed up the situation in *Beppo*:

But "Cavalier Servente" is the phrase

Used in politest circles to express
The supernumerary slave, who stays
Close to the lady as a part of dress,
Her word the only law which he obeys.
His is no sinecure, as you may guess;
Coach, servants, gondola, he goes to call,
And carries fan and tippet, gloves and shawl.

Before the fall of the Republic, when ensuring the purity of family bloodlines was regarded as of paramount importance, it was unusual for the relationship between a lady and her *cicisbeo* to be sexual. No doubt helped along by the years of war and upheaval, this had changed by the time Byron settled in Venice. Indeed, Marianna told Hobhouse that a woman now took a *cavaliere servente* as both *cicisbeo* and lover almost immediately after her marriage, "so that no man can be sure even of his wife's first-born." The custom of having a *cavaliere servente*, long confined to the patrician families, was now widespread among the merchant classes. Pietro Segati knew precisely what his wife's relationship with Byron was: he himself attended another lady.

Byron made it clear to Marianna from the beginning of their relationship that he was happy to be a *cavaliere* but she was not to expect any serving, as it wasn't in his nature. Indeed, on the one occasion when he jokingly tried to hand her into a gondola a combination of the dark night, slippery steps, his lame leg and the fact that his thoughts were elsewhere meant that "I as nearly as possible conveyed her into the Canal." So much, as Byron remarked "for love & all that." However, theirs was a warm and affectionate relationship. It lasted more than a year, from November 1816 until early 1818: longer than his marriage, longer than any of his love affairs until he met Teresa Guiccoli.

Byron soon found that he liked Venice. His original plan had been to stay for a while and then travel on to Rome. However, the city proved to have plenty of attractions besides Marianna. For one thing, what he called "its marine melancholy" appealed to his temperament. He enjoyed the silence and decay that hung over many parts of the city. However, when the mood took him, he also liked to be out and about. Piazza San Marco was still the beating heart of the city. As today, there were shops under the porticoes of the Procuratorie, but there was also a market in the Piazza itself, selling everyday necessities and foodstuffs including live chickens and other birds for the table. The arcades under the porticoes were a favourite place for the *liston*, the Venetian name for the *passeggiata* or evening stroll. What remained of Venetian society could be seen here most evenings, strolling, gossiping with acquaintances and taking refreshments in Caffé Florian under the arcades of the Procuratorie Nuove – loyal Venetians avoided Quadri, on the opposite side of the Piazza, which was favoured by the Austrians. A modern visitor to Venice, who has had difficulty in finding a restaurant or bar still open after 11pm, would probably be surprised to learn that the *liston* often did not begin until after the opera ended sometime after midnight, and continued into the early hours, by which time the ladies and gentlemen going home in their gondolas found the Grand Canal congested with delivery boats bringing fruit, vegetables and fish to the Rialto markets from 3am onwards. Byron enjoyed walking "down St Mark's by moonlight," perhaps with his lady on his arm, meeting his growing circle of acquaintance.[30]

Venetians enjoyed the theatre, and Byron, the former Drury Lane habitué, had eight thriving theatres to choose from in Venice. The season began in October, so by the time of his arrival it was in full swing, and would continue until the end of *Carnevale* on Shrove Tuesday. Byron's Italian was soon good enough for him to make critical judgements of the plays he saw, so that he thought very poorly of a play about the Sacrifice of Isaac, premiered (presumably because of its religious theme) at Christmas 1816. However, he enjoyed Goldoni comedies, in which many of the characters spoke the local dialect of Venexiano. Marianna was teaching him Venexiano, and he was soon proficient enough to understand the plays, even comparing himself to a Goldoni character, the English Milord Runebif from *La Vedova Scaltra* (The Shrewd Widow).

Byron rented a box at Teatro San Benedetto, where both plays and operas were performed, and where he also heard oratorios by Haydn and Handel. However, the chief Venetian theatre in which to see and be seen was La Fenice, and by the time the season opened, to mark the beginning of *carnevale* on 26th December 1816, Byron – clearly well aware of La Fenice's social cachet – had taken a box there, "for two reasons, one of which is, the music is remarkably good."

Byron was welcomed into Venetian society both as an English aristocrat and as a renowned man of letters. In his first winter in Venice, keeping his political opinions firmly in check, he occasionally attended receptions and *conversazioni* given by the Austrian Governor. More to his taste, Madame de Staël had given him a letter of introduction to Madame Albrizzi, "the Madame de Staël of Venice," (although Hobhouse cattily remarked that she was a very poor copy). A collector of art and sculpture and a woman with literary pretensions of her own, she would have been thrilled to welcome the poet to *conversazioni* in her palazzo, a short gondola-ride across the Grand Canal in the San Polo district. Here both literature and politics were discussed – most *conversazioni* concentrated on gossip. Madame Albrizzi was a native of Corfu, and Byron met many Greeks in her salon, so the talk often turned to Greek nationalism, a subject close to his heart. On his first visit to one of Madame's *conversazione*, Byron was shown one of her prized possessions, Canova's bust of Helen of Troy, a gift from the sculptor. He delighted Madame by straight away writing a brief ode in honour of Canova, a great hero to the Venetians not only because of his talent but also for the part he had played in ensuring the return of the horses of San Marco from their exile in Paris to their rightful place on the Basilica. Byron praised Canova by claiming to find his sculpture of Helen more beautiful than any living woman:

> *What Nature* could, *but* would *not do,*
> *And beauty and Canova* can*!*

Byron continued to be a regular guest of Madame Albrizzi over the coming months. Hobhouse, despite his initial poor reaction, also seems to have been a great success with Madame, as she continued to ask about his health and travels long after he had moved on, first to Rome and eventually back to England.

In the midst of this round of pleasure, Byron soon found that his brain also needed exercise, so he began to study Armenian. He and Hobhouse had been rowed out to the Convent of San Lazzaro degli Armeni, near the Lido, when they were sight-seeing soon after their arrival in Venice. Byron, with his ready sympathy for the underdog, was fascinated to learn that the order had been established on the island almost a hundred years earlier by monks fleeing from Turkish persecution. He was also struck by the monks' gentle kindness, both to visitors and to each other, and by the contented simplicity of their lives. The seventy monks looked after the spiritual needs of Venice's sizeable Armenian community of merchants and moneylenders, and made their living by running a printing press – Byron was later to pay for the translation of an Armenian/English grammar and helped the monks to have some rare Armenian versions of early Christian texts published in England.

Byron found learning the 38-character Armenian alphabet "difficult but not invincible" and enjoyed being "studious in the day & dissolute in the evening." Working with his tutor, Father Pasquale Aucher, Byron translated part of a history of Armenia and two epistles, claimed by the Armenian Church to be a third letter from Paul to the Corinthians and their reply, and was very proud of his "scriptural" style:

"But if any of ye, not believing, shall trespass, he shall be judged with the misdoers, and punished with those who have false belief."

A community of Armenian monks still live on the calm and beautiful island of San Lazzaro. The book-lined room where Byron studied Armenian is a high point of the guided tour of the monastery.

Even as Byron made a comfortable life for himself in Venice his old life had not gone away, as he was reminded throughout the winter of 1816-17 by letters from the Shelleys and Claire Clairmont. Shelley's loudly-proclaimed beliefs in free love and the irrelevance of marriage fell by the wayside when the trio returned to England in the autumn of 1816. As Claire's pregnancy became increasingly obvious she and Mary were packed off to Bath, where Claire would barely be noticed among so many ladies in varying degrees of "delicate health." Byron received a series of letters from Shelley, initially solicitous but becoming more and more fretful in the face of silence from Byron, who had given his word to provide for the child and saw no need for further discussion until it was born. He later commented wearily to Hobhouse that "Shelley has written to me frequently."

The letters from Claire were long, passionate and intense: the typical letters of an eighteen year-old girl to her lover. Keeping to his resolve not to have any further contact with her, Byron did not reply. Claire became importunate:

"Indeed, my dearest dear, if you will write me a little letter to say how you are, how all you love are, and above all if you will say to me sometimes that you think of me without anger, and that you will love and take care of the child, I shall be as happy as possible."

Unfortunately for Claire, such letters would instantly bring to Byron's mind the years of over-the-top outpourings he had had to endure from Caroline Lamb.

As the winter progressed and the birth drew closer, Claire began to try to force a response from Byron by making critical remarks about those she knew he cared for. So John Murray is a "mean-spirited paltry soul," Douglas Kinnaird is ugly and Hobhouse unworthy. She even apologises archly because he will be disappointed that a letter is from her and "perhaps... you expected one from Mrs Leigh." She then began to use the unborn child as a stick with which to beat Byron: "if you have little care to prevent any of my sufferings the chance is very small in favour of the affection you may show to the poor little Child."

The winter of 1816 was a momentous one in other ways for the Shelleys. Mary's half-sister Fanny Wollstonecraft committed suicide in October, and Shelley had to make the journey from Bath to Swansea (whence she had travelled from London in the hope of anonymity) to identify the body. Then in December Harriet, Shelley's wife and the mother of his children Charles and Ianthe, drowned herself. The believer in free love hurriedly married Mary before the month was over, in the hope of bringing about a reconciliation with his father and gaining custody of his children.

Byron's continuing respect for at least one member of the Shelley family can be seen in his response on hearing of Harriet's death, "You tell me Shelley's wife has drowned herself – the devil she has – do you mean his *wife* – or his Mistress? – Mary Godwin? – I hope not the last." Fortunately he soon heard from Mary herself, who wrote on 13th January 1817 to inform him of the birth of his daughter and of her own marriage to Shelley. Although she gave Byron the gentle hint that "nothing would give [Shelley] greater pleasure than to receive news of your motions and enjoyments," he clearly did not respond, as in April Shelley sent a very anxious letter, enquiring somewhat urgently about Byron's plans for the baby, then called Alba. The Shelleys were worried that, the longer she remained with them, the greater the risk that someone would work out that she was Claire's illegitimate child and not "the child of a friend in London, sent into the country for her health." Despite Shelley's concerns, the baby was to stay in England for another year.

In Venice, however, Byron was experiencing his first *carnevale*. It began on St Stephen's Day, 26th December, and lasted until Shrove Tuesday, when Lent began. Lasting between six and eight weeks, *carnevale* under the Austrians was a considerably shorter festival than it had been in the latter years of the Venetian Republic, when it had continued for half of the year. Although it has become part of the popular imagination that *carnevale* was a time of excess and sexual licence, for most Venetians (and *carnevale* was very much a Venetian festival both under the Republic and to a greater extent when the Austrian regime discouraged casual visitors) it was a time of equality and freedom, encouraged by the custom of wearing masks. These were not the elaborate sequin and feather affairs beloved of modern tourists, but simple black or white coverings for the upper part of the face, often with a beak to disguise the mouth. A silken hood covered the head and shoulders of both sexes, and the whole thing was topped with a hat. The aim was simple: in a city where everybody knew everyone else's business, a mask gave anonymity and allowed both sexes, all classes to socialise freely on an equal footing. Venetian serving-girls were entitled to a full day off of their own choosing to enjoy the fun, in all probability rubbing shoulders with their masters and mistresses. Even beggars wore masks at *carnevale*.

Piazza San Marco was the centre of most of the entertainments. In his *Memoirs* Goldoni writes of strolling round the square watching the masks and jugglers. There were also musicians, puppet-shows, Harlequin and Pantalone wandering around looking for people to be the butt of their fooling. Byron found "nothing but fiddling and playing on the virginals – and all kinds of deceits and divertissements on every canal of this aquatic city." *Carnevale* continued around the clock, and with invitations to the opera, balls and parties Byron was regularly up until the early hours. He even enjoyed an intrigue. An anonymous lady sent a note inviting him to an assignation. In typical Byron fashion he was unwilling to go out of his way, but replied stating that he would be at home on a certain evening. When the lady arrived however, she turned out to be Marianna's sister-in-law. Hot on her heels came Marianna herself in close pursuit, having spotted her sister-in-law's gondolier on the stairs and knowing the lady well. Byron was then entertained by a bout of screaming, slapping and hair-pulling, after which the lady took flight, Marianna fainted in his arms and Signor Segati came in to see what all the fuss was about. It must have resembled a scene from a Goldoni comedy.

No wonder he felt tired. On Shrove Tuesday he attended a masked ball at La Fenice to mark the end of *carnevale*, "it was a fine sight," he told Augusta, "the theatre illuminated and all the world buffooning," but he felt that the previous six weeks had knocked him up a little and, in reflective mood, he penned one of his most beautiful verses.

So we'll go no more a-roving
So late into the night,
Though the heart be still as loving,
And the moon be still as bright.

For the sword outwears its sheath,
And the soul wears out the breast,
And the heart must pause to breathe,
And Love itself have rest.

Though the night was made for loving,
And the day returns too soon,
We'll go no more a-roving
By the light of the moon.

Byron was unwell through March with a fever, which he said was worse at night. He believed that it was largely the result of too much pleasure and too many late nights during *carnevale*, and refused to see a doctor. He may have felt that a change of scene would be beneficial as, when Hobhouse, who was then in Rome, suggested that Byron join him, he decided to spend a few weeks there. Hobhouse had been rather anxious that he might bring Marianna with him, but Byron was an English gentleman: he might be in love, but he knew what was proper. He also knew that there would be plenty of English visitors in Rome, all more than willing to carry back gossip about him and his doings. They would make things up anyway, no point in giving them extra ammunition.

Leaving Venice in mid-April, he travelled via Padua, Arqua - a diversion so that he could visit Petrarch's house - Ferrara (where he saw Tasso's cell) and Florence, where he saw the tombs of Florentine worthies in the church of Santa Croce. All of these places, along with Venice and Rome itself, would appear in Canto IV of *Childe Harold*, which he wrote on his return to Venice. He found Rome a fine city, but, being definite in his mind that he was there only for a brief visit, behaved like a tourist, seeing the sights and riding out into the surrounding countryside. He made no attempt to describe his impressions of the city to his correspondents, simply saying that they might just as well read the guide-book. Indeed, *Childe Harold* indicates that what struck him most in Rome was the contrast between the ruins of her brutal yet magnificent Imperial past and the modern city, firmly back under the control of the Pope after his exile during Napoleonic rule.

Oh Rome! my country! city of the soul!
The orphans of the heart must turn to thee,
Lone mother of dead empires! and control
In their shut breasts their petty misery."

Byron was impressed by the sight of the Pope, Pius VII, whom he saw conducting the funeral of Cardinal Bracchi. He had been to the cardinal's lying in state. Both live Pope and dead cardinal, he felt, "looked very well." He was glad to see Hobhouse. But he was irritated by the boorish behaviour of some of the English visitors, and he missed Marianna. Three weeks in Rome was enough, and when Hobhouse set off for Naples he returned to Venice.

Back in Venice Byron completed a work which he had begun during the winter, *Manfred*. As his comfortable life with Marianna at last allowed him to relax, so his brain began to unravel and try to make sense of the events of the previous spring and summer: his self-imposed exile from England, his own "half-mad" mental state, the mountainous Swiss scenery. What emerged was a Gothic "dialogue" for several voices. The protagonist, Manfred, is a wizard-philosopher in an Alpine castle who conjures up seven spirits. He converses with them on death and the nature of immortality, much as Byron conversed with Shelley at Diodati in the gloomy summer of 1816. When one of the spirits reveals itself in the form of a beautiful woman, Manfred falls senseless. He is next found alone on the Jungfrau, where his thoughts on Nature:

And thou, fresh breaking Day, and you, ye Mountains,
Why are ye beautiful? I cannot love ye.

recall Byron's Journal written for his sister Augusta, when he admitted being oblivious to the Alpine scenery because of his own inner turmoil. Contemplating suicide, Manfred is rescued by a chamois hunter, whose simple human kindness provides a strong contrast to Manfred's nihilism. Manfred pours out his guilt; although exactly what he is guilty of is never revealed, save that his sister, Astarte, is dead and he believes that he is responsible.

At a waterfall, Manfred conjures up the Witch of the Alps in an attempt to find Astarte's spirit, but his refusal to swear obedience to the Witch leads to failure. He has more success in the Hall of the demon Arimanes, but despite his pleading, all that Astarte says to him is the prophetic: Manfred! Tomorrow ends thine earthly ills!

Back in Manfred's castle, the Abbot of St Maurice pleads with him to save his soul. Manfred kindly but regretfully sends him away. Meanwhile, his fearful servants discuss his long vigils in his tower, when Astarte was his only companion.

Manfred's final soliloquy shows the impact of Byron's recent visit to Rome:

I do remember me, that in my youth,
When I was wandering – upon such a night I stood within the Coliseum's wall,
'Midst the chief relics of almighty Rome;
The trees which grew along the broken arches
Waved dark in the blue midnight, and the stars
Shone through the rents of ruin

The Abbot enters, and he and Manfred contend with spirits who have come to drag Manfred to hell. They vanish, and he dies in the Abbot's arms.

The effect of the "low fever" from which Byron was suffering when he wrote much of the poem is clear: the entire work is very overheated and intense, while the spirits and Arimanes are reminiscent of feverish hallucinations. In fact, believing that the poem was complete, he sent it to Murray for publication. Re-reading it, he realised that Act III, with the Abbot, was "certainly d-d bad;" large sections made no sense at all as he had clearly been delirious, so he re-wrote much of this section on his return from Rome.

Having sent the revised work to Murray along with *The Lament of Tasso*, Byron gave little more thought to it. It was a piece of nonsense which ought to bring him 300 guineas. He had no idea of the fuss that was to follow its publication in the autumn of 1817. On one hand, a number of readers chose to see *Manfred* as a semi-autobiographical work. Manfred's guilt about his sister Astarte was viewed as Byron's outpouring of guilt about his alleged incestuous relationship with Augusta. It was great grist to the mill of Lady Byron and her scandal-mongering friends.[31]

On the other hand, reviewers of the work accused Byron of plagiarism. *Manfred*, it was claimed, was clearly based on the legend of Faust and his pact with the Devil. *The Critical Review* stated that Byron had made use of Marlowe's play *Doctor Faustus*, while others said that he had taken the idea from Goethe's *Faust Part I*, published in 1808.

Some were happy to adopt both views, picturing guilt-ridden Byron the plagiarist. Among them, perhaps surprisingly, was Goethe himself. The sixty-eight year-old Grand Old Man of European Letters, as he was regarded by all in Germany (including himself) had just read *Glenarvon*. Reading *Manfred*, he was not only convinced that it owed a huge debt to his own Faust, but was simultaneously overcome by a fit of sensibility and chose to take Lady Caroline Lamb's book as a biography of Byron and *Manfred* as autobiography. He read Manfred's words about Astarte, "I loved her, and destroyed her," as a straightforward confession of murder. It is hard to credit that the man whose youthful novel *The Sorrows of Young Werther* was widely believed to have led to copy-cat suicides across Europe, and who had written Faust about a man who makes a pact with the Devil, would so easily confuse an author and his work, but Byron was only too used to this sort of confusion. "If I depict a Corsair," he wearily observed, "a Libertine – a Chief of insurgents – or an Infidel, he is set down to the Author."

Byron was at first puzzled, then angry, when he heard of the accusations of plagiarism. He told his publisher that he had not read any of Goethe's works: they had not been translated into English and he did not read German. His only knowledge came from Monk Lewis, who had told him the story of Faust by way of a viva voce translation when he was Byron's guest at Diodati.

The genesis of *Manfred* was his own Alpine journey with Hobhouse, which he had recorded in his Journal for Augusta. As for Marlowe's Faustus, he had no recollection of ever reading it, so "The devil may take both the Faustus's, German and English – I have taken neither."

Byron's return to Venice from Rome at the end of May coincided with the departure from the city of most of the remaining patrician families who could afford a home in the city. Anyone who was able to – landed gentry with estates on the *terraferma* and wealthy merchants who could afford to rent a villa – left Venice during the heat and humidity of June and July, and if they were able decamped from the city again to avoid the autumn gales and *acqua alta* of October and November. The original purpose of the *villeggiatura*, or return to one's villa, was to oversee the harvest and take a hand in the running of one's country estate. However, like much else in Venice, it had turned into an exercise in gossip and socialising: a lady's *cavaliere servente* accompanied her on *villeggiatura*. Goldoni waspishly remarked that "Our ancestors frequented these spots for the sole purpose of collecting their property, and their descendants go merely to spend theirs."

The cream of Venetian society had their villas along the Brenta Canal, which was reached by travelling across the lagoon to Fusina, then up the Brenta in a *burchiello*, or little barge, pulled by horses which walked along the towpath. The journey was slow, but that didn't matter, as a *burchiello* had all the comforts of home, including servants, who travelled in a separate room on the barge. Byron took a small villa (he referred to it as a *casino*, or little house) in the little town of Mira – La Mira as he always called it – midway between Venice and Padua on the Brenta Canal.[32] He rented the villa from the Foscarini family, patricians who were obviously feeling the pinch. By the middle of June 1817 he was installed there with Marianna and her daughter, and stayed at the villa until November. As well as the usual visits and *conversazioni* he was at last able to have his horses with him, and began to enjoy the regular exercise of riding around the countryside in the cool of the evening. Monk Lewis came to stay with him at La Mira, but when Hobhouse arrived at the end of July he insisted on taking lodgings with the local doctor, visiting Byron daily but unwilling to stay under the same roof as Marianna, "a woman living in open adultery." He was shocked to find that she was received in local society and well-regarded by the neighbours, including his landlord's four unmarried daughters, who gave him affectionate messages to pass on.

Pietro Segati came out from Venice once or twice a week to see his wife, and was usually invited to stay for dinner. On one evening he told – he claimed – a true story which had recently happened in Venice. A Turk arrived at a Venetian inn and asked to speak to the landlady, a widow whose husband had been lost at sea some years earlier. He asked about her late husband: did he have any distinguishing marks? Yes, she replied, a scar on his shoulder. The Turk instantly displayed an identical scar before revealing himself as her husband, who had made a fortune in Turkey. He begged her to leave her *cavaliere servente* and return to him. Hobhouse found the story shocking, but it made an impact on Byron: the germ of a new poem was lodged in his brain.

In September Byron's friend Douglas Kinnaird arrived in Venice, with his brother, Lord Kinnaird and a friend, William Stuart Rose, an Italian scholar and translator. They stayed in the city to see the sights, but Byron often came across from La Mira to see them, and they dined at the villa, meeting Marianna. Kinnaird and Rose showed Byron *Whistlecraft*, a poem which Murray had recently published anonymously.[33] The poem purported to be a recently-discovered antiquarian work about the days of King Arthur. Rose liked it because it used the *ottava rima* rhyme-scheme developed by the Italian Renaissance poets he loved. Byron liked it because it was witty. This verse, about ladies who have been captured by ogres and their rescue by Arthur's knights, is a good example both of the poem's humour and of the deceptively simple eight line verse of the *ottava rima* with its internal discipline of rhyme and rhythm:

The ladies? – They were tolerably well,
At least as well as could be expected;
Many details I must forebear to tell,
Their toilet had been very much neglected;
But by supreme good luck it now befell
That when the castle's capture was effected,
When those vile cannibals were overpowered,
Only two fat duennas were devoured.

Byron saw the chance to do something new. He had begun to lose patience with much of the verse written by his fellow English Romantics, which he felt was becoming overblown and self-absorbed. Although he consistently praised Shelley's work he had little time for Keats, comparing his writing to "mental masturbation." Wordsworth ("Turdsworth" as Byron now called him) he despised for turning his back on his youthful radicalism and accepting the patronage of the Tory Lord Lonsdale. Byron had a profound distaste for Southey, the Poet Laureate, on both personal and poetic grounds: Southey was circulating malicious gossip about him in England. From this time onwards, the poet Byron most revered, and viewed as a rôle-model, was Alexander Pope. He sat down one day with a copy of some of his own poems and a copy of Pope's, and found himself both astonished and mortified "at the ineffable distance in point of sense – harmony – effect... & *Invention* – between the little Queen Anne's Man" and himself.

With William Stuart Rose as his tutor, Byron began to study Italian comic verse and the ottavo rima. By the end of October, he was able to tell Murray that he had a new poem ready for publication: *Beppo.*[34] In a chatty, conversational style which draws on Pope but also reflects a *cicisbeo* telling the latest gossip to his lady, Byron tells the story he heard from Pietro Segati, which is probably a Venetian urban myth. The poem is set during *carnevale*:

Of all the places where the Carnival
Was most facetious in the days of yore,
For dance, and song, and serenade, and ball,
And masque, and mime, and mystery, and more
Than I have time to tell now, or at all,
Venice the bell from every city bore, –
And at the moment when I fix my story,
The sea-born city was in all her glory.

Her husband Giuseppe, or *Beppo*, having been lost at sea, the heroine, Laura, has taken a noble *cavaliere servente,*

... a Count, and then he knew
Music and dancing, fiddling, French and Tuscan

Byron takes care to describe the duties of a *cavaliere servente* very clearly, no doubt hoping to shock his English readers in verse in the same way as his rôle as Marianna's *cavaliere* had shocked Hobhouse in reality. At a masked ball Laura observes that a Turk is staring at her, and the man follows her and the Count home, where he reveals himself as *Beppo,*

.... at Venice landed to reclaim
His wife, religion, house, and Christian name.
The poem ends with the aside
I've heard the Count and he were always friends.
This witty, joyous commentary on Venetian life marked
the end of Byron's first year in the city.

Fourth Venetian Interlude

... while this play is presenting with much applause ...

Venice was famous for its thriving theatrical scene. All Venetians went to the theatre regularly, and impresarios competed to make sure that there was something to appeal to all tastes. Doctor Johnson's friend Hester Thrale spent some time in the city in 1785. She was struck by the "many theatres, the worst infinitely superior to ours."

There were in fact eight theatres in the city, seven of which were named for the parish in which they were located. Having so many theatres inevitably led to a cut and thrust atmosphere among theatre owners and managers: a play that was bringing in the punters at one theatre often led to a close imitation hurriedly being presented by a rival.

Teatro San Giovanni Crisostomo was near the Rialto Bridge. It was the chief opera house of Venice until 1792 and the famous castrato Farinelli was among those who performed here. It is still a theatre today, having been renamed Teatro Malibran in honour of the singer Maria Malibran, who appeared there in 1834.

Teatro San Benedetto, where plays, operas and oratorios were performed, was regarded by Goldoni as Venice's finest theatre. A painting in the Fondazione Querini Stampalia shows the auditorium in 1782, ablaze with the light of magnificent glass chandeliers under an elaborate ceiling decorated with huge classical figures. The impresario of the theatre commissioned several operas from Rossini, who conducted the premieres himself. The remains of the theatre have been incorporated into the Punto Simply supermarket and Cinema Rossini which now occupy the site. To confuse the unwary, it stands opposite the Church of San Luca.

The Teatro Sant' Angelo was not large but Goldoni, who wrote several plays for this theatre, said that the receipts were very good. The end of the Venetian Republic in 1797 led to the closure of the theatre, which was housed in what is now the Hotel Manin/Barocci on the Grand Canal.

Teatro San Luca is now the thriving Teatro Goldoni. It was the theatre to which Goldoni moved as playwright in residence from the Sant' Angelo. Actors liked to work there as they all took a share of the evening's takings. During his visit to Venice in 1786 Goethe watched and hugely enjoyed both a Goldoni comedy and the audience participation in the action. He was struck by their "ecstasy of joy" to see "them-

selves and their families so realistically portrayed on the stage." Venetian audiences were notoriously noisy, and Goldoni thought it was a notable event when one of his plays was listened to in silence – he was very relieved to hear loud applause between the acts.

The only theatre on the San Polo side of the Grand Canal was Teatro San Cassiano, famed for its comedies. The theatre is remembered today solely in street names, the Corte del Teatro and Calle de la Commedia.

Teatro San Samuele's leading lady in the 1720s was Casanova's mother, Zanetta Farussi, and young Giacomo grew up in the area around the theatre. The theatre as it was in 1753 is captured in another painting in the Querini Stampalia, showing that a performance here was quite an occasion. The audience, in private boxes or the capacious pit under a ceiling glittering with stars, enjoyed performances on a stage decorated with crystal panels, lit by banks of tall candles. The theatre closed in the late nineteenth century, and today a school stands on the site. The theatre's existence is recalled in the street name Ramo del Teatro.

Teatro San Moise, near to Piazza San Marco, was home to both theatre and opera. Goethe saw an opera here which he did not care for, although he had to admit that the ballet was most enjoyable, as the dancers "considered it their duty to acquaint the audience with every beautiful part of their bodies." Performances were given into the early years of the twentieth century. A plaque commemorating the theatre can still be seen on Calle del Teatro, just off Calle Larga XXII Marzo on the approach to the Church of San Moise.

However the chief theatre in Venice was and is Gran Teatro La Fenice, opened in 1792. Despite the ravages of two fires, in 1836 and 1996, this magnificent building is still very much the one designed by Gianantonio Selva. Its classical façade dominates the small Campo San Fantin, but most members of Venetian Society, disembarking from their gondolas to attend a performance, would have been more familiar with the water entrance. The theatre was built just before the fall of the Republic by a group of wealthy families known as the Nobile Società, and was always the most exclusive of Venice's theatres, designed with the maximum number of private boxes, which were available only by subscription. These rise up in three tiers encircling the compact auditorium, the most luxurious boxes being closest to the stage. Each box has its own lockable door and curtains which can be closed for privacy or opened if one wishes to view one's neighbours, be viewed by them, or watch a popular aria or the ballet.

When Byron and Hobhouse arrived in Venice in November 1816 the theatrical season, which began in October, was in full swing, and they soon began to enjoy the variety of what was on offer. The first theatre they visited was San Benedetto, which had a very varied programme: everything from operas by Rossini to Goldoni comedies to translations of plays first performed on the London stage. Hobhouse attended the theatre almost every evening, but the first play that Byron saw at San Benedetto was Aristodemo, a rather gory tragedy by the pair's Milanese literary acquaintance, Vincenzo Monti. For friendship's sake, Hobhouse allowed that it was a fine piece of writing, but both he and Byron felt that it was very poorly performed. A few days later Byron wrote to his fellow Drury Lane habitué Douglas Kinnaird to say that he had just been to a farce which he had originally seen in London when Kinnaird had helped present it at Drury Lane a couple of years earlier, and wondered what the odds were "against me seeing the same farce at Venice?" The audience at San Benedetto was very enthusiastic: when Hobhouse attended a benefit concert here, as well as the usual applause and cheering, some went so far as to throw sonnets of praise onto the stage. Byron soon took a box at San Benedetto, where he enjoyed a number of Goldoni comedies as well as operas, especially works by Rossini.

An Italian theatrical institution was the improvvisatore, *or extemporiser, an actor who performed a one-man show around topics suggested by the audience. The most famous Italian extemporiser in Byron's time was Tommaso Sgricci. Sgricci was very talented, hugely popular and extremely eccentric, appearing on stage in whatever he happened to be wearing at the time, usually including his yellow slippers. Byron and Hobhouse had seen a performance of his in Milan where he declaimed lengthy speeches and improvised verses on topics as diverse as mythological themes, historical events and current affairs, written on scraps of paper by the audience and pulled at random from a vase by a small boy. Hobhouse saw Sgricci again at Teatro San Luca in Venice, where improvisation seems to have been something of a tradition – Goethe had seen the actors here improvise an entire comedy, to great acclaim. On this occasion Sgricci extemporised only one piece, the story of Elizabeth I and the Earl of Essex, but it must have been a bravura performance as it lasted for two hours, included verse interludes and Sgricci represented five characters, male and female, in a range of voices. No wonder Byron said of him "his fluency astonished me."*

Teatro La Fenice was a place where Byron soon felt at home, declaring that it was a "finer theatre" than his old stamping-ground of Drury Lane. All of Venice's theatres drew part of their audience from members of the patrician class. Hobhouse had noticed the numerous wax candles and mirrors at Teatro San Benedetto, "in which the society adjust their hair." However, the opulent La Fenice was the place where everybody who was anybody met, entertained each other in their boxes between (and during) acts and observed the progress of each other's love affairs. Byron took a box here for the season beginning on December 26th 1816, and was pleasantly surprised by the cost, the equivalent of about £14.00 for what, he was sure, would have cost at least £400 in London. In Venice he had "a better box and a better opera."

On the first night of the season, Byron was greatly diverted by two events. The first was the behaviour of the principal dancer in the ballet. A dance interlude was at that time shoe-horned into the action of every opera and play: the gentlemen in the audience expected it. The ballerina went, says Byron, "into convulsions" because she was applauded on her first appearance, whether from first-night nerves or an attack of sensibility is unclear. Her attack was so extreme that the action had to be stopped. The manager stepped forward with the timeless request for a doctor in the house. Byron, who (somewhat prophetically) held doctors in low esteem, drily noted that, had the one who was sitting in his box offered his services "these would have been the last convulsions which would have troubled the Ballerina."
The second episode which amused him came at the end of the piece. The first night crush was so great that it became impossible to find a way out of the theatre. Byron, mindful of his lady companions, took the law into his own hands and brought into play his boxing skills. Like many other members of the bon ton, he had been coached by the famous "Gentleman" John Jackson at his boxing studio in Bond Street, London, and on this evening Jackson's training paid off. A man foolish enough to stand in Byron's way was treated to "an English punch in the guts – which sent him as far back as the squeeze and passage would admit – he did not ask for another – but with great signs of disapprobation and dismay appealed to his compatriots – who laughed at him."
No wonder Byron came to enjoy Goldoni's plays so much. Both men found great humour in everyday situations and ordinary people. Let them bring the curtain down together: "Good bye – I am just going to a comedy of Goldoni's."

Chapter Five

Don Juan

"… since last year I have run the gauntlet; – it is the Taruscelli – the Da Mosti – the Spineda – the Lotti – the Rizzato – the Eleanora – the Carlotta – the Giulietta – the Alvisi – the Zambieri – The Eleanora da Bezzi – (who was the King of Naples' Gioaschino's mistress – at least one of them) the Theresina of Mazzurati – the Glettenheimer – & her Sister – the Luigia & her mother – the Fornaretta – the Santa – the Cagliari – the Portiera – the Bolognese figurante – the Tentora and her sister …"

Byron's second experience of the Venetian *carnevale* was very different from his first. He still went to the opera, the ball, the ridotto, but instead of returning to the calm comforts of Marianna in the Frezzeria he threw himself into a round of womanising and whoring which was to last for almost a year.

The trigger for this was the end of his relationship with Marianna. Pietro Segati's drapery business had been feeling the pinch for some time: Austrian taxes on one hand, poor harvests on the other, meant fewer customers with less to spend. Byron seems to have given money to bail him out on one or two occasions; Hobhouse believed that this added up to as much as £500 altogether, a very substantial sum. Byron also presented Marianna with a set of diamond jewellery, the sort of handsome gift which a gentleman would offer to his lady. Whatever Marianna's feelings for Byron, the crisis in her husband's business and the need for financial security for herself and her child proved stronger than sentiment. The diamonds were exchanged for hard cash. Byron would probably have been none the wiser had not the jeweller to whom Marianna sold the diamonds thought of the English Milord as a likely purchaser. Byron bought them back and gave them to Marianna once again, with a little joke, but the unwelcome revelation of a more mercenary side to his lady seems to have been the beginning of the end.

The fading attractions of the Frezzeria and news from England of the impending arrival of Allegra, his daughter with Claire Clairmont, provided twin stimuli for Byron to look for new lodgings. He was optimistic about his financial situation, as it seemed that a buyer had at last been found for his ancestral home Newstead Abbey. So, spending the money before it was in his pocket, he began to consider living in style in a palazzo on the Grand Canal. He almost took Count Gritti up on the offer of his palazzo on the Grand Canal near the Church of San Marcuola,[35] but he and the Count disagreed about the terms of the lease. Hearing on the grapevine that Lord Byron was willing to pay the very high sum of 200 louis a year – which was the rent he had agreed with Count Gritti – Countess Lucia Mocenigo offered him the tenancy of her private apartments in the imposing Palazzo Mocenigo, on the bend of the Grand Canal as it turns between Rialto and the *bacino*.[36] Byron signed a three-year lease, rent payable in advance every June (Lucia Mocenigo was clearly an excellent business-woman) and took up residence in the *piano nobile* of the central twin *palazzi*, known to locals as Ca' Nova, on June 1st 1818.

His relationship with Marianna had finally fizzled out by March 1818 and "I have taken a dozen instead." The compulsive womanising in which Byron indulged throughout 1818 is just one symptom of a manic phase, apparent in many areas of his life at this time as his mental health once again took a downward turn. Having slipped easily into a comfortable relationship immediately on his arrival in Venice, he had been able to put from his mind the horrors of his broken marriage, the poor state of his finances and the unlikelihood of his ever being able to play an active part in the upbringing of his daughter Ada. The break with Marianna, coupled with news of the likely sale of Newstead, seem to have brought his true situation to the forefront of his mind Anger at Marianna became mixed with anger at the "cold-blooded animal... Miss Milbanke." All women – except his sister – were whores, and for a time he treated them as such. On one hand, the news about Newstead was good: the estate had been on the market for some time and Byron was sorely in need of the money. On the other, he had a great sentimental attachment to the Abbey and the prospect of losing it meant the cutting of one of his last remaining ties with England. The sale worried Byron to such an extent that he went through a period of writing to Douglas Kinnaird, his banker, and John Hanson, his solicitor, on an almost daily basis, allowing no time for replies to reach Venice. He was clearly very agitated about the sale, his debts and money he believed was owed to him. The loss of his English home (even though he had not lived there for some years, or even visited since before his marriage) made him all the more determined to settle permanently into a Venetian one. He told several friends that he planned to stay in Venice for the foreseeable future and had no desire to even visit England. Indeed, when his solicitor had important papers relating to the sale of Newstead for Byron to sign he stubbornly refused to leave the city, "were it even as far as Fusina or Maestri,"[37] and John Hanson had to make the journey to Venice.

Byron had also given up his lowering diet and was eating and drinking a great deal. This had a considerable impact on both his mental and physical health. A few years later, a more self-aware Byron wrote that too much alcohol made him "sullen and savage to ferocity," and his behaviour in 1818 bears this out. Mentally, he became irritable and self-pitying. On hearing of the suicide of the lawyer and politician Sir Samuel Romilly, who had represented Lady Byron during the Separation, he wrote a rare letter to that lady. Romilly took his own life whilst in a state of extreme grief following the death of his wife. Byron was unable to feel any pity for the dead man, only for himself, and he expressed himself unusually harshly, almost exulting in Romilly's death. "This Man little thought when he was lacerating my heart according to law – while he was poisoning my life at its sources… that in less than thirty-six Moons… a domestic affliction would lay him in the Earth – with the meanest of Malefactors – in a Cross road with the Stake in his body."

When Hanson reached Venice in November he found Byron very nervous and on edge. This could perhaps be explained by his anxiety at having to sign papers which would hand Newstead Abbey to a new owner once and for all, yet a puzzled Hanson found that Byron barely wished to discuss the sale or the financial implications: Mr. Kinnaird would sort all of that out back in London. All he was interested in was whether Hanson had brought a large consignment of books and periodicals from John Murray and various medicaments he had requested. He dismissed Hanson as quickly as possible and wrote a long, manic letter to Hobhouse complaining that the lawyer had left "every thing except his legal papers" in London and Hobhouse must engage a courier immediately, regardless of expense, to bring the books to him. Hanson, who had travelled to Venice on Byron's behalf, was no better than a "Monster" on whom Byron would have revenge.

Among the items Byron was so anxious to receive were corn rubbers, as his feet were giving him trouble. This was because, as a result of abandoning his lowering diet, Byron had gained a great deal of weight. Hanson found him fat, pale, bloated and looking much older than thirty, as did another acquaintance who met him at this time, Mary Montgomery, a friend of Lady Byron. She saw a man who had completely lost his famous good looks as a result of his weight gain.

Byron must have been eating a prodigious amount, as he gained weight despite taking a great deal of exercise. Not wishing to give up the daily rides he had enjoyed so much during his stay at La Mira, on his return to Venice in November 1817 he moved his horses to the Lido. Today, the Lido is a luxurious summer beach resort where Italian families and wealthy foreigners spend a great deal of money whilst developing incipient skin cancer. In Byron's day this long spit of sand, which protects the Venetian lagoon from the worst of the Adriatic storms, was home to nothing except a few fishing villages, the Jewish and Protestant cemeteries and several Austrian forts. Byron rented a stable at the fort on the northernmost point of Lido from the Commandant.[38] He went to the Lido for a daily gallop from the fort down towards the village of Malamocco, roughly half way along the sand-bar. Sometimes he rode as far as that village; usually he rode along the sand dunes as far as another small defensive fort about five kilometres from his starting-point. It is often said that today nothing remains of the Lido Byron knew, and this is certainly the case in the busy town of Lido itself. However, it is possible to re-create Byron's Lido. The northernmost point of the island, where Byron began his daily ride, remains bleak, windswept and untouched by modern development. Moving south, past the hotels and private beaches of Lido, the sea-defences run in an unbroken line as far as Malamocco, visited by few except the occasional jogger or the modern cousin of the horse-rider, the cyclist. The Adriatic on one side, dunes of scrubby grass and tough plants on the other; Byron would have had a remarkably similar view as he galloped along the shore. The remains of the fort which was his regular turning-point can still be visited. Byron once told his friend Hoppner that he wanted to be buried in the vegetable-gardens surrounding it.[39]

As his mood became even more manic, the daily ride was not enough. Together with riding, swimming had long been a favourite way of exercising: in the saddle or in the water his lame leg was neither on display nor a handicap. Swimming also lifted his spirits, something of which they were sorely in need in the spring of 1818. Byron had always been unable to resist the challenge of a wide expanse of water: at Lisbon in 1809 he had swum across the estuary where the River Tagus meets the sea and in Turkey the following year had swum the Hellespont from Sestos to Abydos in imitation of Leander. He now began to swim across the lagoon from Lido to Venice after his ride, leading to one of his best-known Venetian exploits.

The British Consul to Venice, Richard Belgrave Hoppner, introduced Byron to Angelo Mengaldo. Mengaldo was only a few months older than Byron, and had also idolized Napoleon as a young man. In 1806 he had volunteered to serve in his hero's army, seeing action in Dalmatia, Albania and Hungary, where he had led a secret attack on the Austrians by swimming across the Danube with his men. Understandably proud of this exploit, he recounted at every possible opportunity. Byron was also rightly proud of his achievements and something of a war of words began. The gentlemanly one-upmanship between Byron and Mengaldo is easy to imagine, and resulted in a challenge. On 15th June Byron, Mengaldo, Hoppner and Alexander Scott, a Scottish gentleman living in Venice, all entered the water together at Lido with the aim of swimming across the lagoon to the Riva degli Schiavoni, the long promenade running from the Doge's Palace towards the Arsenale. Only Byron swam the entire distance, the other three being forced to give up halfway. However, Mengaldo's pride was obviously piqued by Byron's easy victory, and he challenged Byron to a return match, this time from Lido to the Grand Canal. The swim took place on 25th June, and Scott again joined in. This time all three men fared somewhat better, as Mengaldo and Scott swam from Lido across the lagoon and then up the Grand Canal as far as Rialto. Byron, however, continued swimming right to the end of the Grand Canal, as far as the canal of Santa Chiara.[40] He covered a distance of four and a half miles (seven and a quarter kilometres) and was in the water for almost four hours. However, he wrote to Hobhouse on the same evening, "I could not be much fatigued having had a piece in the forenoon – & taking another in the evening at ten of the Clock."

The compulsive womanizing which Byron so casually refers to, often several different women in a day, was another symptom of his mania. By September 1818 he estimated that he had slept with over 200 women, from all classes of Venetian society, "some noble – some middling – some low – & all whores." It is not surprising that he picked up a dose of the clap during *carnevale*, despite having a supply of "cundums" which Hobhouse had brought out for him from England. At this date condoms, made of sheep-gut and designed to be re-usable, were used as a protective against disease rather than as a contraceptive. English condoms were considered the best. However, since the lady who infected Byron came from a well-known patrician family, perhaps he had considered their use unnecessary. He couldn't say that he hadn't been warned, as the Venetian censor Signor Petrotini had told him that the girl "Elena da Mosta – a Gentil Donna… was clapt - & she has clapt me – to be sure it was gratis, the first Gonorrhoea I have not paid for."

The ensuing treatment, the painful injection of mercury into the urethra, clearly did not deter Byron from further adventures, as

he rented a small apartment for the sole purpose of womanizing. It was a common Venetian practice to have a *casino*, or "little house," somewhere in the city. *Casini* came in two varieties. Some were simply cosy places where Venetian patricians could relax and be warm, which is not always easy in a draughty palazzo. Whereas a palazzo was the place for formal evenings and *conversazioni*, the *casino* was somewhere for friends to meet and unwind; "these snug retreats are intended for the relaxation of those who inhabit the more splendid apartments and are fatigued with exertions of dignity and necessity of no small expense." Other *casini* were kept solely for sexual assignations. Casanova describes a *casino* belonging to the British Ambassador to the Republic which was decorated with pornographic pictures made from Chinese tiles. Most were small, just one or two rooms perhaps with a discreet servant.
Byron's *casino* was near the church of Santa Maria del Giglio. Its exact location is unknown, as Byron only seems to have shown it to one acquaintance, Angelo Mengaldo, who later claimed be shocked by the place. It seems likely that the *casino* was on one of the waterways running from the Grand Canal in the direction of the Giglio, a short gondola-ride from Palazzo Mocenigo. Byron could leave his gondola and enter his *casino* from the narrow *fondamenta*, knowing that he could rely on the professional discretion of his gondolier. The *casino* was also close to Teatro La Fenice, handy should Byron arrange an assignation before or after the opera.[41]

The only woman who seems to have held his attention for any length of time during this spell of casual womanising was Margarita Cogni, *La Fornarina* (the Baker's Wife). Byron had first met her when he was still involved with Marianna. One evening at La Mira, when he and Hobhouse were riding along the Brenta Canal, they spotted two very pretty girls among a group of country people. There was a great deal of rural distress at the time, a combination of the poor harvests brought about by the bad weather of 1816, high Austrian taxes and the sudden influx of soldiers returning from the Napoleonic Wars. Byron, always a generous and charitable man, had done what he could to help the peasants around La Mira. Margarita, a spirited woman, clearly knew of this and when the two gentlemen rode past she asked them for money. Byron made a jest that she was too lovely and too young to need his help, but a few days later he and Hobhouse met the two girls – Margarita and her cousin – again. Byron seems to have begun a casual affair with Margarita in the late summer of 1817. He was amused by her fiery temper, displayed to great effect when Marianna, learning of a rival for

Byron's affections, told her publicly to stay away from Milord. Margarita did not mince her words. *"You* are *not* his wife: *I* am *not* his wife – *you* are his Donna – and *I* am his *donna* – your husband is a cuckold – and mine is another."

When Byron returned to Venice she followed, and she remained a regular, though casual, amour among all the rest. At this time Byron found her displays of temper, such as snatching the *carnevale* mask from the face of a lady leaning on his arm, entertaining. When he moved into Palazzo Mocenigo, however, she left her husband and joined him. Her husband brought the police to take her back; Byron said he did not want her; she refused to return to a "consumptive cuckold." Restored to her long-suffering husband by order of a legal commissioner she ran back to Byron, and was allowed to remain for a while: because she made him laugh and because the servants were so terrified of her that the quality of housekeeping at the palazzo improved overnight.

The surviving portrait of Margarita, an engraving used by Murray as a frontispiece to Byron's play *Marino Faliero*, shows an unexpectedly demure young lady, her eyes cast modestly down. Byron had this sketch made of her wearing the *fazziolo*, the scarf or kerchief worn over the head by working-class women. In this, he said, she was beautiful. Margarita, however, had other ideas. Now she was the mistress of an English Milord she should have a hat with feathers and a dress with a train. The sight of Margarita parading about the palazzo, dragging her train behind her, or trying to read his letters (she was unable to read) to work out whether or not they were written in a feminine hand made Byron laugh – he welcomed anything which lightened his mood in the spring and summer of 1818.

Byron retained very clear memories of Margarita's time at Palazzo Mocenigo. One evening, returning from the Lido, a sudden storm blew up over the lagoon, putting his gondola briefly into difficulty. Reaching the safety of the Grand Canal at last, "I found her on the open steps of the Mocenigo palace… with her great black eyes flashing through her tears and the long dark hair which was streaming drenched with rain over her brows and breast… the lightning flashing around her – with the waves rolling at her feet – made her look like Medea alighted from her chariot – or the Sibyl of the tempest that was rolling around her."

Eventually the displays of temper began to bore Byron and he told Margarita that it was time to go back home. She began melodramatically to threaten knives and revenge, to which Byron equably replied that there was a knife and fork on the table as he was about to eat his dinner. Next day at the same hour she forced her way into Byron's presence with the promised knife.

Disarmed by Fletcher, she was escorted out. "She seemed quiet and walked downstairs. – I resumed my dinner. – We heard a great noise. – I went out – and met them on the staircase – carrying her up the stairs. – She had thrown herself into the Canal," giving considerable entertainment to the neighbours. Byron's landlady – "Mother Mocenigo" as he called her – was watching from the window of her apartment. To Byron, the incident was an unwelcome reminder of another lover given to melodrama; the whole episode, he noted, "was in the Lamb style." It certainly gave more grist to the Venetian gossip-mill, and a garbled version of the story spread far and wide. When Tom Moore heard it in Geneva the following year Byron had become the villain of the piece, having seduced and abandoned an innocent young girl, who had thrown herself into the Grand Canal in despair and was now confined in the lunatic asylum. This was the Byron legend the world preferred.

Although Margarita was ejected for good after this episode in the autumn of 1818, she continued to boast of her relationship with Byron well into her old age. A French visitor to Venice found her running an oyster-stall and using her status as a selling-point for, as long as she talked about Byron, the Frenchman continued to eat oysters! When William Dean Howells was American Consul to Venice in 1862, the balcony overlooking the Grand Canal from which Margarita threw herself ("the hideous basket-balcony" as Howells described it) was still pointed out to visitors, and it may well have been the lady herself who, having moved on from oysters, kept a butter and cheese shop in the Calle de la Mandola, leading from Campo Sant' Angelo to what is now Campo Manin, "a fat sinner, long past beauty" yet still visited by curious literary tourists on the look-out for interesting relics of Byron.

Byron, always self-aware, knew that he was behaving badly in 1818. He also knew that he was experiencing a mental breakdown as, in reply to an enquiry about his health, he replied that "poets especially seem to be a marked race" mentioning the idiocy of Swift, the melancholy of Johnson and the madness of Cowper. Yet his period of mania and dissipation was, at least in a poetic sense, a cleansing one for Byron. He emerged on the other side with a clarity of vision due, at least in part, to a growing physical and emotional distance from England. His letters to Hobhouse and Kinnaird, who were both standing for Parliament during this period, show that he was losing patience with English politics. The struggle for Italian freedom would soon appear much more immediate and more important. He already believed that English Romantic poetry was stuck in a perpetual adolescence, and his reply to this was to experiment, as he had done in *Beppo,* with a completely new style. By mid-July, the worst of his mania over, Byron paused, took stock of his life and, as normality slowly returned, began to write his work of mature genius, *Don Juan*. He began writing Canto I in July 1818 and had completed it by September when he confided to Tom Moore that his new poem was "meant to be a little quietly facetious upon everything," although he felt (correctly as it turned out) that it might be "too free for these very modest days."

The character of Don Giovanni was, of course, well-known throughout late eighteenth and early nineteenth century Europe. The story of the serial seducer given his come-uppance by the statue of a man he has killed, the father of one of his cast-off lovers, originated in Spain in the seventeenth century and was soon widely-imitated. In London, Byron had seen Carlo Antonio Delpini's pantomime based on the traditional version of the story, complete with the Don dragged to hell. In Venice, the story was hugely popular. Goldoni's *Don Giovanni Tenorio,* first performed in 1738, a comedy in which the Don was shipwrecked – a mishap which *Don Juan* also experiences – may well have influenced Byron.

In 1787 at least three composers wrote operas called *Don Giovanni*. The only version still performed today is the one by Mozart. However, in Venice both Gardi (barely-known to modern audiences) and Giuseppe Gazzaniga composed their own versions, with very similar plots.[42] Gazzaniga's *Don Giovanni,* commissioned by Teatro San Moise, was a great success and stayed in the repertoire in Venice until 1821. It was just the sort of opera to appeal to Byron. Indeed, he seems to teasingly quote from it in a letter of January 1819 when, after talking of his new poem, he lists his conquests for the benefit of Hobhouse and Kinnaird. In Gazzaniga's opera Don Giovanni's servant, Pasquariello, gives a detailed list of his master's conquests.

Ladies, townswomen,
Artisans, peasants,
Chambermaids, cooks and scullery-maids,
It is enough that they are women
To make him amorous…
I tell you that he loves all women
Whether beautiful or ugly
Only by old women
Does he not feel inflamed.

Byron's own list, "some of them are Countesses – & some of them Cobblers wives – some noble – some middling – some low," jokingly recalls Pasquariello.[43]

It is not hard to see similarities in the close relationship between Byron with his valet William Fletcher, who had been in Milord's service since Byron was sixteen and was privy to most of his secrets and all of his love-affairs, and that of Don Giovanni and his devoted, conniving servant. Fletcher was also involved with a lady at this time. Her name was Tiretta and it seems to have been a serious and long-standing relationship. Late in 1819, Fletcher suddenly remembered that he already had a wife. Byron was considering returning to England and Fletcher came to him in something of a panic: Tiretta was making plans for their new life together: what about Mrs Fletcher and the children? Milord must do all he could to prevent Tiretta from getting a passport.[44]

Byron remained faithful to the original Spanish setting of *Don Juan*, at least in Canto I of the poem. However, his hero differs from the earlier incarnations of *Don Giovanni* in one major respect: Giovanni is a rapacious serial seducer; Juan is an innocent abroad. Women throw themselves at him and make the running, beginning with Donna Julia, a married woman of twenty-three to Juan's sixteen, who manages to be alone with him in an arbour at twilight, and:

One hand on Juan's carelessly was thrown,
Quite by mistake – she thought it was her own

She leads Juan into kisses and embraces until

A little still she strove, and much repented,
And whispering "I will ne'er consent" – consented.

This, at least in Byron's own estimation, was how many of his own love affairs had begun. He felt that in his own case the woman usually took the initiative: Caroline Lamb and Claire Clairmont both began with anonymous letters; in 1812 Lady Oxford, sixteen years his senior, invited the twenty-four year-old Byron to her country home in her husband's absence; Marianna Segati explained the rules of a *cavaliere servente* and made it clear that her husband would not be jealous; Margarita Cogni followed Byron to Venice from La Mira. Even his last attachment, Teresa Guiccioli, would be the protagonist of their relationship, calling out to him "Mio Byron" at a *conversazione* and scandalizing the other ladies and their whispering *cicisbei*.

On publication in July 1819, the first part of *Don Juan* would also scandalize many. As Byron began to write it, another female was taking centre-stage: his daughter Allegra. Shelley had continued to write regular letters keeping Byron informed about the child's health and development, and she was obviously a much-loved member of the Shelley household. However, Shelley's attempts to gain custody of his two children by his first wife Harriet had ended in failure. In March 1817 the Court of Chancery granted custody to Harriet's family: Shelley, a professed atheist, was considered an unfit father. He was worried that his own estranged father, Sir Timothy Shelley, might use the Chancery judgment in an attempt to gain custody of William, Shelley's son with Mary. The last thing he needed was gossip of an irregular household, especially since it was widely believed that Claire was, or had been, his lover. Since the Poet Laureate, Robert Southey, was already busy spreading gossip about Shelley and Byron's so-called "league of incest" in Geneva when, so Southey claimed, they had shared Mary and Claire between them, it was clear that alternative arrangements had to be made for Byron's daughter, whom the Shelleys called Alba. Byron rejected Shelley's initial suggestion, to farm the child out to nursemaids in Marlow, where the Shelleys were then living. Shelley made a new proposal: to bring the child out to Italy, at least as far as Pisa, himself and spend the winter of 1817-18 there. This plan in turn came to nothing as Shelley had no money and Mary had recently given birth. The baby, Clara, was too frail for such a long journey. Shelley now proposed that the baby might be entrusted to "any friend, or person of trust, who is leaving England for Italy," like a parcel, as Byron wryly noted in a letter to Hobhouse, "pray – desire Shelley to pack it carefully."

Byron also continued to receive letters from Claire. On Alba's first birthday, 12th January 1818,she sent a detailed description of the child, everything from her dimples to her digestion before slipping once more into bitterness, "I so fear she will be unhappy, poor little angel! In your great house, left perhaps to servants, while you are drowning sense and reason in wine," and self-pity; "Find me some other human being who has borne unkindness and injustice with the patience and gentleness I have. I have a child, and show me a more attentive and fond mother."

In March 1818 the child was baptized at her father's express request. Her certificate of baptism gives her name as Clara Allegra. The Shelleys, despite being unbelievers, had their two children baptized at the same time as an insurance against Sir Timothy and the Court of Chancery. Allegra finally began her journey to her father when the Shelley ménage set out for Italy.

Shelley wrote to Byron from Milan, would he come and collect the baby and see her mother? But Byron, given a clear reminder of Claire in full flow from her recent letter, was adamant in his refusal ever to see or speak to her again. Allegra was sent to Venice with her nurse Elise, a Swiss girl who had been with the Shelleys since their stay at Geneva in 1816. The two of them arrived in early May and stayed with the British Consul, Richard Hoppner, and his wife until Byron moved into the Palazzo Mocenigo. Byron found the child "healthy, noisy and capricious," and she was soon petted and admired by the local ladies on her daily airings in Piazza San Marco. When Allegra joined him in the Palazzo Mocenigo, however, both he and Fletcher were struck by a most peculiar resemblance. Allegra had clearly been doted upon and given her own way by both her mother and the Shelleys, and as a result had become an imperious and demanding child, "much more like Lady Byron than her mother – so much so as to stupefy the learned Fletcher – and astonish me." Byron also noted "I suppose she must resemble her sister Ada," the arrival of his illegitimate child having brought his "little legitimacy" into the forefront of his mind. Ada was now two and a half years old, and Byron was constantly anxious for news of her. His only source was Augusta, who acted as a conduit of communication between his wife and himself, and even she found it hard to find out a great deal, "the moral Clytemnestra is not very communicative of her tidings."[45] The lack of information about Ada, the growing realization that he would have little, if any role in her upbringing, was doubtless a factor in his determination to have Allegra with him in Italy. Lady Byron might rob him of one daughter; he would not be deprived of two.

The early years of the two girls make an interesting contrast. Allegra had the run of the Palazzo Mocenigo and made frequent visits to the Hoppners, who had a little boy of a similar age. Byron was clearly very proud of her although, like all men of his time and social class, he had little to do with the practicalities of child-rearing. From her arrival in Venice until she began her convent education when she was aged four and a half, Allegra was indulged (perhaps over-indulged) and was given to frequent displays of what her proud father considered to be the Byron temper. Byron described her looks, health and manner in letters to his friends, and was pleased when Hoppner, who may not have intended it as a compliment, commented that "her temper and her ways... are like mine."

Lady Byron, on the other hand, was a cold and unemotional mother. A fear that Ada would grow up like her father "... a fancy that her youthful imagination will be led astray by the poetical colouring of circumstances," motivated her, from Ada's earliest years, "to provide against the contingency by every means in my power." She changed Ada's nursemaids frequently so that the child would not develop an attachment to any of them. Her governesses (Lady Byron began a strict and utilitarian system of education when Ada was four) were expected to teach her the importance of "pleasing Mamma by doing her duty." Should Ada fidget, she was locked into a dark cupboard for half an hour. Good behaviour was rewarded by half an hour with a botanical picture book, but never by a cuddle. Her grandmother's will even contained a clause forbidding Ada to ever see the famous portrait of her father in Albanian dress until she was twenty-one years old.

Allegra's short life is usually seen as tragic. Yet she was spoiled by Byron; indulged by Teresa Guiccoli in whose carriage she rode as part of the Ravenna *carnevale* procession; adored by the nuns in her convent, who were inconsolable when she died and kept her clothes as a memento. Ada, on the other hand, grew up to mathematical fame – she was a collaborator of Charles Babbage and wrote programs for his Difference Engine, the forerunner of modern computers – marriage to an earl and splendour. Yet she endured poor mental and physical health and used her mathematical skills to help indulge her gambling addiction. She never succeeded in winning either her mother's affection or approval.

As the summer of 1818 moved towards autumn, Byron was once again threatened by a visit from Claire Clairmont. The Shelleys had settled for the summer at Bagni di Lucca, in Tuscany, and the nurse Elise sent Claire regular bulletins about Allegra's health. In one of these she implied that Byron planned to bring up Allegra to be his future mistress. She may have written this out of spite because Byron, feeling that she lacked experience, had put both Allegra and Elise under the control of Mrs Hoppner. Claire, unaware that Elise was feeding the Hoppners with similar tales about herself and Shelley (Elise told the Hoppners that Claire was Shelley's mistress and, at a later date, that Claire had gone to Naples to give birth to Shelley's child) instantly demanded that Shelley take her to Venice to rescue Allegra.

Leaving Mary alone in Bagni di Lucca with William and the baby, Claire and Shelley set out for Venice, arriving on 22nd August. Allegra was staying with the Hoppners at that time, as Claire had no doubt been informed by Elise. Perhaps Elise had made arrangements with Mrs Hoppner for Claire to see her child, as the travellers went straight to the Hoppners' home as soon as they arrived in Venice. The Hoppners, "the most amiable people I ever knew," strongly advised Shelley to keep Claire's presence in Venice a secret from Byron, so Shelley went alone to the Palazzo Mocenigo. He told Byron "who was delighted to see me" that he had come to Venice on an errand from Claire to see Allegra.

Byron was just about to set out for his daily ride on Lido, and invited Shelley to go with him. "He took me in his gondola across the laguna to a long sandy island which defends Venice from the Adriatic. When we disembarked, we found his horses waiting for us, and we rode along the sands of the sea, talking." Shelley later immortalized this conversation, and the Lido as it then was, in his poem, *Julian and Maddalo*:

I rode one evening with Count Maddalo
Upon the bank of land which breaks the flow
Of Adria towards Venice: a bare strand
Of hillocks, heap'd from ever-shifting sand,
Matted with thistles and amphibious weeds

The two men continued their conversations from Diodati,

Concerning God, freewill and destiny

although by this time they seem to have agreed to differ: to Shelley's annoyance, Byron continued to believe in God and "the delusions of Christianity, which, in spite of his reason seem perpetually to recur," while one of Byron's reasons for not wanting Allegra to be brought up in the Shelley household was that he did not wish her "to be taught there is no Deity."

Returning across the lagoon, they

saw the city, and could mark
How from their many isles, in evening's gleam,
Its temples and palaces did seem
Like fabrics of enchantment pil'd to Heaven.

Shelley's poem includes a description of Count Maddalo's child, in reality Allegra:

A lovelier toy sweet nature never made,
A serious, subtle, wild yet gentle being…
She was a special favourite: I had nurs'd
Her fine and feeble limbs when she came first
To this bleak world.

The poem concludes with a lengthy meditation on life and suffering, put into the mouth of an inmate in the lunatic asylum on the island of San Servolo. Byron's gondola passed close to the island on the way to Lido, although there is no record that Shelley paid a visit.[46]

Although Shelley said that Mary, Claire and the children were staying at Padua, Byron was not fooled, and was well aware of Claire's presence in Venice, "she came prancing over the Apennines – to see her *shild…* – and I was in a pucker until I got her to the Euganean hills." Byron had rented Hoppner's summer villa at Este in the Euganean hills south of Padua, but had never stayed there. Now he invited the Shelleys and Claire to make use of it. Claire could have Allegra to stay with her, but was under no circumstances to come anywhere near him in Venice.

Shelley immediately accepted Byron's offer, but was now faced with the difficulty of actually getting Mary and the children to Padua and then to Este to give credence to his story. He wrote to Mary that she was to "come instantly to Este," leaving her to make the long journey across Italy in August with two small children and only their Italian manservant to assist her.

What Shelley did not know was that the baby, Clara, always frail, was ill and feverish. When Mary finally arrived in Este the baby was so sick that Shelley went to Venice to ask Byron's advice. Byron had a good opinion of Doctor Aglietti, who had attended the Byron household and had been recommended by him to English visitors. The Doctor was a kindly man who would sit up all night with his patients if necessary; Byron, who had little time for doctors in general, no doubt felt his bedside manner was more effective than his prescriptions. Shelley wrote to Mary telling her to bring the baby to Venice. She was also to bring his manuscript of *Prometheus Unbound,* about which he expressed especial concern. All in vain. The baby died in Mary's arms before they reached Doctor Aglietti. She was buried on Lido in the Protestant section of what was primarily the Jewish cemetery.

Mary remembered Byron's kindness at this time for the rest of her life. Understanding that the best occupation for a grieving person is a mechanical and routine task which gives occupation and distracts the mind, however briefly, from their loss, he asked her to make fair copies of two poems he had recently written. He also asked her to read the memoir he had begun to write. Thus Mary Shelley was one of the few people to read the manuscript, famously burned in John Murray's offices after Byron's death. Tom Moore, to whom Byron entrusted it for posthumous publication, said that it dealt largely with Byron's marriage and the Separation. When Moore was writing Byron's biography, Mary was able to offer a great deal of assistance. She always had a high opinion of Byron, and kept a lock of his hair until her death.

The Shelleys remained at Este until late October, enabling Claire to spend two months with her child. Shelley, no doubt grateful for Byron's kindness at this time, wrote to his friend, the novelist Thomas Love Peacock, that Byron was "changed into the liveliest and happiest-looking man I ever met," an interesting contrast to Byron's lawyer John Hanson, who only a few weeks later found him bloated and fat. However, when Shelley wrote to Peacock again from Rome he took a very different tone. Already his memories of their conversations on Lido had become transformed from what he had recorded in *Julian and Maddalo*. He had remonstrated with Byron in vain, he wrote, on his "tone of mind" and "obstinate and self-willed folly;" and he described with horrified relish the "contemptible" Italian women, who "smell so strongly of garlic," with whom Byron was associating, ending piously, "I do not doubt, and, for his sake, I ought to hope, that his present career must soon end in some violent circumstance."

Shelley, despite his much-trumpeted beliefs in free love and open marriage, was in many ways very priggish. He was always recommending courses of improving reading to Mary, in spite of the fact that her novel *Frankenstein*, published in the spring of 1818, had attracted considerable attention while he remained largely unknown. His desire to lecture Byron, whether on religion or on the need for Byron to write a great and serious poem, would have awoken Byron's delight in teasing. He often teased and played practical jokes on his friends, from the time he had taken a tame bear into his college rooms at Cambridge (the regulations forbade dogs but, as Byron pointed out, bears were not mentioned) to the letter he had recently sent Hobhouse, purporting to be from Fletcher and announcing the death of "my late dear Master – my Lord." Now, as his mental health improved and his good temper returned, so did his spirit of mischief.

Shelley had shown Byron his own work in progress, *Prometheus Unbound*, and Byron no doubt returned the compliment with *Don Juan*. Shelley was shocked by the poem, telling Peacock that Byron was "contemplating in the distorted mirror of his own thoughts the nature and destiny of man." Similar comments made face-to-face could well have awoken a desire to provoke Shelley with shocking tales of the whoring he had indulged in during his mania, and "practices which are not only not named, but I believe seldom even conceived in England" which, tantalizingly interesting as they sound today, seem to have horrified Shelley. His attitude to Byron certainly became very ambivalent from this time onwards.

The Shelleys departed to spend the winter in Rome and Naples, and as 1818 drew to a close Byron concentrated on poetry. The two poems he had given to Mary Shelley for copying were *Ode on Venice* and *Mazeppa*. The *Ode* is a meditation on Venice's past glory and present subject state. In the light of modern concerns about a changing climate and the effect that rising sea-levels may have on the city, the opening lines are prophetic:

Oh Venice! Venice! when thy marble walls
Are level with the waters, there shall be
A cry of nations o'er thy sunken halls,
A loud lament along the sweeping sea!

Byron laments Venice's lost greatness, replaced by "the harsh sound of the barbarian drum" as Austrian soldiers march through the city. He then moves on to lament the never-ending victories of Tyranny over Freedom, contrasting these with Venice in her days of glory, when her navies protected Europe from the Ottoman Empire. With Europe "clothed in chains" the only hope for freedom lies in the west over "the far Atlantic" in America, whose citizens had freed themselves from British rule only thirty years earlier. Europe's oppressed citizens must

Fly, and one current to the ocean add,
One spirit to the souls our fathers had,
One freeman more, America, to thee!

Byron briefly considered taking his own advice after meeting a young American man who had fought with Simon Bolivar for Venezuelan independence from Spain. In 1819 he made plans, later abandoned, to buy a farm in Venezuela and settle there with Allegra, "I want a country – and a home – and if possible – a free one… There is no freedom in Europe, that's certain."

In *Mazeppa* Byron attempts to return to the romantic tales which had made him famous, and it makes a striking contrast to the lightness of his other Venetian poems, *Beppo* and *Don Juan*. It tells of Mazeppa, a Cossack warrior who falls in love with a married woman. Her powerful husband causes Mazeppa to be tied to a horse and sent on an epic ride, described in laboured rhyming couplets

The wood was past; 'twas more than noon,
But chill the air, although in June;
Or it might be my veins ran cold –
Prolonged endurance tames the bold

After reading it Hobhouse confided to his diary, "Of *Mazeppa*… I do not think much."

Fortunately, Byron soon returned to the lighter touch of ottavo rima and the poem he called Donny Johnny. He had more or less completed Canto I by September. After the Shelleys' departure he revised and added to it, and by November was ready to send it – along with *Mazeppa* and the *Ode* – to Hobhouse, whose critical opinion he relied on, along with that of Kinnaird. Byron knew Hobhouse well, and must have expected his strait-laced friend to be shocked by the poem. He may not have expected Hobhouse to start drawing parallels between the characters and the author's own experience as soon as he started to read. *Don Juan* opens with an exploration of the unhappy marriage of the hero's parents, Don Jose and Donna Inez, a blue-stocking:

> *Her favourite science was the mathematical,*
> *Her noblest virtue was her magnanimity;*
> *Her wit (she sometimes tried at wit) was Attic all,*
> *Her serious sayings darkened to sublimity.*

In fact, she is so "perfect past all parallel" that her husband's eye wanders, they quarrel and she

> *… tried to prove her loving lord was mad,*
> *But as he had some lucid intermissions,*
> *She next decided he was only bad.*

Hobhouse, reading the poem together with the quotation from Horace which Byron originally wanted for the epigraph, *domestica facta* ("household facts," although Byron insisted that he meant "common life") was convinced that Donna Inez was a caricature of Lady Byron. So was Hookham Frere, to whom Hobhouse showed the poem. When Cantos I & II were published, *Blackwood's Edinburgh Magazine* denounced Donna Inez as "an elaborate satire on the character and manners of his [Byron's] wife." Byron always insisted that she was "not meant for Clytemnestra," but if people chose to read the poem that way it was not his fault; "is a ludicrous character of a tiresome woman in a burlesque poem to be suppressed or altered because a contemptible and hypocritical wretch may be supposed to be pointed at?" Luckily for Lady Byron, her learning did not extend to self-knowledge. On reading *Don Juan* she complacently remarked, "As for myself, I do not think that my sins are in the pharisaical or pedantic line."

In the poem, Don Jose conveniently dies, leaving Donna Inez to bring up their only child, Don Juan. At sixteen, the handsome Juan is seduced by his mother's friend, Donna Julia. Her much older husband, Don Alfonso, deeply suspicious, arrives at her bedchamber at midnight with witnesses and his attorney, determined to catch Julia and Juan *in flagrante*. In a scene reminiscent of a Goldoni comedy, they search the room:

He search'd, they search'd, and rummaged everywhere,
Closet and clothes-press, chest and window-seat.....
Arras they prick'd and curtains with their swords,
And wounded several shutters, and some boards.

Julia berates her husband at great length for his lack of faith in her fidelity until, humiliated, he stammers his excuses and departs. No sooner is the door closed than "Juan slipp'd, half-smother'd from the bed," before being hidden again in the wardrobe as Don Alfonso returns, alone, to apologise once more. Julia accepts his apologies very prettily until, departing, "he stumbled o'er a pair of shoes" and pandæmonium breaks out.

Dire was the scuffle, and out went the light;
Antonia cried out 'Rape'! and Julia 'Fire'!
But not a servant stirr'd to aid the fight.

Juan escapes from the bedroom, but neither he nor his mother can escape from the ensuing scandal. Don Alfonso's divorce proceedings against his wife "Were in the English newspapers, of course," while the canto ends with Juan sent on a long journey with a tutor,

... through
All European climes, by land or sea,
To mend his former morals and get new,
Especially in France and Italy.

As Byron slyly implies, the journey will be one of self-discovery, not self-improvement.

Byron always affected surprise that anyone could be shocked by *Don Juan*, but the poem's moral framework is one which was becoming distinctly outmoded in England, where the social climate had already undergone a sea-change in the brief period of Byron's absence. The sun was setting on the lax morals of the Whig aristocrats such as the Melbournes and the Devonshires, the social set in which Byron had been at home during his time in England between 1811 and 1816, and of the Prince Regent and his circle. Indeed, the casual acceptance of a married woman taking a lover (it was widely-believed that none of Lady Melbourne's children, apart from the eldest, were fathered by her husband) had never extended far beyond that small and very exclusive Metropolitan set. The influence of the Evangelical Movement, which would soon drop its dead hand over early Victorian life, was already apparent, especially among the growing urban middle class of the northern and Midland manufacturing towns. Evangelical teaching focussed on the concept of Sin and the need for self-examination and repentance. Good works among the poor were central, as was the importance of education and self-improvement. Lady Byron was greatly influenced by the Evangelical Movement, using the ideas of the Evangelical writer Hannah More in her educational programme for Ada. The Evangelical emphasis on the importance of preaching the Gospel to others and pointing out to them the error of their ways dovetailed precisely with Lady Byron's constant urge to interfere in the lives of others: her persecution of Augusta sprang from her belief that Augusta had "sinned" and must be made to understand, and be given the chance to confess, the error of her ways.

The wind of change was even being felt on the London social scene, where "a blanket of propriety" seemed to fall after the season of 1817-18. The loose morals which had seemed so appropriate during the long years of war suddenly tightened, a change physically reflected in fashion: the loose-fitting empire-line, which had freed women from the tight-lacing of the eighteenth century, fell out of vogue and a more closely-corseted style returned.

The raffish ways and salty language of the older generation were often regarded with a shudder. For example, Henry Fox, the son of Byron's friend Lord Holland, was unwilling for his young sister Mary to spend too much time with their grandmother as "she talks so terribly indecently before poor Mary that it quite shocks."

The intended audience for the "burlesque poem," world-weary men and women who, like the author, held that "pleasure's a sin, and sometimes sin's a pleasure," were slipping out of existence. Byron was writing the epitaph of the eighteenth century. The Victorian era was just around the corner.

Fifth Venetian Interlude

Oh! the long evenings of duets and trios!

Byron loved music. One of his most popular works was the Hebrew Melodies, *published in 1815. Hoping to emulate the success of his friend Tom Moore's* Irish Melodies *Byron had worked with a Jewish composer, Isaac Nathan, writing twenty-three verses with settings based on traditional Jewish music. The collaboration was a close one, and Nathan always retained fond memories of Byron, who had not behaved as a poetical prima donna but had been ready to take the musician's advice when it came to adapting his verses to the demands of the music.*

Once settled in Venice, a city with a long-standing reputation across Europe for the quality of its music, Byron was soon enjoying to the full everything that was on offer. He often went to the opera as well as to performances of oratorios by Haydn and Handel at the Teatro San Benedetto.

Something Byron would no longer able to hear, however, was the type of music on which Venice's reputation had so long rested: sacred music. Although Venetians had a well-deserved reputation for not being unduly pious, all social classes were happy to attend a mass lasting up to four hours if it meant the chance to hear good music, such as that written by Vivaldi for the female orphans of the Pietà, or the antiphonal chants composed by Monteverdi to be sung across the galleries of the Basilica of San Marco.

Venice was unusual in allowing women and girls to perform sacred works – they were not even allowed to appear in secular theatre or opera in the Papal States – and the female musicians (who performed behind screens, either to preserve their modesty or to prevent male members of the audience entertaining lewd thoughts) were famous for their high musical standards. Goethe had attended an oratorio in the Ospedale di San Lazzaro dei Mendicanti in 1786, and was more than impressed, "the church was filled with listeners, the music beautiful and the voices superb. An alto sang the part of King Saul, the protagonist of the work. I have never heard such a voice."

Alas, Goethe was among the last auditors of Venetian sacred music. The tradition came to an abrupt end when the religious houses, including the Pietà and the Mendicanti, were closed by order of Napoleon. Although the Austrians allowed monasteries and convents to re-open, the teachers and musicians had scattered throughout Europe, finding work in monasteries and royal courts. The impetus for religious music in Venice was lost; indeed even today there is a dearth of liturgical music in the city.[47]

Byron instantly recognised the plot of the first opera he saw at Teatro La Fenice, as it was based on an episode from Livy's *History of Rome*. The in-depth study of Greek and Roman writers had comprised the major part of his curriculum at Harrow. They also provided a valuable resource for composers in the early nineteenth century, when all things classical were popular – whether in fashion, sculpture or design – as a result of Napoleon's promotion of himself and his Empire as "the heir of Rome." The work Byron saw was a premiere, *Le Daniadi Romani* (The Roman Danaides), by the popular composer Stefano Pavesi. It had been commissioned to open the *carnevale* season of 1816-17 at La Fenice. The title refers to the Danaides, the fifty daughters of King Danaus, who killed their husbands on their wedding-night. Livy tells of a group of Roman matrons plotting to poison their husbands, and Byron summarised Pavesi's operatic version thus:

"a hundred and fifty married ladies having poisoned a hundred and fifty husbands in the good old times – the bachelors of Rome believed this extraordinary mortality to be merely the common effect of matrimony or a pestilence – but the surviving Benedicts[48] being all seized with the colic examined into the matter – and found that 'their possets had been drugged' the consequence of which was much scandal and several suits at law. – This is really & truly the subject of the Musical piece at the Fenice – & you can't conceive what pretty things are sung and recitativoed... the conclusion was a Lady's head about to be chopped off by a lictor – but (I am sorry to say) he left it on – and she got up and sang a trio with the two Consuls – the Senate in the background being chorus."

Sounds like quite an evening.

Byron made a new musical discovery in Venice, a composer still unknown outside Italy, Gioacchino Rossini. Three days after arriving in Venice, Byron and Hobhouse saw Rossini's *Tancredi*, set at the time of the Crusades and based, almost inevitably since he seemed to be waiting round every corner during Byron's first winter in Venice, on Tasso's *Gerusalemme Liberata*. Rossini's opera clearly made an impact, since the two friends went to see it five times in the next two weeks. The following year, when they saw Il barbiere di Siviglia, with which Teatro San Moise opened the 1817 season, Hobhouse immediately compared it to what was patently his operatic gold standard: *Tancredi*.

The composer of these operas was still in his twenties. Rossini was an extremely prolific composer, premiering twenty-nine works between

1810 when, aged eighteen, he was commissioned to write a one-act opera for Teatro San Moise, and 1819, when Byron attended a premiere of one of his works at Teatro San Benedetto. Tancredi, *which had its premiere at La Fenice in 1813, was his first big success, and remained hugely popular in Venice – as did its composer, who was straightaway given a commission by Teatro San Benedetto, writing* L'italiana in Algeri *and thus achieving two Venetian premieres in one year.*
Unfortunately, Byron didn't enjoy his next Rossini opera a great deal, but the fault (if there was one) lay with the libretto rather than the score. When he found out that Otello *was to be performed he was immediately drawn to it, as it brought together so many of his own areas of interest. "It will be curious to see in Venice – the Venetian story itself represented – besides to discover what they make of Shakespeare in music."*
Alas, Byron was distinctly unimpressed by what they made of Shakespeare in music. Rossini's librettist, the dilettante aristocrat Marchese Francesco Berio di Salsa, felt that the barbarities in the plot of "the ferocious Shakespeare" needed to be toned down to make the story acceptable to a civilised Italian audience. So most of the meat of the piece was discarded, leaving behind a pretty tale focussing on Desdemona. Although Byron conceded that the music was excellent, he felt that Shakespeare's play had been crucified: "All the real scenes with Iago cut out – and the greatest nonsense instead: the handkerchief turned into a billet doux, and the first singer would not black his face, for some exquisite reasons assigned in the preface."
It is interesting to compare Byron's reaction to Otello *with that of a composer, Rossini's contemporary Giacomo Meyerbeer, who also attended a performance at Teatro San Benedetto. He records that Acts I and II were not well-received, but that the piece was rescued by the third act, a touching scene between Desdemona and her confidante Emilia which climaxes in Desdemona singing the lovely Willow Song before her death. The performance of Isabella Colbran, Rossini's mistress, as Desdemona not only saved the opera, it caused a sensation.*
Byron was much more impressed by the next Rossini opera he saw, telling Hobhouse, "There has been a splendid opera lately at San Benedetto, by Rossini – who came in person to play the Harpsichord - the People followed him about, – crowned him – cut off his hair "for memory" he was Shouted and Sonnetted and feasted – and immortalised much more than either of the Emperors"[49]
The opera was Eduardo e Cristina, *commissioned by the impresario of the Teatro San Benedetto, Signor Cortesi, who wanted Rossini to create a role for his daughter Carolina, a contralto. The part that Rossini wrote for Carolina Cortesi was that of the hero, Eduardo. These "breeches roles," a male character sung by a woman, were very popular. Rossini had written* Tancredi *as a breeches role and although the*

title-role in Otello *was written for a tenor, it was also sung by women. Maria Malibran, one of the most popular divas of the 1820s and 1830s, was famed for alternating the roles of Otello and Desdemona.*

Although ostensibly set in Sweden, Eduardo e Cristina *is in many ways a very Venetian opera. It is an intimate work, with only five main characters. However, any resident of Venice would smile in recognition at the way in which all of their private moments, from bedchamber to prison cell, are watched over by a chorus of servants, guards and hangers-on. Cristina, daughter of the king of Sweden, has secretly married the king's general, Eduardo, and is the mother of his child, a fact which only comes to light when her father plans to betroth her to the king of Scotland. The theme of a clandestine marriage and a secret child would no doubt strike a chord with many in the audience. The offspring of similar liaisons, from all classes of Venetian society, had been cared for and educated in institutions such as the Pietà until their closure by order of the French Viceroy Eugene Beauharnais a mere ten years earlier. In this case, however, everything ends well for all concerned – Rossini was well-aware that happy endings went down well with a Venetian audience.*

The premiere of Eduardo e Cristina *took place on 24th April 1819. The audience loved both composer and work so much that the relatively short opera (a little over two hours) lasted from 8pm until 2 o'clock the next morning due to the applause, the number of encores and the repeated calls for the composer, who was directing the orchestra from the harpsichord, to take bows on stage.*

Byron left Venice a few months after seeing Rossini at the premiere, but he continued to take an interest in the composer. One of the leading divas of the day, Giuditta Pasta, was famous as an interpreter of Rossini. Early in 1820 the theatre in Ravenna, where Byron was then living, planned a subscription to pay for Madame Pasta's engagement to sing there for a season. Byron immediately offered to contribute £200 towards the subscription (a huge sum of money, but the likes of Madame Pasta could name their own price). Unfortunately, the chair of the Ravenna Theatre Committee was Count Alessandro Guiccoli, and relations with him were a little tricky at the time: Byron had come to Ravenna as the accepted cavaliere servente *of the Count's wife Teresa, and Alessandro was not a happy man. He interpreted Byron's offer not as the generous gesture of a music-lover but as another attempt to muscle in on his territory. The affair ended in a rancorous dispute and the music-lovers of Ravenna lost the chance to hear Madame Pasta in their theatre.*

Byron's fondness for Rossini was not a one-way street, since the composer also admired the poet. For one thing, their political views were remarkably similar. Like Byron, Rossini believed that foreign oppressors should be driven out of Italy, although as his fame grew he often

had to swallow his principles, as in 1822 when, during a gala banquet in his honour in Vienna, he was presented to Metternich.
However, in 1824 Rossini was able to pay his own tribute to Byron. By co-incidence, he was in London when he heard the news of Byron's death. Rossini had just enjoyed a successful season of his operas at the King's Theatre and endured a musical evening at the Brighton Pavilion in the presence of George IV. The composer sang some of his own works and the king insisted in accompanying him on the piano, but was unable to keep time. Rossini made a great impression at evening parties, at one of which he met Byron's friend Tom Moore, another regular performer in Society drawing-rooms. Moore's expert eye and ear noted that Rossini's "mastery over the pianoforte" was "miraculous."
News of Byron's death, on 15th April 1824, reached England by the middle of May. On 11th June Rossini gave a concert in the presence of the bon ton at the exclusive Almack's Assembly Rooms in St James's. Many of those present would have known Byron personally. They heard Rossini's short cantata Il pianto delle Muse in Morte di Lord Byron *(The muses weep at the death of Lord Byron). After a short orchestral introduction a solo harp is heard, recalling Apollo's lyre and symbolising Poetry. The tenor, representing Apollo, and the chorus sing that a great voice has been stilled, a great son of his country lost. There are no operatic trills or cadenzas, just a simple expression of heartfelt grief at Byron's loss.*
Rossini himself sang the role of Apollo, and although The Examiner *(a paper which was no friend to Byron)*[51] *found "something very foreign" about his style of singing the evening was clearly a moving one. Rossini would later re-use motifs from the cantata in an opera with the Byronic title* Le Siege de Corinthe. *The theme of the opera was, all things considered, an apt one: the Ottoman siege of the city of Corinth, part of the on-going struggle for Greek freedom for which Byron gave his life.*

Chapter Six

Teresa

Could Love for ever
Run like a river
And time's endeavour
Be tried in vain –
No other pleasure
With this could measure;
And like a treasure
We'd hug the chain.

Whilst Hobhouse fretted over Canto I of *Don Juan*, Byron immediately began work on Canto II, which he started to write just before Christmas 1818 and had completed by late January 1819. He seems to have spent a somewhat quieter *carnevale* than the previous year now that his mania had passed, only taking part in the last ten days of festivities. One reason for this was that his physical health was not good: stomach problems caused repeated bouts of sickness, and as a result Byron began to lose some of his excess weight – his famed good looks slowly returned in 1819. The gossips put his illness down to too many women but, having calculated that he had spent over £2,500 on women since arriving in Venice, Byron may simply have decided to cut down on his casual encounters. It is certainly true that, once the money from the sale of Newstead was in the bank, he was far more careful with his finances than in the days when he was living on credit. He also seems to have greatly enjoyed writing his poem, which would reach seventeen cantos and remain incomplete by the time he left Italy in 1823. He extended more paternal care to Donny Johnny than to any of his other poems. He showed very little interest in most of them once he had sent them to Murray, often refusing to bother with correcting proofs when Hobhouse could do it just as well. In contrast, his letters to Murray and Hobhouse from this time on were full of the poem and his defence of it, what cuts he would and would not allow, changes and additions which Murray must at all costs include.

The second Canto has a macabre black humour which, although in tune with modern tastes, disgusted Hobhouse a great deal when he read it. Byron begins with a final sideswipe at Donna Inez, whose Sunday School gives pause for thought about just how much Byron knew about the education being inflicted on his daughter.

Infants of three years old were taught that day,
Dunces were whipt, or set upon a stool:
The great success of Juan's education
Spurr'd her to teach another generation.

The poem then turns to Juan's adventures. Sailing from Cadiz with his valet and tutor, their ship is caught in a violent storm and sinks. Thirty survivors, including Juan, his spaniel and his tutor, manage to stay afloat in the rough seas in a lifeboat,

But man is a carnivorous production,
And must have meals, at least one meal a day

and thus it turns out that, on the fourth day without sight of land, the survivors eat the dog, and on the seventh day the tutor. Luckily, Juan refuses to "dine with them on his pastor and his master" as all who do go mad and die. One by one, those in the boat die of thirst, heat, starvation, until only Juan remains. The boat runs ashore in Crete where a naked Juan swoons elegantly on the beach, his beautiful white skin miraculously untouched by the blazing sun and open boat,

His slender frame and pallid aspect lay,
As fair a thing as e'er was formed of clay.

He is discovered by Haidée, the daughter of the pirate ruler of the island, and her maid, who care for Juan in a hidden cave. The canto ends as Juan and Haidée consummate their love,

And thus they form a group that's quite antique,
Half naked, loving, natural and Greek.

No sooner had Byron put down his pen than he received Hobhouse's letter advising in the strongest possible terms against the publication of Canto I. He had shown the poem to their mutual friend Scrope Davis and to Hookham Frere, the author of *Whistlecraft*. Both were men of the world. Both agreed with Hobhouse that *Don Juan* was unpublishable in its present form. On the one hand, it was indecent, licentious and wholly unworthy of Byron, whose friends persisted in wanting him to write a serious epic. On the other hand, the gossips would have a field-day, doing exactly what Hobhouse himself had done and drawing parallels between the poet and his hero. "All the idle stories about your Venetian life will be more than confirmed, they will be exaggerated."

Byron stuck to his guns, even when his friend and fellow-poet Tom Moore joined in the fray. He accepted that the poem would lead to "a war of Criticism and Methodism," but insisted that there be no "cutting and slashing" of the poem, "You sha'n't make Canticles of my Cantos." He accepted that Cantos I and II should be published anonymously, not because he considered them indecent but because he was aware that certain sections of the reading public would do so, and this could give Lady Byron ammunition against him. His daughter Ada was already a Ward in Chancery. Byron was only too aware of what had happened to Shelley, denied parental control of his two older children because of his atheism, which he had made public in his poem *Queen Mab*. He most definitely did not want to give his wife grounds for a Chancery injunction taking away paternal authority if *Don Juan*'s author, as well as the poem, was seen as "indecent and blasphemous."

However, if Cantos I and II were to be anonymous, Byron accepted that some stanzas would have to be omitted, although not on moral grounds. The poem began with a savage dedication to the Poet Laureate, Robert Southey. Byron had long despised Southey for turning his back on his youthful Radicalism in order to write sycophantic verses about George III, but Southey had attracted his particular ire for spreading rumours about the Villa Diodati. "The Son of a Bitch on his return from Switzerland two years ago – said that Shelley and I had 'formed a league of Incest...' – he lied like a rascal – for they *were not Sisters*...[and] there was no promiscuous intercourse – my commerce being limited to the carnal knowledge of the Miss C – I had nothing to do with the offspring of Mary Wollstonecraft – which Mary was a former Love of Southey's – which might have taught him to respect the fame of her daughter." Byron had confined his poetic attack to Southey's politics,

BOB SOUTHEY! You're a poet – Poet-laureate,
And representative of all the race;
Although 'tis true that you turn'd out a Tory at
Last, – yours has lately been a common case.

However, he accepted that he could not "attack the dog so fiercely without putting my name – that is reviewer's work."[52] He also agreed to omit stanzas attacking his political bête noir, the "intellectual eunuch, Castlereagh," the Foreign Secretary, who had represented Britain at the Congress of Vienna,

> *States to be curb'd, and thoughts to be confined,*
> *Conspiracy or Congress to be made –*
> *Cobbling at manacles for all mankind."*

Byron's reasoning here was that Castlereagh had every right to challenge him to a duel for what he had written, and at the moment he was too far away to accept such a challenge. Should he ever return to England, it would be a different matter, and he would publish the verses straight away.

So it was that *Don Juan* Cantos I and II were published, anonymously and without even a publisher's name on the title-page, on 15th July 1819. For days beforehand mysterious advertisements had appeared in the press, "In a few days *DON JUAN*," and the authorship was an open secret. The poem immediately became infamous. All the usual suspects queued to condemn it, so that to Southey it was "A foul blot on the literature of the country, an act of high treason on English poetry," while Wordsworth believed it would "do more harm to our English character than anything of our time." The members of the Newcastle-upon-Tyne Literary and Philosophical Society worked themselves into such a state of righteous indignation that they called a special meeting to vote for the removal of the poem from their library shelves. The finest response, however, came from Caroline Lamb, who attended a masquerade at Almack's dressed as *Don Juan* surrounded by a host of devils.

By the time it was published, however, Byron had far more important things to think about than the public reaction to his poem. In the autumn of 1818, at one of Madame Albrizzi's *conversazioni*, he had given his arm to a newly-married young lady, recently-arrived in Venice and attending her first Venetian social event. However, because of either tiredness or shyness on the lady's part, she said very little and, Byron noted, her husband never took his eyes off her. He thought no more of the encounter. When the two next met, at Countess Benzoni's at the beginning of April 1819, it was a very different story: the attraction between them, although instant, was to prove long-lasting.

The young lady was Countess Teresa Guiccioli, in Venice with her husband Alessandro, who had estates in and around Raven-

na, a hundred miles south of Venice in the Papal States. Teresa, aged eighteen, was the fifty-seven year old Count's third wife. She was fair-haired, pretty and vivacious, though she regretted the fact that she was not very tall (as their relationship progressed, Byron would tease her affectionately about her short legs). Despite the great differences in their ages, Teresa seems to have been quite content with her husband, until that evening at Ca'Benzon, which she later described to Tom Moore.
"More fatigued than usual, that evening, on account of the late hours they keep at Venice, I went with great repugnance to this party, and purely in obedience to Count Guiccioli. Lord Byron, too, who was averse to forming new acquaintances, – alleging that he had entirely renounced all attachments, and was unwilling any more to expose himself to their consequences, – on being requested by the Countess Benzoni to allow himself to be presented to me, refused, and at last, only assented from a desire to oblige her. His noble and exquisitely beautiful countenance, the tone of his voice, his manners, the thousand enchantments that surrounded him, rendered him so different, and so superior a being to any whom I had hitherto seen, that it was impossible he should not have left the most profound impression upon me. From that evening, during the whole of my subsequent stay in Venice, we met every day."

The impact seems to have been just as great for Byron. On 6th of April, only two or three days after the meeting at Countess Benzoni's, he was writing to Hobhouse, "I have fallen in love with a Romagnuola Countess from Ravenna."[53] Teresa, who had spent the years leading up to her marriage in a convent acquiring the education required in the future wife of a nobleman, could quote Dante by the page but knew little of the ways of the world. She was totally lacking in the discretion needed to conduct an extra-marital affair, calling her lover "Mio Byron" loudly in public, but Byron was smitten, and considered this to be a long-term relationship from the very beginning, "I am in love – and tired of promiscuous concubinage – & have the opportunity of settling for life."
Teresa knew that she and Byron had only a few days before her husband left Venice to return to Ravenna, so the affair progressed rapidly. Since she was already carrying Count Guiccioli's child and there was no danger of becoming pregnant by Byron, she embarked on a sexual relationship within a few days of their meeting. Teresa was taking a risk – there were rumours that neither of the Count's two previous wives had died of natural causes – and Byron was well-aware of the Count's involvement in

the assassinations of two men who had stood in his way (in matters of law rather than love), but "everything is to be risked for a woman one likes."

Count and Countess Guiccioli left Venice for Ravenna in mid-April, and Byron soon began to send love-letters, which Teresa carefully preserved. He wrote in somewhat flowery Italian, and often resorted to the kind of sentiments a lady would expect to receive from her lover, so they are more florid and less immediate than his English letters. However, his elaborate language expressed genuine regard, as the regularity of his correspondence and the constancy of his feelings both show. From this time until he set sail for Greece he wrote to Teresa whenever they were separated for more than a few days. "Perhaps," Byron tells her in his first letter, "if I loved you less it would not cost me so much to express my thoughts, but now I have to overcome the double difficulty of expressing an unbearable suffering in a language foreign to me. Forgive my mistakes."

With Teresa out of Venice Byron, although in love, felt under no obligation to be monogamous at this early stage in their relationship, and embarked on a small adventure. During the previous winter he had begun an intrigue with a young lady from one of the Venetian patrician families – Byron is careful not to identify which one, naming the girl only as Angelina – who had even proposed marriage to him, recommending that he either divorce his wife or have her poisoned. Her father found out what was afoot and, according to Byron, "locked the Girl up – and gave her prayers and bread and water" while sending the family priest to either threaten or counsel the English Milord, who received him civilly and offered him coffee. Teresa's absence co-incided with the girl's father being taken ill, resulting in her being less closely watched. Byron took the opportunity to resume the liaison, having himself rowed to her palazzo after midnight and climbing, Romeo-like, to her balcony. On his way to an assignation "My foot slipped in getting into my Gondola to set out (owing to the cursed slippery steps of their palaces) and in I flounced like a Carp – and went dripping like a Triton to my Sea-nymph – and had to scramble up to a Grated window," where, from either gentlemanly good manners or self-interest, he sat for an hour and a half soaking wet rather than "miss my appointment by the delays of changing." Byron does not refer to Angelina again; a young woman willing to have Lady Byron poisoned clearly had a strong will and forceful personality, so it is unfortunate that her reaction on discovering that her erstwhile lover was now the *cavaliere servente* of a married Italian lady is not recorded.

Meanwhile, Byron sat in the Palazzo Mocenigo composing regular love-letters to Teresa and keeping up with English affairs through the weekly newspaper to which he subscribed. This was *Galignani's Messenger*, an English-language digest of British and European news published in Paris and anodyne enough to get past the Austrian censors.

As April 1819 progressed Byron was puzzled to see his name mentioned frequently. This was not unusual, as news of him, real or imagined, appeared regularly in the public prints – the latest snippet was that he had become religious and given up going out into Society – and he usually chose to ignore it. However, almost every issue of *Galignani's Messenger* spoke of Lord Byron's new book, a work of fiction entitled *The Vampyre*. Intrigued, Byron wrote to the Messenger's editor in order to put the record straight, "if the book is clever it would be base to deprive the real writer – whoever he may be – of his honours; – and if stupid – I desire the responsibility of nobody's dullness but my own."

His friends in England were similarly puzzled by advertisements for Byron's new work, about which they knew nothing. Douglas Kinnaird wrote to Byron to ask about *The Vampyre* and received the testy reply "Damn *'the Vampire'* – what do I know about Vampires?" Only Hobhouse seems to have actually read the book, an overheated novella narrated by a young gentleman named Aubrey, the travelling companion of the mysterious Lord Ruthven who – by the author's deliberate design – shares his name with another Byronic figure in fiction, the protagonist of Lady Caroline Lamb's *Glenarvon*.

Debt forces Lord Ruthven to travel abroad, and he crosses Europe leaving a trail of tragedy and sadness in his wake. Aubrey and he part company in Rome, after Aubrey reveals Ruthven's plan to seduce a young lady. Aubrey travels on to Greece, where he falls in love with the lovely Ianthe. She tells him lurid tales of "the living vampyre" who haunts the countryside, before dying with the marks of vampiric teeth on her neck.

Ill with grief, Aubrey is cared for by Ruthven, who "chanced at this time to arrive in Athens," and the two men journey together into the wilder parts of Greece where Ruthven is shot by bandits. After making Aubrey swear to keep his death a secret, he expires and Aubrey returns alone to London, just in time for his sister's presentation at Court. Who should appear in the Royal drawing-room but Ruthven, who whispers "remember your oath."

Ruthven now begins to pay court to Aubrey's sister while Aubrey, torn between his oath and love for his sister, sinks into madness. Kept under lock and key, he is unable to warn his sister of Ruthven and she dies on her wedding-night: "… it was too late. Lord Ruthven had disappeared, and Aubrey's sister had glutted the thirst of a VAMPYRE!"

It was immediately clear to Hobhouse that this nonsense could not be by Byron. It had the fingerprints of Doctor Polidori all over it. Hobhouse wrote to the doctor, demanding to know what he was up to and received a full confession by return of post, "he owned it upon my writing to him, and Murray got out the whole story." Polidori then wrote to the newspapers claiming that the story was his own, although based on a story that Byron had begun to write at the Villa Diodati. Hobhouse was surprised that anybody could be fooled into thinking that *The Vampyre* was Byron's work, "I, who like all coxcombs know you by your style, swore the whole to be a vile imposture, and Dolly's whole and sole doing."[54] He also warned Byron that Polidori had kept a diary during the time they travelled together, and had offered this to the publisher of *Glenarvon*. Public demand for Byron-related gossip was so great that it would probably have been a best seller, but Hobhouse stepped in and warned him not to publish. He was unable to resist an "I told you so" to Byron, "I fear he is a sad scamp, but you know I told you that you were wrong in taking him, you know I did."

Polidori did not invent the legend of the vampire. There had long been a widespread belief in, and fear of, vampires both in eastern Europe – where they were usually portrayed as wizened, decaying undead, unable to rest and craving the blood of living creatures – and also in Greece. Indeed, Goethe had made use of Greek tales of the vampire, or *vrykolakas*, in his 1797 poem *The Bride of Corinth*, in which an undead girl returns to claim her bridegroom on their wedding-night.[55] Polidori did, however, more or less create the suave vampire of popular nineteenth and twentieth century imagination, as well as adding considerable grist to the mill of Byronic legend with his tale of the handsome, bored Ruthven. Although "invited to every house," he "gazed upon the mirth around him, as if he could not participate therein," before spreading a trail of vice across Europe.

The book, partly because of the clever publicity campaign linking it with Byron, sold in huge quantities. However, Polidori made very little money from it, having sold the copyright to his publisher for just £30. Unable to settle down – he asked Byron for a reference when he was considering a move to Brazil as physician to the Danish Consul – he moved first to Norwich, then back to London where he abandoned medicine and planned to study law. He took his own life by drinking prussic acid in 1821. Byron, by then living in Pisa, was not particularly surprised to hear of his former doctor's death, perhaps remembering Polidori's plan to commit suicide after their quarrel at the Villa Diodati. "When he was my physician," Byron remarked, "he was always talking of Prussic acid."

In May 1819, Byron's attention was distracted from Doctor Polidori by news that Teresa was ill. Fanny Silvestrini, a friend of Teresa's, was the conduit through which they communicated. She made sure that letters from Byron to Teresa did not fall into the wrong hands, and also delivered Teresa's messages to Byron. She now brought the news that Teresa had suffered a miscarriage on her journey and Byron began to make plans to visit Ravenna in order to be near her. Apparently on the mend and worried about gossip and scandal in her home-town Teresa sent several contradictory messages: he should stay in Venice; no, she wanted him with her straight away; he should travel as far as Bologna; no, he should stay at an inn in Ravenna and await instructions, so that Byron almost decided to stay in Venice. Then, at the end of the month, he heard that Teresa had suffered a relapse and was feverish. He set out immediately for Ravenna, travelling by way of Bologna.
During his journey, Byron wrote verses for Teresa, *Stanzas to the Po*. Count Guiccioli had a villa on the banks of the River Po, midway between Venice and Ravenna, and in the verses Byron imagines that Teresa is there:

River, that rollest by the ancient walls,
Where dwells the lady of my love, when she
Walks by thy brink, and there perchance recalls
A faint and fleeting memory of me;
What if thy deep and ample stream should be
A mirror of my heart, where she may read
The thousand thought I now betray to thee
Wild as thy wave, and headlong as thy speed!

He speaks of his love for Teresa, but while she belongs to the land of Italy, he never can:

A stranger loves the lady of the land,
Born far beyond the mountains…"

The verses end on a prophetic note, although as Byron was writing in a state of some distress about Teresa's prospects of recovery it would be wrong to read too much into the words:

'Tis vain to struggle – let me perish young."

He arrived in Ravenna on 10th June and immediately wrote to Teresa.

"My Treasure – Here I am, in Ravenna. If you can arrange to see me I shall be happy – if not, I have at any rate not broken my word – and I hope at least to hear that your health is better. Always, B."

Teresa, meanwhile, had to play a careful game. Her husband knew Byron already – indeed the two met on Byron's first evening in Ravenna and he was invited into the Count's box at the theatre – but her family knew nothing of the English Milord except for the usual gossip. Teresa's brother, Pietro, wrote a long letter warning her that Byron "is the husband of a young woman full of innocence and affection like yourself; and not satisfied with having abandoned her to give himself up to a life of disorder, he keeps her shut up in a Castle, of which many dark and mysterious tales are told."

Pietro was in Rome, where the English visitors and residents would be only too happy to fill his head with highly exaggerated Byron gossip. Teresa's father, Count Ruggero Gamba, in Ravenna with his daughter, was also very suspicious of the Englishman. Teresa, still bedridden, had to engineer a meeting with Byron under the jealous gaze of her husband and father and in the full awareness that the prying eyes of Ravenna society were watching her every move. Teresa was certainly ill, and had undergone the ministrations of the local medical men, who felt that the best remedy for the blood loss caused by her miscarriage was to bleed her again. However, it seems likely that she exaggerated her illness somewhat in order to see her lover. She could clearly wrap both husband and father round her little finger, as on the day after Byron's arrival in Ravenna the Count himself drove to Byron's lodgings and escorted him personally to Teresa's bedside where he was able to pay his respects. He found his lady surrounded by her family and friends, and could only hope that "time will teach me hypocrisy" in order to behave correctly in such a situation.

Now able to see her lover every day, Teresa miraculously began to recover rapidly, and was out of bed when Byron visited her on 14th June. He, however, was bored, having soon exhausted the sights of Ravenna with a visit to Dante's tomb and several evening rides in the local pine-woods. He already felt trapped, both by the claustrophobic little town and the intensity of his relationship with Teresa, and was well aware that both his lady and her husband were easing him gently into the accepted modes of behaviour for a married woman's *cavaliere servente*. He had always treated the *cicisbei* he had met at Venetian *conversazioni* as figures of fun who whispered gossip, handed out coffee, elegantly draped a lady's shawl. Now, he realised with some panic, he was on the road to becoming one himself. "I should not like," he told Hobhouse, "to be frittered down into a regular *cicisbeo*," an emasculated state "which is to be condemned." Yet what could he do, in a small town where his every action was observed and where he stood out as a foreigner far more than he ever had in Venice; where Teresa, although making it clear that her recovery was dependent on him – on June 16th she tottered downstairs for the first time, leaning on Byron's arm – was already treating him as a conventional *cavaliere*. In her twice-daily letters she would work herself up into fits of pretended jealousy before playfully accusing him of not loving her enough. When he replied full of ardour she would change the topic to a discussion of his poetry instead. Her husband seemed to be acting as a pander, complacently seating his wife in Byron's carriage for a ride in the pine-woods before asking Byron's help in being made British Vice-Consul. For a man who had already spent time in the papal prison of Castel Sant' Angelo on suspicion of murder, a sinecure which put him under the British Government's protection would be a useful asset. Byron wrote to his publisher John Murray asking him to call in a few favours among his Tory friends, but the plan came to nothing.

Byron made an attempt to put his relationship with Teresa back onto a footing he was comfortable with. He began to make vague suggestions about their future life. Would it not be pleasant if they could travel together? He also wrote to Augusta telling her "If you see my Spouse, do pray tell her that I wish to marry again – and as probably she may wish to do the same – is there no way in *Scotland*? without compromising HER immaculacy – cannot it be done there by the *husband* solely?" However, these tentative hints of a possible elopement were enough to give Teresa a relapse, and she took to her bed with a cough and fever, thus throwing all the men in her life: her lover, her husband and her father, into a state of panic. "Her symptoms," wrote Byron, "threaten Consumption."

Convinced that the Ravenna doctors were doing more harm than good, Byron insisted on sending for the only doctor he had any faith in: Doctor Aglietti from Venice. He in turn had to apply to the Austrian Governor for permission to travel, and finally arrived in early July. The doctor was a man who did not suffer fools gladly. Contemporary accounts record that, faced with a hypochondriac or fit of the vapours, he would sit at the patient's bedside and pretend to fall asleep until, realising their foolishness, they rallied without assistance. Although, having travelled to Ravenna at Byron's expense, he was too polite to doze off on this occasion, he certainly seems to have had the measure of Teresa, informing the family "She may be cured if she likes," before prescribing leeches, Peruvian bark (quinine) and a complete change of scene. From this time onwards Teresa's father, Count Gamba, regarded Byron in a completely different light as the man whose decisiveness had saved his daughter's life. The two men were to become close friends.

Teresa decided that she did like to be cured, and the two lovers soon fell into the habit of meeting every evening to take the air in Byron's carriage. Count Guiccioli's apparent complacency in the face of this excited much local gossip and even anonymous letters so that, in August, he used the pretext of business in Bologna to remove his wife from the city. But not from Byron, who not only followed his lady to Bologna but was soon installed in an apartment in Count Guiccioli's palazzo there.

Byron stayed in Bologna for just over a month. His daily routine was carefully noted in the book of gossip in which an Italian Count, Francesco Rangone, was assiduously recording the doings of the English Milord. "He is invisible till three pm. At four he goes to see his lady, and remains there until six. He rides for an hour, always in the great Cemetery. At eight he dines, at nine he goes to his Amica[56] and remains there until midnight. He studies till dawn. What he does until three remains a mystery. He eats and drinks little." What Byron did until three, mysterious to Count Rangone, was sleep. He had long preferred this semi-nocturnal lifestyle, writing poetry (he was working on the third canto of *Don Juan*) through the night and sleeping during the morning. He was also back on his lowering diet, as his mental health was once more disturbed, largely by his uncertain and cicisbean state. During an evening at the theatre with the Guicciolis he had succumbed to an hysterical fit.

When Teresa and her husband were away from Bologna for a few days, Byron sat in the gardens of their palazzo and abandoned himself to melancholy. He had always thought of himself as a decisive man, whether in choosing to leave England for the East in 1809, to marry in 1814 or to travel abroad at the time of his bankruptcy in 1816. He had been, for good or ill, master of his own fate. Now, however, he felt that he had lost control of his life. He was unable to make plans for the future, as everything now depended on the wishes of someone else. He tried to explain this in a note he wrote in Teresa's copy of Madame de Staël's novel *Corinne*. "You will not understand these English words… but you will recognise the hand-writing of him who

passionately loved you… I feel that I exist here – and I fear that I shall exist hereafter – to what purpose – you will decide – my destiny rests with you." He almost wished that Teresa were still in the Convent, or that their paths had never crossed, but it was too late for such might-have-beens, his future lay entirely in her hands," I more than love you – and cannot cease to love you. – Think of me sometimes when the Alps and the Ocean divide us – but they never will – unless you wish it." It was in this mood that he wrote to Murray, "I am out of sorts – out of nerves – and now and then – (I begin to fear) out of my senses."
Byron found some relief from his confusion and mental turmoil in the melancholy calm of the Certosa Cemetery a short ride from the centre of Bologna. Originally cared for by the Carthusian monks of the adjacent monastery, the cemetery had become wild and overgrown since the closure of the monastery by order of Napoleon in 1797. Byron had first visited it in June, on his way to Ravenna, and had been very taken, not only with its air of Romantic neglect, but also by the simple epitaphs he found there. He quoted two in a letter to Hoppner, the British Consul in Venice:

"Martini Luigi
Implora pace.

Lucrezia Picini
Implora eterna quiete.

that was all – but it appears to me that these two and three words comprize and compress all that can be said on the subject… They contain doubt, hope and humility… they have had enough of life – they want nothing but rest – they implore it." Byron then made a request which Hoppner would sadly prove unable to fulfil. "Pray – if I am shovelled into the Lido Church-yard – in your time – let me have the 'implora pace' and nothing else for my epitaph." This was part of an on-going discussion with Hoppner, who later told Tom Moore that Byron "repeatedly told me" of his desire to be buried on Lido. "I was to overcome whatever difficulties might be raised on this account. I was not to allow his body to be removed to England, nor permit any of his family to interfere with his funeral."

Although Byron and Count Alessandro Guiccioli were on the most amicable terms – indeed the Count was at this time trying to borrow a sizeable sum of money from his wife's lover – Teresa felt the need for some time alone with Byron. When her husband decided to return to Ravenna she reminded him of Doctor Aglietti's advice that she needed a complete change of scene in order to make a full recovery. What if a too-sudden return to

Ravenna led to a relapse? Either he fell for the tale or the fear of losing Byron's loan compelled him to agree. In any case, as Teresa set off for an extended stay at Byron's villa at La Mira, to enable her to consult Doctor Aglietti and to enjoy the change of scene he had recommended, the gossips had a field-day. An Austrian spy based in Bologna reported "Lord B. departed suddenly with Madame Guiccioli, who was therefore said to have been either carried off by him or sold to him by her husband."

The prospect of a more settled lifestyle for the foreseeable future gave Byron the chance to include Allegra in his household again. He no doubt felt that Teresa's presence would prove a calming influence on the child who, he told Augusta, "has a good deal of the Byron… frowns and pouts quite in our way." On his departure from Venice in June, he had left Allegra in the care of the Hoppner family. Mrs Hoppner in particular found the child temperamental and difficult. Feeling that the child needed a more settled existence, Hoppner had suggested that adoption might be the solution: a rich and childless English widow then living in Venice, a Mrs Vavassour, had offered to bring Allegra up as her daughter. While Byron prevaricated about making a decision, Claire Clairmont got wind of the suggestion and sent a particularly bitter letter. "Do not make me mention," she wrote, "what you *ought* to do for her, for I know that every word that falls from my mouth is serpents or toads to you, like the wicked sister in the fairy tale. It is not mine, but your fault that they are not pearls and diamonds. Pray think of the child's miserable condition if you were to die, without anyone to take care of her but her mother, who is hated and detested by everybody." Given food for thought by his former lover's way with words, Byron declined Mrs Vavassour's offer, and also a further suggestion from the Hoppners to take Allegra with them on their summer trip to Switzerland (Mrs Hoppner was Swiss) and leave her to be educated there where, they felt, the bracing climate would be rather better for her health than that of Venice.

In August, Byron wrote, in Hoppner's absence, to Henry Dorville, the British vice-consul in Venice, asking that Allegra and her nurse should make the journey to Bologna to stay with him. It was only now that he learned that the Hoppners had been a little selective in the information they had given him: Mrs Hoppner had (unsurprisingly, given the girl's fondness for inventing tall stories about her employers) dismissed Allegra's nurse Elise some months earlier, and the child had been cared for entirely by the Hoppner's Venetian servants. Thus it was that, when she arrived in Bologna, Allegra could speak nothing except Venexiano. Although Byron found this amusing, he realised that she needed to be taken in hand. A nurse was appointed and by the end of September Allegra was settled at La Mira with Byron and Teresa.

Even though Byron still had the lease of Palazzo Mocenigo, he and Teresa spent most of their time at La Mira. Teresa made occasional visits to Venice to consult Doctor Aglietti – after all, she had to keep up the pretence that she was at La Mira because of her health – and Byron went occasionally to one of Countess Benzoni's *conversazioni*, but by and large they avoided Venetian society, knowing full well that they were its chief subjects of gossip. The Venetian ladies and their *cavalieri* strongly disapproved of both Byron's and Teresa's behaviour: she for leaving her husband's protection, he for inviting her to stay, unchaperoned, under his roof. This really was a most improper way to conduct a liaison. Behaviour like that of Byron and Teresa showed the cracks in the whole carefully constructed edifice of married lady and accepted *cicisbeo* approved by her husband and family. Marina Benzoni in particular lost no time in making her displeasure felt. "Until this unfortunate affair," she pronounced, Byron had "conducted himself so well."

As far as Teresa was concerned, Byron was determined to continue conducting himself well. He ignored the invitations and temptations of Venice to spend quiet evenings at La Mira, a model of devotion. Yet the sensation of being trapped, which he had felt so strongly in Bologna, had not diminished. He wrote to Hobhouse, the only friend in whom he was truly able to confide, explaining his frustration, "a man must be a *Cicisbeo* and a singer in duets and a Connoisseur of operas – or nothing here – I have made some progress in all these accomplishments – but I can't say that I don't feel the degradation." He even began to make plans to leave Italy, not to return to England – he seems to have regarded a country occupied by Lady Byron with something approaching horror – but to settle in South America with Allegra. He shared this idea with several correspondents, but only explained his true reasons to Hobhouse. "Better be an unskilful planter – an awkward settler – better be a hunter – or anything than a flatterer of fiddlers – and a fan-carrier of a woman."

The country Byron had in mind was Venezuela, which in 1819 was in the process of emerging as an independent nation, fighting for independence from Spain. Byron had great admiration for the hero of the Venezuelan struggle for independence, Simon Bolivar (in 1822 he would name his newly-built schooner *Simon Bolivar*), and had read that Bolivar was encouraging European settlers to move to the new country. He asked Hobhouse to use his influence among friends with South American contacts to obtain letters of

introduction to Bolivar, and made plans to buy land. "I want a country – and a home – and if possible – a free one."
The prospect of Lord Byron, South American planter, is an intriguing one, but in the end the plan came to nothing. Byron found release by becoming involved in struggles for independence nearer to hand.

For the moment, however, more immediate relief was in prospect: Byron's friend Tom Moore was about to arrive on a visit. Moore's works may be little-read today, but he was one of the few contemporary poets whose fame and popularity rivalled that of Byron. Byron teasingly wrote to his friend that he would not "allow the Miss Byrons (legitimate or illegitimate)" to read Moore's poetry, "that they mayn't discover that there was a better poet than papa."
Born in Dublin into a Roman Catholic family in 1779 Tom Moore had had to make his own way in the world at a time when Parliament and many of the professions were closed to Catholics. Like Byron, he supported Irish Home Rule and Catholic Emancipation. However, as a student at Trinity College, Dublin Moore had seen at first hand the punishments meted out to supporters of Wolfe Tone's rebellion against British rule in 1798, and had even been taken in for questioning himself. After settling in England in 1799 he chose a more subtle path: on the surface, he was the friend of peers and the darling of Society; yet his most popular poems, The *Irish Melodies,* recalled Ireland's mythical past and heroes. Singing the melodies in Society drawing-rooms, as he was often called on to do, Moore encouraged a sentimental attachment to an imaginary Ireland among the British ruling classes. His poems, set to music, could be found on most drawing-room pianos: countless young ladies trilled their way through *The Harp That Once Through Tara's Halls* and *She is far from the land where her young hero sleeps,* a lament for the Irish rebel Robert Emmet, executed by the British for treason. These verses were, in the opinion of Daniel O'Connell,[57] more effective in the long run in changing British attitudes to Ireland than violence or open rebellion. O'Connell said of Moore, "I attribute much of the present state of feeling, and the desire for liberty in Ireland, to that immortal man."
Moore and Byron had first met in 1811 at the home of their mutual friend Samuel Rogers. The younger poet had been rude about Moore in his juvenile work *English Bards and Scotch Reviewers* (as he had about every other poet he could think of: the mature Byron considered it a dreadful piece) and Moore had challenged him to a duel. The challenge, issued in 1809, was not

delivered until Byron returned from the east two years later, and Rogers had taken it upon himself to smooth the ruffled feathers of both men. They soon became firm friends, Moore's light-hearted, easy going personality often being just what was needed to shake Byron out of melancholy and make him laugh at himself. Since leaving England, Byron had written regularly to Moore, congratulating him on the births and condoling with him on the deaths of his children, and eager for news of *Lalla Rookh*, Moore's epic attempt to emulate the success of Byron's eastern romances such as *The Giaour*.

Now, after three years, Moore was on his way. He travelled as far as Milan with his friend Lord John Russell, and the two men were shown round that city by Douglas Kinnaird's brother, Lord Kinnaird, who lived there with a dancer. On his travels Moore had heard a great deal of Byron gossip of varying degrees of veracity, tales of seduction, despair and madness which would have done credit to the pens of Polidori or Caroline Lamb. Lord Kinnaird would be able to give Moore a clearer picture of Byron's true situation and his relationship with Teresa, so that Moore was not taken by surprise on his arrival at La Mira on 8th October 1819. In his *Life of Byron* Moore gives a very vivid description of his time in Venice and his pleasure at seeing Byron again. He was forcibly struck by the physical changes in his friend: although he was once more following his lowering diet (Moore watched him eat two raw eggs, a cup of black tea and a piece of dry biscuit for his 4pm breakfast) Byron still bore some signs of the weight he had gained the previous year, so that his face, Moore felt, had lost "some of that refined and spiritualised look, that had, in other times, distinguished it." He had also given himself what Moore could only describe as "a foreign air" with longer hair and side-whiskers. Byron was still undeniably handsome and Moore felt that the change suited him, "whatever his features had lost of their high, romantic character, they had become more fitted for the expression of that arch, waggish wisdom… which he had shown to be equally inherent in his various and prodigally gifted nature." In other words, Byron was now more *Don Juan* than *Childe Harold*.

Byron introduced his friend to Teresa straight away, and in the Life Moore smoothly recalls her as "fair-complexioned and delicate," leaving an impression of "intelligence and amiableness." However, Byron confided some of his inner turmoil to Moore, who recorded it in his private journal. "If you had come here a little sooner," Byron told him, "I'll be damned if I would have run away with a red-haired woman of quality."

Then, like two naughty schoolboys off on a jolly, the two friends

set out for Venice. Doing his best to evoke a grand, Romantic impression of his first arrival in the city for his readers, Moore has to admit that "The exuberant gaiety of my companion, and the recollections – anything but romantic – into which our conversation wandered, put at once completely to flight all poetical and historical associations; and our course was, I am almost ashamed to say, one of uninterrupted merriment and laughter."
Tom Moore's account of his time in Venice with Byron has a valedictory air: it is as if Byron sensed that his own final departure from the city was imminent, and by visiting beautiful and favourite spots with his friend he was saying his own farewells to a city with which he had a complex relationship. He had fallen a little out of love with Venice as he cast a cool and objective eye over his behaviour there the previous year, almost as if he blamed the city for his own excesses. Yet as he made his tour with Moore, and saw Venice afresh through his friend's eyes, his original affection for the melancholy, beautiful, crumbling city briefly revived.
Byron insisted that Moore, who wanted to go to a hotel, should stay in Palazzo Mocenigo even though, he explained, he would be unable to spend his own nights away from La Mira. Having been instrumental in Teresa leaving her husband's protection, he clearly took his own role as her *cavaliere* very seriously and was determined not to give the gossips of Venice the slightest opportunity to say that he had abandoned her. A couple of overnight stays in Venice with Moore would, he was well aware, be more than enough grist for their mill.
Moore left a marvellous description of his arrival at his friend's "damp-looking mansion" as evening drew on. Neither lights nor any of Byron's fourteen servants were visible. The *cortile* had been left to the mercy of Byron's menagerie. Wherever he went he acquired creatures of a faintly exotic nature and as well as the loyal and ancient Mutz his animals at this time included a bulldog, a tame raven, a fox and a couple of monkeys, one of which gave Moore an uncomfortable few moments as Byron blundered about looking for the stairs.
Once upstairs, Byron was unable to find the key to his apartment. Servants having by now materialised, none of them could find it either and Tom Moore thought longingly of the Hotel Gran Bretagna until, "Impatient of the delay of the key, my noble host, with one of his humourous maledictions, gave a vigorous kick to the door and burst it open."
Having kicked the door down and ordered dinner, Byron took Moore out onto the magnificent stone balcony of his apartments to enjoy the Grand Canal in the twilight. Moore, once again

striving to evoke a Romantic atmosphere, began to speak of the rosy hue of Italian sunsets, but Byron was in no mood for that, rallying is friend with "Damn it Tom, *don't* be poetical." Spotting a gondola party of what he assumed were English visitors, well aware that the gondolier was probably pointing him out as one of the sights of Venice, he adopted a swaggering pose up on the balcony so as not to disappoint them.

Byron's friend Alexander Scott had been recruited as Moore's guide around the city, and he took charge of filling up the mornings and afternoons, when Byron was still in bed, with a tour of Venetian art and architecture; the evenings with visits to the theatre and *conversazioni*. Scott introduced Moore to Countess Benzoni, who took it upon herself to deliver a lecture about Byron's moral conduct which, Moore reports, provoked "a smile and a sigh" from his friend when he was told of it. Moore also visited Madame Albrizzi, who was pleased to meet a friend of Byron's now that Byron no longer attended her salon. She was trying to compile a pen-portrait of him (Byron, hearing of this, asked her not to publish. She waited until after his death) which, despite being written by a woman who knew him personally, was littered with errors and exaggerations which have now come to be part of the Byron legend. Madame Albrizzi first told the world that Byron was never seen on foot anywhere in Venice (which must have made getting from his gondola to his opera box difficult) and only ever saw Piazza San Marco from a window. Little wonder that the subject asked for it to be suppressed.

As was always the case with Byron, the presence of a visitor from England brought English affairs to the forefront of his mind, and when the two friends were alone together they spent a great deal of time discussing Byron's marriage. Byron gave Moore the full story of its failure; Moore told Byron what had been, and still was, said of him in England. As a result of these conversations, Byron gave his friend the *Memoirs* which he had begun to write in 1818 and which now ran to 78 pages. Moore later said that the *Memoirs* dealt almost exclusively with the events of Byron's marriage. Mary Shelley had already read them, and Byron told Moore that he was free to show them to any of their circle of friends in England, even Lady Byron if she wanted to read them. Moore was to think of the *Memoirs* as a gift. Byron knew that a growing family had put a strain on his friend's finances, and that he had recently suffered a serious loss when a money-making scheme in the West Indies had gone badly wrong. Moore was free to sell the *Memoirs* to a publisher, with the proviso that they were not to be published during Byron's lifetime. On his return to London, Moore was able to raise £ 2,000 by selling the *Memoirs* to Byron's publisher Murray. Unfortunately, this took them out of his control and they were destroyed after Byron's death, burnt in Murray's office fireplace through the combined efforts of Lady Byron's solicitor and of Hobhouse, jealous both of his friend's posthumous reputation and of his closeness to Tom Moore.[58]

On what was to be Moore's last evening in Venice, Byron arrived at Palazzo Mocenigo in naughty schoolboy mood once more, announcing gleefully that "the Contessa had given him leave to 'make a night of it." He took his friend to the opera, where he enlivened the performance with anecdotes about the love-lives of various members of the audience and of the diva, a fiery lady who was rumoured to have stabbed one of her lovers. From there the friends went to Piazza San Marco and sat in Caffé Florian, "drinking hot brandy punch and laughing over old times" till two in the morning. The evening ended with a farewell gondola ride by moonlight around the lagoon; both men were moved almost to tears by the melancholy beauty of the sleeping city.

The following day, after calling at La Mira for a farewell dinner "favoured by the presence of Madame Guiccioli" Tom Moore set out for Rome. The two friends would not meet again.

As the autumn progressed, letters began to arrive from Ravenna indicating that Alessandro Guiccioli felt it was high time his wife came back. Although he, a man of the world, must have been only too aware of the nature of her relationship with Byron, Teresa's father was only too happy to believe what his daughter told him: that the arrangement at La Mira was purely platonic and she was chaperoned at all times (in fact Fanny Silvestrini, the friend who acted as so-called chaperone, had long since been sent to stay in Venice). Teresa had kept up a lengthy correspondence with both husband and father, with detailed accounts of the state of her health, including a description of her piles which must have been rather more than Alessandro wanted to be told. By late October, however, he had tired of the charade, and Teresa received a letter informing her that he would arrive in Venice on All Saints Day to accompany her back to Ravenna. To confound the gossips, the Count wrote, he would receive her back under his protection at Palazzo Mocenigo, where the two of them would then remain as Byron's guests for two nights.

When Alessandro arrived, his wife was already at the Palazzo, having hurried there to nurse Byron through a tertian fever – probably a recurrence of the malaria he had picked up on his eastern journey – which had come on after he was caught in a thunderstorm while out riding on Lido. His delirium was so bad that he believed that his mother-in-law was in the room with him, "and on my senses coming back – found Fletcher sobbing on one side of the bed – and la Contessa G weeping on the other – so that I had no want of attendance."

Having tasted freedom and life with Byron, Teresa was in no mood to go home with her husband, particularly after he presented her with a list of "Indispensable Rules" for her future conduct, covering everything from what time she should get up in the morning to her control of the household economy to a request (perhaps from bitter experience of their former life together) that she should not argue or make a fuss. Most telling are the Count's demands that she should live quietly, receiving few visitors, and give up "her longing for travel or for dwelling-places which do not suit her husband's or her family's arrangements… let her be completely docile with her husband." Teresa, a long way from docility, replied with a list of counter-demands, including "to receive, without discrimination, any visitor who may come."

Having laid their cards on the table about future relations with Byron, both husband and wife refused to back down. Byron, trying to keep a low profile while Count and Countess argued under his roof, was surprised to receive a visit from Alessandro Guiccioli, asking him to intercede, "He actually came to *me* crying about it." He told the Count very definitely that, should he decide to separate from his wife, "I will take her undoubtedly – it is my duty – it is also my inclination." If, however, they were reconciled, Byron would "not carry further disturbance into your family" and would give serious consideration to leaving Italy. Teresa was persuaded "with the greatest difficulty" to return to Ravenna with her husband, although with her Byron had to hint "that I might come there again – else she refused to go."

Byron, in his suddenly empty palazzo in the gloom of a Venetian November, began to fulfil his promise to Alessandro Guiccioli by beginning to pack up his household and leave Venice. His plan was to briefly return to England before journeying on to settle elsewhere: he still had South America in mind. Everything was brought to a halt, however, when Allegra became seriously ill with *doppia terziana*, double tertian, a virulent form of malaria. Byron, who had refused to see a doctor during his own illness (and was still suffering feverish attacks as a result) sent for Doctor Aglietti to attend his child and endured several weeks of anxiety as his plans were "lulled upon the feverish pillow of a sick infant."

In a low physical state, worried about his daughter, in emotional turmoil about what seemed to be the end of his relationship with

Teresa and with his future life uncertain once more, Byron turned to verse in an attempt to clarify his feelings with the stanzas *Could Love Forever*. He tried to put a brave face and positive slant on the events of the past few months, claiming that it was better for a love affair to end in the first flush of passion rather than wither and die through weariness and over-familiarity:

Wait not, fond lover!
Till years are over,
And then recover
As from a dream,
While each bewailing
The other's failing
With wrath and railing
All hideous seem –
While first decreasing,
Yet not quite ceasing,
Wait not till teasing
All passion blight:
If once diminish'd
Love's reign is finish'd –
Then part in friendship and bid goodnight.

At last, by the middle of December, Byron seemed ready to leave. The lease of Palazzo Mocenigo was given up, the menagerie arranged, Allegra was well enough to travel, his goods were packed. On December 9th 1819, almost exactly three years since Byron first arrived in Venice, Tita waited with the gondola at the steps of the palazzo. Within, Byron was putting on his gloves and picking up his cane. "At this moment Mylord, by way of pretext, declares that if it would strike one o'clock before everything was in order… he would not go that day. The hour strikes and he remains. Evidently he had not the heart to go."

Going back into the palazzo, Byron wrote to Teresa to tell her that he could not leave her, "Love has won." By the middle of the month he was in Ravenna in order to be near her. He never came back to Venice.

Sixth Venetian Interlude

... there are one or two *Conversazioni* ...

Conversazioni *were a Venetian institution, fined-tuned to an exquisite degree during the last hundred years of the Republic. They were by and large uncomfortable, tedious evenings but, should one belong to a patrician family, one's attendance at* conversazioni *was an expected part of social life. Imagine the scene: guests arriving by private gondola enter the palazzo via the* portone, *the water-gate directly from the canal. As they climb the elegant sweeping staircase up to the first floor* piano nobile, *the rustle of the ladies' silk dresses against the marble steps can clearly be heard. The* conversazione *itself takes place in an elegant* salone, *the walls usually covered in marble or damask. Above, the cavorting* putti *or allegorical figures of the ceiling fresco look down on the guests who, lit by Murano glass chandeliers, perch uncomfortably on gilded, spindly armchairs. Most guests are probably cold – if the high and echoing* salone *has a fireplace it is inevitably at the opposite end of the room and too small and over-decorated to cope with the demands of its job – and cannot even gossip for their supper as it is highly unlikely that anything more substantial than coffee or fruit is offered.*[59]

Eighteenth century frescoes in the Palazzo Grassi show uniformed flunkies bearing salvers of tiny coffee-cups whilst gentlemen vie against each other to entertain a veiled lady who tries to conceal her smiles (or yawns) behind her fan. At conversazioni *the* cicisbeo *was expected to live up to his name: it was a place for gossip. Tittle-tattle and amusing stories, and perhaps card games, were the order of the evening. The ladies sat in small circles, the gentlemen gathered into groups near each, circulating as the evening progressed. As in so much Venetian Society, one attended not to enjoy oneself, but to be seen.*

In common with many other Venetian institutions, conversazioni *were in decline by the time Byron arrived in the city: the war, high taxes and patrician poverty had seen to that. However, there were still two or three places where a noble Venetian or a celebrated visitor should expect to be seen. Byron told his friend Sam Rogers, "there are one or two* Conversazioni *– where I go regularly – just to keep up the system – as I had letters to their Givers – & they are particular on such points – & now and then – though very rarely – to the Governor's."*

In his first winter in Venice, in his character as an English Milord, Byron attended a few conversazioni *given by the Austrian Governor,*

Count Goetz. Politics aside, one could meet interesting people of all nationalities there, and Byron seems to have got on well with the Governor's Lady, with whom he had literary discussions about the origins of the story of Romeo and Juliet.

The leading conversazioni, *however, were presided over by two society ladies. Madame Albrizzi's* conversazioni *tended to be literary, artistic and at times even political. They took place in the famed* Salone di Putti *of Palazzo Albrizzi, which boasted a ceiling of pleated stucco with disporting cherubs. The Countess Albrizzi*[60] *prided herself on her literary reputation, not only as a friend of Alfieri and Ugo Foscolo, but also as an author in her own right, having published a collection of pen-portraits of some of the famous people of her acquaintance. Byron attended quite a few* conversazioni *at Palazzo Albrizzi, and seems to have enjoyed them initially. He and Madame could gossip about their literary acquaintance, including Madame de Staël and the Milanese literary set, and he could hear up-to-date information on the Greek nationalist movement from the Greeks who attended the salon: Madame was Greek by birth and Venice had a sizeable Greek community. However, as time passed and no new faces were seen, no new topics introduced,* conversazioni *at Palazzo Albrizzi lost their sparkle for Byron. He showed renewed interest in the spring of 1818, noting that "Madame Albrizzi's* Conversazioni *are greatly improved, there have been some pretty women there lately," and he continued to have great personal affection for Madame. His letter requesting that she should not publish a pen-portrait of him in her new volume was a model of courtesy and good manners, in contrast to his reply to an Italian who, at about the same time, wished to publish his own translation of* Manfred*: he was offered 200 francs and a horsewhipping.*

The other lady famous for her conversazioni *was Countess Marina Benzoni whom Byron compared to his friend Lady Melbourne; with just cause, as both had been* grandes horizontales *in their youth. Although now happy to use her Austrian title of Countess, in 1797 Marina Benzoni had danced with Ugo Foscolo around the Tree of Liberty which the French had erected in Piazza San Marco: gossip said that she had danced with such gusto that her Grecian tunic flew up, revealing both her legs and her lack of underwear. Approaching sixty when Byron met her, the Countess was greatly changed from the girl whose behaviour had inspired the barcarole La Bondina in Gondoleta, but was still well-known to all the gondoliers, albeit for a very different reason. She was very fond of her food, especially polenta and, when out in her gondola, would keep a hot slice in her embonpoint to nibble at should she feel peckish. The rising steam led to gondoliers who saw her approach calling to each other "Xe qua al fumeto" – "Here comes the little cloud."*

Byron was introduced to Marina Benzoni by the British Consul, Richard Belgrave Hoppner, and he became a regular visitor to her conversazioni *after he moved to the Palazzo Mocenigo. Ca'Benzon was a short gondola ride, a few hundred metres up the Grand Canal not far from the Rialto. Byron found her* conversazioni *more entertaining than those of the Governor and Madame Albrizzi, probably because they were about gossip, pure and simple. The Countess was like Lady Melbourne in other ways, as both were very kind and generous women. She and Byron became great friends. Guests at a* conversazione *at Ca'Benzon were assured of a warm welcome from the Countess and her* cavaliere servente, *Count Giuseppe Rangone, whose devotion was famed throughout Venice.*[61]

One disadvantage for Byron of attending conversazioni *where gossip was top of the agenda was that he became a popular topic of discussion, especially during the spring and summer of 1818 when he gave himself up to the soft underbelly of Venetian life. Giuseppe Rangone's brother Francesco even kept a notebook of every bit of Byron-related tittle-tattle he could lay his hands on,* Peep at a very cultivated and rich, but strange Mylord. *His women, his diet, his politics, recorded with greater or lesser degrees of accuracy, were all grist to the Venetian gossip-mill.*

And it was not only the Venetian gossips who were at work. English visitors to Venice were eager to attend conversazioni *during their stay in the city, and Countess Benzoni's was the place, if one could gain an introduction. Thus it was that, in May 1818, Lord Byron met a friend of his wife at Ca'Benzon. He was his usual charming self and, although such an unexpected meeting must have been difficult, went out of his way to be agreeable. Lady Byron's friend, Miss Montgomery, was unable to look him in the eye, but lost no time in sending a breathless account of the encounter back to England:*

"he crossed the room to come and sit next to me, said he was afraid I did not recollect him, hoped travelling had benefitted my health, asked how long I proposed staying at Venice, whether I was going to England… he seemed quite unembarrassed as far as I could judge from the tone of his voice, for his countenance I could not distinctly see… as I am not blessed with much presence of mind and felt a little oddly at being addressed by him."

Miss Montgomery was only too happy to pass on any gossip to Lady Byron, the more malicious the better, "His beauty is quite, quite gone. He is enormously fat, his face bloated and complection pasty.[62] *Nothing remains of that fine antique outline so peculiar to his head. His dress is very much neglected… He is not known to have had any liaison with the ladies of Venice – the person known as his favourite was the wife of a shopkeeper who received considerable pecuniary remuneration for the loss of her affection."*

It is not hard to imagine Lady Byron's schadenfreude *on reading the letter. Nor is it hard to understand Byron's decision, later in the same year, to give up going into Society as "It distresses me."*

Chapter Seven

Byron after Venice

"I always fear that you will die suddenly of a fever, knowing the life you lead."

By Christmas Eve 1819 Byron was back in Ravenna, where he found a warm welcome, not only from Teresa herself, but also from her family. As he settled into his new life during the cold winter gripping Emilia-Romagna several threads which had first been woven into his life in Venice, continued to be of importance. Most obvious was his relationship with Teresa, her husband, father and brother. There were also questions about Allegra's future to be settled. And Byron's interest in the Italian struggle for freedom, little more than dilettante awareness in Venice, was about to ripen into fully-fledged involvement.

He immediately found that there was no escape from the role of *cicisbeo* which Teresa had prepared for him. He was paraded in front of Ravenna society at a New Year's Eve party given by Teresa's uncle, and wrote ruefully to Hoppner about his growing skill in folding a shawl. He felt like a caged animal and could see no sign of escape, as in Ravenna "a man actually becomes a piece of female property." The cage doors closed with a clang when Alessandro Guiccioli, noticing (or so he claimed) that the inn where Byron was lodging was less than adequate for the needs of an English Milord and his entourage, invited him to stay in the Palazzo Guiccioli itself. All Ravenna looked on with fascinated interest as "dogs, monkeys, house-servants, a little girl – said to be his offspring by a girl in London – and Mylord, took up their abode in this delightful new inn." The gossipy Francesco Rangone noted that Byron "became an accomplished *cavaliere*," accompanying Teresa to the theatre and to *conversazioni*, both of which he found somewhat dull after Venice, complaining that, while at the theatre everybody talked, in society conversation was rare and the only entertainments were cards or *lotto reale*, a board game with numbers that was an ancestor of bingo.

Meanwhile, in his apartment on the first floor of the Palazzo

Guiccioli there was little to do except wait for the snow to melt so that he could go riding, and communicate with Teresa, living on the floor below, by letter: the kind of intrigue she so enjoyed but which quickly began to pall for Byron.

Largely confined to his apartments in the palazzo and to the quiet streets of the dull little town, he returned to writing to divert himself. He finished Cantos III and IV of *Don Juan* and parcelled them off to Murray. He completed *The Prophecy of Dante,* a poem begun during his time in Ravenna the previous year which Teresa – proud, like all citizens of Ravenna, that Italy's national poet had found refuge in their town – had asked him to write. Local legend claims that Byron would doff his hat whenever he passed the poet's tomb. In the poem Dante, exiled in Ravenna, foresees the state of Italy as Byron knew it.

Beholding with the dark eyes of a seer
The evil days to gifted souls foreshown.

Looking back on his sojourn in Venice, and especially on his debaucheries, of which his inner Aberdeen Calvinist now felt deeply ashamed, he was inspired to write something new, a play rather than a poem, based on the life of Doge Marino Falier. Byron had first learned about the tragic death of this Doge in 1817 and, with his ready interest in flawed and fallen heroes, read all he could in histories of the period, both English and Venetian. The historical Marino Falier was Doge for a brief period in 1354-55, at a time of considerable unrest in the Republic as a result of economic decline, brought about by interminable wars with the city of Genoa, Venice's rival for control of Mediterranean trade. At the time, Genoa had the upper hand. As a result, trade was slow, unemployment high, and the people of Venice blamed their rulers. Doge Falier, angered by the constraints of his position (the Doge was little more than a ceremonial figurehead) took advantage of the civic unrest by plotting to overthrow the Great Council of Venetian patricians and become sole ruler. He was beheaded on the steps of the Giant's Staircase in the Palazzo Ducale, a symbolic act as this was the site of every doge's coronation. In the Great Council Chamber, where portraits of all the Doges are displayed, Falier's image was replaced with a black veil and the words "This is the space reserved for Marino Falier, beheaded for his crimes."

Byron's play, *Marino Faliero, Doge of Venice,* followed the historical events closely. However, socio-economic unrest would make an unlikely background for a tragedy, and he preferred the apocryphal story that Falier's actions resulted from an insult to his wife, called Angiolina in the play. Byron makes her a young and attractive woman, married to a much older husband of uncertain temper: a situation with which he was becoming all too familiar. The Venice portrayed in *Marino Faliero* is not the powerful *Serenissima* of the fourteenth century but the decayed, decadent Venice with which Byron was so out of love, blaming the city, the "sea-Sodom," for his own dissipations. In *Marino Faliero* the Republic and its officials stand as representatives for the oppressive regimes Byron saw all around him, across Italy and Europe. In one particularly moving scene the play's chief conspirators, ordinary Venetian working men, discuss their plans. Their aim is to purify not only their own city but all "corrupted commonwealths." Although the men are fully aware that arrest, torture and death (which await them at the climax of the play) are ever-present possibilities, they are ready. "They never fail who die in a great cause," says the conspirator Israel Bertuccio,

> *They but augment the deep and sweeping thoughts*
> *Which overpower all others, and conduct*
> *The world at last to freedom.*

The play was completed by the middle of June 1820. By then, Byron was himself actively involved in the "great cause." He had become a member of the Carbonari.

"Carbonari," or charcoal-burners, were a network of loosely-linked secret societies which had originally spread across Europe in the 1790s and early years of the nineteenth century. Inspired by the French Revolution and by the career of the young Napoleon Bonaparte their aims were freedom from oppression and to give ordinary citizens a voice. Carbonari were found across Europe, in France, Spain and London, as well as in Italy. The activities of the Italian Carbonari remain the best-known because their ranks included a number of men, such as the politician and philosopher Giuseppe Mazzini, who spent their lives working for the liberation and unification of Italy.

In the first decades of the nineteenth century Carbonari cells were established in Sicily, Naples, the Papal States, Piedmont and Tuscany. Each was a more or less independent entity and, because secrecy was of prime importance when government spies – in the pay of the Pope, the Austrians, the King of Naples – were everywhere, communication between cells was erratic and ad hoc.

Emilia-Romagna, one of the Papal States, had a flourishing Carbonari network. Teresa's father, Count Ruggero Gamba, was a member. As a youth he had been a supporter of the French

Revolution, and when French troops invaded in 1797, freeing Emilia-Romagna temporarily from papal rule, he had helped set up a Tree of Liberty in Ravenna's central piazza where the "Golden Book," a list of the Romagnuola aristocracy, had then been ceremonially burned. Teresa's younger brother Pietro belonged to the Carbonari. So did Lega Zambelli, an employee of Count Alessandro Guiccioli who began to look after Byron's finances at about this time. It is not clear which of them first approached Byron about becoming a member, or introduced him to the local network, but by April 1820 he had joined their ranks.

Becoming a member of the Carbonari was an elaborate procedure which involved a complex initiation rite. The blindfold initiate was led into the meeting-room, where his hand was placed on a dagger-blade while he swore loyalty to Italy. As his eyes were uncovered, he found himself surrounded by drawn daggers, a visible reminder that all Carbonari should protect each other, but anyone who betrayed his oath could expect only death.

The schoolboy in Byron would no doubt relish the ritual and secrecy, the regularly-changed passwords and secret signals and handshakes. He would also welcome a chance of closer friendship with Teresa's father and brother, of whom he was becoming genuinely fond, and his sense of mischief would have been piqued by the awareness that becoming a carbonaro would, should he ever hear of it, cause great annoyance to the deeply conservative Alessandro Guiccioli. It also gave him a chance to be active, to do something that didn't involve assignations, folding a shawl or undergoing the trials of yet another lovers' quarrel. Above all, Byron had found a cause the aims of which he passionately supported. Like Count Gamba, he had idolised the young Napoleon and hoped he would bring freedom to Europe, hopes dashed first by Napoleon's imperial ambitions and then by the Congress of Vienna, which had re-imposed the *status quo* of oppressive rule across France, Italy, and the Austrian Empire, not to mention Great Britain.

Back in England, Hobhouse was undergoing his own trials due to his Radical opinions at the same time as Byron was becoming active in the Carbonari. Throughout the previous year he had written to Byron frequently about the unrest and political turmoil in Britain, brought about by a combination of post-war unemployment, poor harvests and an economic downturn. Hobhouse was determined to become an MP – he stood as a candidate for the constituency of Westminster three times between

1818 and 1820, when he was finally elected – and urged his friend to return to England and become active in politics once more. "England is in such a state of ferment" he wrote, "that perhaps you may find some interest in it." Byron, however, had been away from England for too long, and was out of touch. He found it difficult to accept that the Whig aristocracy where he had found his natural home was losing influence. Opposition to the seemingly endless succession of repressive Tory administrations now came from the urban middle-classes of the northern and midland industrial towns and from those sections of the working-class who were seizing the opportunities for education and self-improvement offered by the nonconformist churches. Many members of the landed gentry, both Whig and Tory, found this hard to stomach. The French Revolution was still fresh in their minds, and the new Radical leaders were a clear reminder of the Parisian mob. Byron was critical of Hobhouse both for leaving the Whigs – "you were the founder of the Whig-Club at Cambridge" he reminded his friend rather plaintively – and for taking up with "blackguard Reformers," such as Sir Francis Burdett who supported such extreme Radical measures as universal male franchise and a secret ballot.

Hobhouse was right about England being in a state of ferment. In August 1819 a large crowd (some estimates claim as many as 80,000 people) gathered at St Peter's Fields in Manchester to listen to the famous Radical Henry "Orator" Hunt, who was to speak in favour of granting all men the right to vote. There were many family groups in the crowd, which was well-organised and peaceful. However, this did not prevent local magistrates, in a panic that such a large number of working people should have gathered together, ordering mounted troops to charge into the crowd with drawn sabres in an attempt to arrest and silence Henry Hunt. The "Peterloo Massacre" killed fifteen people and injured up to 700 more. In the ensuing outcry the Tory Government, fearful of mounting unrest, passed the Six Acts. The Acts banned large public meetings, gave magistrates the right to order a search of any private property and aimed to silence the growing number of small-circulation Radical newspapers by increasing the stamp duty which had to be paid on all newspapers.

One result of the Government's panic was that Hobhouse was arrested and imprisoned under the terms of one of the acts, The Blasphemous and Seditious Libels Act. In the aftermath of Peterloo he had published *A Trifling Mistake*, a political pamphlet condemning the Six Acts in which he asked "What prevents the people from walking down to the House, and pulling out the members by the ears, locking up their doors and flinging the key into the Thames?" Even though Hobhouse answered his own question by noting that the protectors of Parliament were to be found a stone's-throw away "at the Horse Guards, and the Knightsbridge barracks," he spent six weeks in Newgate Gaol on a charge of libelling Parliament. He was never formally charged and was released when Parliament was dissolved due to the death of George III in February 1820.

Byron responded to his friend's imprisonment by writing a satirical ballad. It was probably intended to be a witty "I told you so" to be read in the light of the letters the two had exchanged throughout the previous autumn and winter, in which Byron had not minced his words about Hobhouse's political associates. Had the ballad been sent directly to Hobhouse it may have brought a wry smile to lighten his imprisonment. However, perhaps in a bid to avoid having the letter opened, as something addressed to Newgate Gaol almost certainly would have been, Byron chose instead to send the ballad to Murray, with instructions to give it directly to Hobhouse. Instead, in a cruel and unnecessary move, the publisher chose to circulate it among his Tory friends for their sniggers.

Byron begins by asking

How came you in Hob's pound to cool,
My boy Hobbie O?
Because I bade the people pull
The House into the Lobby O.

He goes on to criticise Hobhouse's aspirations to become a radical MP

You hate the House – why canvass, then
My boy Hobbie O?
Because I would reform the den
As member for the Mobby O.

And concludes with a warning to Hobhouse about his chosen constituency (Westminster was a famously radical seat)

When to the mob you make a speech,
My boy Hobbie O,
How do you keep without their reach
The watch within your fobby O?

Hobhouse was deeply upset when he read the ballad, but behaved with great dignity, confiding his feelings only to his

diary, and when he received a friendly letter from Byron congratulating him on his release he chose to view it as an apology, saying no more to his friend than "Oh you shabby fellow – so you strike a man when he is down do you?"
In the general election which followed the death of the King, Hobhouse again stood for Westminster. In a small act of revenge for the ballad, he could not resist telling Byron that the sitting MP was one of "your friends, the Whigs." He was George Lamb, Lady Caroline's brother-in-law, and that lady turned up at the hustings where she did her best to drum up support by going into the local taverns to buy drinks for the electors and dance with them, so that eventually George Lamb was greeted with cries of "Where's Caroline?" Hobhouse conceded that "the mad skeleton" worked hard to keep the seat for George, she "kissed, canvassed, & cuckolded, but all in vain," as Hobhouse and Sir Francis Burdett were duly elected. Byron and Fletcher followed Hobhouse's parliamentary career with interest, and in August Byron teased his friend, "Fletcher reads you in Galignani – and comes grinning over your speeches to me – he has already noted Seventeen."

In Ravenna, meanwhile, Byron's attention was temporarily diverted from his involvement with the Carbonari by yet another crisis in the Guiccioli marriage. Count Alessandro, who had not only turned a blind eye to the relationship between his wife and Milord but had, at times, actively seemed to pander to it, especially when trying to extract a loan or a favour from Byron, and who had invited Byron to be his permanent house-guest a few months earlier, now executed a complete *volte-face*. Returning home one evening to find his wife and her lover spending a quiet evening together as usual, he told Byron that such visits made him unhappy and uncomfortable: would Milord please bring them to an end? Byron replied calmly that, as the Count's guest, he must defer to his wishes, and went to his own apartment. Left alone with his wife, Alessandro ranted, raved and threatened to such an extent that next morning Teresa sent for her father and, after giving a detailed account of husband's behaviour, declared that she could no longer live with him and wished to return home.
Count Gamba, by now firm friends with Byron, not only agreed to his daughter's request but went much further and sent a petition to the Pope – who was, conveniently, a close friend of Teresa's grandmother – requesting a formal separation. Alessandro Guiccioli retaliated by sending the testimonies of his household staff to the Holy Father, giving details of occasions when Teresa

had been discovered in Byron's apartments (and vice versa) and of their being found *in flagrante* in Byron's bedchamber. The Pope, however, seems to have agreed with public opinion which was, according to Byron, that Count Alessandro "had no business to take the business up now after a year of toleration. – The law is against him – because he slept with his wife after her admission – all her relatives… are furious *against him* for his conduct – & his not wishing to be cuckolded at threescore – when everyone else is at one." On 6th July 1820 Pope Pius VII issued a decree granting Teresa a formal separation from her husband, who was to pay her a handsome monthly allowance. Teresa, in turn, was to return to live at her father's home in "a manner which befits a respectable and noble Lady separated from her Husband." In other words, she was expected to conduct herself discreetly and not appear in public with her lover.

Since her father was living in his summer villa at Filetto, in the countryside about thirteen kilometres from Ravenna, Teresa was left with little option except that of avoiding Byron's company. While she settled back into life surrounded by her younger siblings (Teresa was the eldest of six children: the youngest was at this time less than a year old[63])Byron remained in his apartments at Palazzo Guiccioli. Count Alessandro gave him notice to quit, but he was comfortable there and the apartments were convenient for the limited social life Ravenna had to offer, for his daily rides into the pine-woods and for his Carbonari meetings, so he simply ignored the Count and stayed put. He knew that the Papal decree had effectively made his relationship with Teresa a permanent one: it would be impossible for a gentleman who had been the cause of a lady's separation from her husband to then move on – he would be considered to have abandoned her. However, he seems to have appreciated the breathing-space granted to him by the distance to Filetto and by the Pope's desire that Teresa live respectably as he did not visit her for almost two months, although he wrote to her regularly, keeping her abreast of palazzo and town gossip.

He was becoming a well-known, even a popular, figure in the small town. With Teresa away and the bones of the Guiccioli separation picked clean by the gossips, the people of Ravenna began to notice another side to the English Milord in their midst: his kindness and generosity. He had always been charitable, even when he had little to spare, and as his fortunes improved during his time in Venice he was able to give more money away. His friend Hoppner, the British Consul in Venice, had noted that he was always ready to help the needy, but tried to do so without attracting attention, and since he tended to simply use the ready cash in his pocket little record of his Venetian charities remain. Hobhouse noted in his diary that Byron gave money to the distressed peasants around La Mira in the summer of 1817, resulting in his first meeting with Margarita Cogni. He also helped a stranded English sailor called John Dodd, whom he met in 1819, giving him money for his passage back to England and a letter of recommendation. However, on settling in Ravenna in 1820 he began to employ the very efficient Lega Zambelli as his steward, and Lega's account-books give a very clear picture of Byron's spending. Byron was certainly very generous, as Lega records sixteen separate donations in a single month, including:

March 1st: to a poor old lame woman.
March 5th: to three old men and a lame woman.
March 23rd: borrowed from Fletcher for charity to a poor man.
March 31st: to the Capuchin monks.

Byron himself records, in the journal he kept for the first two months of 1821, meeting an old lady of ninety-five who subsisted by gathering firewood in the pine forest which surrounded Ravenna. He was so taken with her that he invited her to Palazzo Guiccioli where he talked to her about her life, ordered new clothes for her and put her on a weekly pension.

The secret police, however, placed a different interpretation on Byron's charity. He gave money, they reported, only "to the bad characters who form his society," and did so "in order to create a following" among the people. They clearly suspected that he was involved with the Carbonari, and so began a campaign of petty harassment in the hope that he would leave Ravenna. First he was told that he must change the colour of his servants' uniforms as they were too similar to those worn by the papal *carabinieri*. "I have sent a trenchant reply," he noted. "My liveries are of the colours conforming to my arms and have been in the family hue since the year 1066." He also decided to arm his servants "in case of accident or treachery," resulting in an order direct from the Vatican that any of Byron's Italian servants who carried arms should be arrested. The order was not carried out, although Byron was warned privately and noted that in the current atmosphere of suspicion: "they seem to dread my influence."

The Pope was not the only ruler keeping a close eye on the English Milord. Grand Duke Ferdinand, the ruler of Tuscany and brother of the Austrian Emperor Francis, sent an agent to Emilia-Romagna in 1819, who filed reports on Byron's activities over the next two years. The agent, Valtancoli, had a cover-story to explain his interest in meeting liberals and Carbonari sympathisers: he had been sent (he claimed) on a secret mission to sound out support for the Grand Duke's plan to annex the Romagna as part of his Tuscan domains. Ferdinand was (by the standards of the day) an enlightened ruler, so this plan – had it been true – would have been far preferable to continued rule by the Vatican, which grew more oppressive with the passing years. Not only were any attempts at modernisation frowned upon (street-lighting and vaccination had both been banned as un-Catholic), but many political activists, and a large number merely suspected of involvement with the Carbonari, were arrested, interrogated and held indefinitely as ferment for change became more intense throughout 1820 and 1821. One man, Luigi Galassi, was asked about Byron during his interrogation, and replied that the English milord was known in Ravenna as a very sincere man, "uno dei Capi, e che spendesse molto per la Societa" [one of the leaders who spent a great deal on the association [the Carbonari].

In the fearful atmosphere created by this crackdown Valtancoli found many ready listeners for the Grand Duke's alleged scheme, and he was able to send detailed reports back to Tuscany on the opinions and activities of the liberal leaders in the cities of Bologna, Ferrara, Forli as well as Ravenna, from whence he wrote of Ruggero and Pietro Gamba and their close associate Lord Byron.

Unfortunately, like many others before and since, the Grand Duke's agent fell hook, line and sinker for stories from the wider realms of Byron legend. The milord, he reported was, in common with many other English travellers in Italy at that time, a Romantic. These people might claim to be students of literature, but were in fact very high-ranking Freemasons.[64] Byron, Valtancoli claimed, was the leader of a Masonic sect called "The Romantic Society" and had written not only the Society's statutes and rules, but also a number of revolutionary pamphlets "inciting the people to rise up against tyranny, shake off their lethargy and become like new Brutuses, making a vendetta against the tyrants."

In many ways, reports like this provided Byron with ideal cover: while the secret police regarded him as some kind of demon-king, his genuine involvement with the Carbonari, which deepened as 1820 progressed, seemed to pass almost unnoticed under their noses. It is possible, however, that both the Vatican and Austrian secret police were aware of the precise extent of Byron's Carbonari activities, but were reluctant to take any action against him.[65] The arrest and detention of a British Peer, even if this was due to activities which would be illegal in his home country, would have provoked a diplomatic incident, and the British navy still maintained a strong presence in the Mediterranean.

Hopes for change in Italy were at this time focussed on Naples where, in July, a small band of Carbonari began a rebellion demanding a constitution. The King of Spain had been forced to grant one a few months earlier, and now a group of five Carbonari strolled to the royal palace, asked politely to see the King (also, confusingly, called Ferdinand), and within two hours had been given both a royal audience and a constitution. Ripples of revolt spread first to Sicily, then to Piedmont. In the Romagna, an uprising, both supporting and emulating that in Naples, was planned, and Carbonari activities increased.

The Ravenna Carbonari was divided into three sections: Protettrice (Protectress) was the name given to the leaders, the youth-wing was known as *Speranza* (Hope), while the *Turba* (Mob) were ready-for-action troops. Byron was given command of a band of *Turba*, who called themselves the *Cacciatori Americani* or American Hunters, in honour of the revolutionaries who had won freedom from their British rulers just forty years earlier. The '*Mericani* met in the pine-woods surrounding the town – handy for Byron as he was known to ride there every evening, so his movements attracted less suspicion. Well-aware that his letters were opened, Byron rarely wrote of his Carbonari activities to his English friends, but he did tell Murray, "The "*Mericani*" of whom they call me – the "Capo" (or Chief) mean "Americans" – which is the name given in *Romagna* to a part of the Carbonari – that is to say of the *popular* part, the *troops* of the Carbonari. – They are originally a society of hunters in the forest – who took the name of Americans – but at present comprise some thousands &c. but I shan't let you further into the secret, which may be participated with the postmasters."

Byron began to buy guns, bayonets and bullets to arm his troop. Looking for a safe place to store them he hit upon the ideal location: Count Guiccioli's cellar. Whether he felt that the house of a well-known conservative and loyal son of the church was unlikely to be searched, whether it simply appealed to his sense of mischief to keep them there, he was happy to offer "my house" as a hiding place. "If they are denounced or discovered," he noted laconically in his journal, "I shall be in a scrape."

The Romagna uprising was planned for early September, but unfortunately the leaders of the Bologna Carbonari got cold feet when the Austrians, who kept a garrison stationed at Ferrara with papal consent lest swift intervention be needed in the Papal States or the south of Italy, began to marshal their troops along the River Po, a day's march from Bologna and little further from Ravenna. Even though Pietro Gamba, among others, argued strongly for carrying on with the planned revolt, cooler heads prevailed and the rising was "postponed," much to Byron's annoyance. "Every thing was ready – and we were all in our bandaliers," he told Douglas Kinnaird, "but it was all the bloody Austrians on the Po." Writing to Hobhouse he felt that the blame should be laid at the door of Bologna, "all of a sudden the *City of Sausages* (do you understand me?) withdrew from the league… of course without B – the Romagnuole towns can do but little… and so here we are the principals liable to arrest every day."

Byron was right in that the arrests of suspected Carbonari continued, and a number of younger men decided to journey to their country estates, or to pay visits elsewhere in Italy, until the situation cooled down. The guard on the Papal Legate's palace was doubled and there was, Byron noted "a little stabbing and shooting – but in a small way." He, however, continued to pin his hopes on the Neapolitans. A parliament met in Naples on 1st October, to great public rejoicing. King Ferdinand, however, appealed for help to the Holy Alliance of Austria, Prussia and Russia, who were meeting at that time at Troppau in Austria. The Alliance decided to send an Austrian army to Naples. The parliament replied by declaring war on Austria, even though they could call upon an army of less than 40,000 men, miniscule when compared to the unlimited resources of the Austrian Empire.

Eager to help the Neapolitan struggle, Byron wrote offering financial and personal help. "An Englishman, a friend to liberty, having understood that the Neapolitans permit even foreigners to contribute to a good cause, is desirous that they do him the honour of accepting a thousand louis, which he takes the liberty of offering. Having already, not long since, been an ocular witness of the despotism of the Barbarians in the States occupied by them in Italy, he sees, with the enthusiasm natural to a cultivated man, the glorious determination of the Neapolitans to assert their well-won independence."

He went on, "if, as a mere volunteer, his presence were not a burden to whomsoever he might serve under, he would repair to whatever place the Neapolitan Government might point out, there to obey the orders and participate in the dangers of his commanding officer, without any other motive than that of sharing the destiny of a brave nation, defending itself against the self-called Holy Alliance, which but combines the vice of hypocrisy with despotism."

Written, with Teresa's help, in formal Italian, the letter was entrusted to one Giuseppe Gigante, who claimed to be an emissary of the Neapolitan parliament. He had been, he said, arrested and questioned by the Austrians on his way north, and they had taken his documents and all of his money. He must have been very convincing, as Byron gave him not only the letter and the 1,000 louis, but also money for his return journey. The man was a double agent, although whether he was in the pay of the Austrians or the Vatican is unclear. Neither letter nor money ever reached Naples.[66]

As 1820 drew to a close Byron, waiting to hear news about or from the Neapolitans, had plenty to occupy him in Ravenna. In November the Gamba family returned to Ravenna from their summer villa in Filetto. With Teresa living nearby, Byron visited her almost every evening, after his ride in the pine-woods. She would sing and play the piano, they talked about Italian history and literature, she corrected the proofs of his writings and helped him with his Italian correspondence. Teresa had given up trying to provoke lovers' tiffs and petty jealousies: perhaps she had realised that they served only to exasperate Byron rather than bring about declarations of undying devotion. So the two of them spent a winter of great contentment, more like an old married couple than a lady and her *cavaliere servente*.

A growing awareness of Teresa's many accomplishments provoked an idea in Byron's mind as he pondered on Allegra's future. Allegra was now nearly four years old. She, her nurse and two maids occupied a nursery in the Palazzo Guiccioli. She was known as "Miss Biron" to distinguish her, Byron said, "from little legitimacy," and he planned to bring her up as an Italian young lady with a sizeable dowry of ?5,000 so that she could make a good marriage. She was petted and made much of in Ravenna, "being a great favourite with every body on account of the fairness of her Skin," and when Teresa was in the city she took the child for a daily drive in her carriage. She was, as Byron admitted to Hoppner, thoroughly spoiled and in need of firmer discipline, "as obstinate as a Mule… she thinks herself handsome – and will do as she pleases."

He was also aware that his own future plans were uncertain – his offer to serve as a volunteer for the Neapolitan insurgents had been a genuine one, and he still hoped for an uprising in the Romagna – and that Ravenna was becoming an unsafe city. In December Captain Luigi Dal Pinto, the commander of the detachment of Papal troops billeted in Ravenna, was shot outside the Palazzo Guiccioli. A curious and hostile crowd gathered, but no-one offered help until Byron, hearing the shots, ran outside with Tita and had the man carried into the palazzo, where he died on Fletcher's bed, "shot in five places – three mortal with Slugs." Although Cardinal Rusconi, the Papal Legate, offered a reward, the assassin was never discovered. Byron now found himself in the unusual position of receiving letters of thanks from the Cardinal and from the dead man's comrades and family while at the same time becoming the victim of a whispering campaign that a man who ran to the aid of one of the enemy was perhaps not as true a friend to freedom as he claimed.

It was clear then to Byron that, both for her discipline and her security, a decision about Allegra's future had to be reached. Her mother, living in Pisa with the Shelleys, had written repeatedly asking to have the child with her. Typically of Claire, her letters became more importuning and hysterical as the weeks passed without a reply from Byron. When she threatened to come to Ravenna in person he wrote a brief but desperate letter to Shelley, "I should prefer hearing from you – as I must decline all correspondence with Claire who merely tries to be as irrational and provoking as she can be."

Byron's reluctance to send Allegra for a long stay with the Shelleys was not entirely due to his distaste for her mother. He also had concerns about her physical well-being. Mary Shelley's little boy, William, had recently died when the family were in Rome; she had now lost three children in infancy. Byron laid the responsibility for this partly at the door of the Shelleys' diet: they were strict vegetarians at a time when fresh produce was often hard to come by, and spent the winter months of every year living on potatoes, carrots and turnips, perhaps supplemented with little preserved fruit. So, Byron told Hoppner[67] "I so totally disapprove of the mode of Children's treatment in their family – that I should look upon the Child as going into a hospital."[68] Remembering his conversations with Shelley about the existence of God, he goes on, "the Child shall not quit me again – to perish of Starvation, and green fruit – or be taught there is no Deity." He was determined that Allegra "shall be a Christian and a married woman – if possible," and in a Catholic country like Italy the latter was contingent on the former.

So, as Byron relaxed in the glow of his lady's convent-taught accomplishments, the ideas began to form: why not a similar education for Allegra? The convent of San Giovanni at Bagnocavallo, about 18 kilometres from Ravenna, was selected. It was new (the school had been opened in 1818) and had a good reputation – the wealthy families of the locality sent their daughters there. The school had pupils near Allegra's age, and she was enrolled on 10th March 1821. She seems to have settled in quickly, as the brother of one of the nuns, who acted as the convent's steward, soon wrote to let Byron know that she was happy, sleeping well and making friends.

When Claire heard the news however, she reacted in a way which might be expected of a young woman with Romantic sensibilities who had read a great deal of sensational Gothic fiction. Heroines cruelly imprisoned in convents where they were ill-treated by heartless nuns were a staple for authors such as Mrs Radcliffe in her *Romance of the Forest*, published in 1791, and of course Byron's friend Matthew Lewis, whose sensational best-seller *The Monk*, published in 1796, not only featured a ghostly vampiric "Bloody Nun" but had one of the leading characters sent to a convent to prevent her marriage to her lover. Here she was ill-treated, apparently poisoned and finally buried alive by a cruel Abbess. In the 300 years since the Reformation, enclosed religious orders had become an unknown quantity to the vast majority of people in the United Kingdom, and Catholic Europe had been largely closed to British travellers since 1789. Gothic novelists could create over-heated plot-lines well-aware that their readers, lacking first-hand knowledge, would swallow their tales hook, line and sinker, a situation famously parodied by Jane Austen in *Northanger Abbey*.

On receiving the news that Allegra was to be educated in a convent, Claire had an attack of sensibility which would have done credit to Catherine Moreland. Byron, she believed, had robbed Allegra "of her liberty and shut her up in a building dark, gloomy and forbidding – she was never allowed to see a glimpse of the outer world, never a field, a wood, a rivulet – she was cut off from nature which is the great Nurse, Comforter and delight of Children – an hour every day she might enter the garden of the Convent which was surrounded by high gloomy walls and looked upon the burying place of the Nuns."

She immediately sent Byron one of her "provoking" letters, in which she managed to criticise both him, for placing Allegra in a convent, and Teresa who had, she knew, been educated in one herself, writing that convent-bred Italian women were " bad wives, most unnatural mothers, licentious and ignorant, they are the dishonour and unhappiness of society."

Even though Shelley felt obliged to write a letter of apology for Claire's outburst, he seems at this time to have shared her over-wrought views of convent life. In Pisa he had developed an attachment to a young lady called Emilia Viviani, who was engaged to be married. When her parents decided to place her in a convent out of harm's (and Shelley's) way until her wedding, he began to make elaborate plans to "free" her. The only member of the Shelley household to take a sensible view of the situation was Mary, who felt that the healthy air of Bagnocavallo would be good for the child, who had suffered greatly from fevers in both Venice and Ravenna.

With Allegra safely provided for, Byron was able to focus his attention on the planned Carbonari uprising. He still pinned his hopes on the Neapolitans, hoping that the embryo constitutional parliament would succeed and would spread its influence across Italy. The rulers of Italy, however, had other ideas. The Holy Alliance of Austria, Prussia and Russia had already made plans to send an army to crush the Neapolitan insurgents. In January 1821 the Austrian Chancellor, Metternich, invited Ferdinand, the king of Naples, to a congress at Leibach (the modern Ljubljana in Slovenia) in order to "advise" him on how to restore order to his kingdom. Many members of the Neapolitan parliament, seeing which way the wind was blowing, were reluctant to allow the king to leave. The duplicitous Ferdinand gave assurances at home that he would guarantee the constitution, whilst begging Metternich for help in restoring the *status quo*.
The Romagna Carbonari groups again agreed on an uprising to co-incide with the Austrian troops' passage the Papal States on their way to Naples. Byron, who had begun a private journal in January 1821, recorded the progress of the planned revolt, albeit with some scepticism. On 5th January he noted that it should begin in March, "in which appointment I should trust, had it not been settled that it was to have broken out in October 1820." By 9th January the Carbonari of Ravenna, at least, seemed fully committed, as Pietro Gamba informed Byron that "they mean to *insurrect* here, and are to honour me with a call thereupon. I shall not fall back; though I don't think them in force or heart sufficient to make much of it." He noted of the Congress, "the interests of millions are in the hands of about twenty coxcombs, at a place called Leibach." By 23rd January the Austrians were building a pontoon bridge to move their troops across the Po, yet "the Carbonari seem to have no plan… how, or when, or what to do," although he still pinned his hopes on the Neapolitans beating the "bloody butchers of the crown and sabre" and was meeting his "*Americani* in the forest, all armed." On 30th January he received the new Carbonari passwords and a few days later a shipment of arms for storage in his cellar, but to his annoyance the Ravenna leaders "are gone on a shooting, are not yet returned…

they have been out for five days buffooning, while the interests of the country are at stake," and when the Austrians marched through the Papal States in early February nothing happened. New orders arrived that they were to be attacked on their return, leaving the Ravenna Carbonari with little to do except invite Byron to a dinner in the forest, where he planned to "get as tipsy and patriotic as possible."

News from Naples when it came was not what Byron had hoped for, but probably much as he feared. The ill-disciplined and quarrelsome Neapolitan army were unable to present any ordered resistance to the well-drilled Austrians, who advanced rapidly and entered the city on 23rd March 1821. Dreams of freedom had been soundly crushed.

Byron was in despair. Even though he was fully aware of the reluctance of the Romagna Carbonari leadership to move against the Austrians, he chose to pin the blame firmly on the Neapolitans, ignoring the fact that they had at least attempted to overthrow their rulers. "The *real* Italians," he insisted, "are not to blame – merely the Scoundrels at the *Heel of the Boot* – which the *Hun* now wears and will trample them to ashes with for their Servility."

The Vatican chose this moment, with the liberals and Carbonari disheartened and in disarray, to launch a crackdown. There were many arrests, rumours of exile, and new attempts to force Byron out of Ravenna. The Papal Legate, Cardinal Rusconi, informed him that an enquiry would be launched into his dealings with Giuseppe Gigante, the double-agent to whom he had entrusted his letter and donation meant for Naples, but Byron pretended ignorance of "Signor Giant," claiming that he was simply a poor unfortunate who had asked for charity after being robbed by the Austrians. Next, a member of the Cardinal's guard picked a quarrel in the street with Tita, who was arrested, causing Byron to write in great indignation to the Legate's secretary, "I wish to know what is to be gained by it? – If they think to get *rid* of me – they shan't."

The authorities now chose to use the only weapon they had left against Byron: on 11th July Ruggero and Pietro Gamba were told that they had twenty-four hours to leave Ravenna and go into exile. Teresa, who had been instructed by the Pope to live in her father's house, would have to go with them. As the Gambas set out for exile in Tuscany, the Papal Legate must have prayed that Byron would follow. Teresa, desperate to stay with her lover, remained for a few days longer under the pretext of packing up the household. Byron wrote to his friend and former landlady Elizabeth Duchess of Devonshire. She was a close friend of Pius

VII and was then living in Rome. Byron hoped that she could influence the Pope to repeal the exile, but it was to no avail. Count Guiccioli also made representations to the Pope, and Teresa was informed that unless she followed her father immediately, she must "either return to him [Guiccioli] or be shut up in a convent." On 25th July she, too, left Ravenna.

Contrary to the hopes of both Teresa, to whom he sent regular letters promising that they would be reunited soon, and of the authorities in Ravenna, Byron showed no sign of leaving Palazzo Guiccioli and following the Gambas, who had temporarily settled in Florence while considering their options. His ostensible reason was that he was expecting a visit from Shelley, on a commission from Claire to see Allegra and make sure that she truly was not locked in a windowless convent cell. However, he chose to remain in Ravenna for three months after the Gamba's departure, giving a clear signal to the authorities that he was immune to pressure and that the choice of going or staying remained in his own hands.

He occupied himself, apart from his daily rides in the pine-forest, with writing. He had put *Don Juan* aside as the result of a promise to Teresa, who had read Cantos I and II in a French translation and was shocked, not by the morality of the poem but, according to Byron, because it stripped away the sentimental illusions of love-making and showed women to be as lustful as men. Byron predicted that all women would dislike the poem for this reason.[69] At this time he was still finding great enjoyment in writing plays, even though he kept up a pretence to Murray and others that he did not want any of them to be performed, going so far as to write to the Lord Chamberlain asking him to refuse a licence for *Marino Faliero* on the London stage.[70]

Byron the playwright put his experience as a member of the Drury Lane committee to good use, especially the time he had spent studying the five hundred manuscripts of plays he found on the theatre shelves, all unfit for production. His aim as a playwright, somewhat vague at the time he wrote *Marino Faliero,* had now developed into a more definite plan. He felt that the English stage needed to move away from melodramas, which were popular with actors as they presented numerous opportunities for high drama and over-acting, and he aimed in his plays to present an alternative, "to dramatise like the Greeks (a *modest* phrase!) striking passages of history." His plays, he hoped, were "simple and severe."

After completing *Marino Faliero,* Byron had written a play about the final days of Sardanapalus, the last ruler of Assyria. He returned to Venice for the plot of his new work, *The Two Foscari*, which deals with the fifteenth century Doge Francesco Foscari. Like Marino Falier, Foscari was Doge at a time of war and unrest, and after a conspiracy to assassinate him was discovered he asked the Great Council's permission to abdicate. They refused, and he became one of the city's longest-serving Doges, in office for thirty-four years.[71] His son, Jacopo Foscari, was implicated in various plots and intrigues serious enough to require the death-penalty. However, perhaps out of respect to his father's high office and long service to the Venetian state, Jacopo escaped every time with the far lighter sentence of exile to one of Venice's *terraferma* provinces. However, after reports that, even in exile, he continued to conspire against the state, he was recalled to Venice to stand trial in 1456. This time he was sentenced to a year in prison followed by a return to exile. Jacopo reportedly begged his father to obtain a pardon for him, but was told to accept the will of the Venetian state without protest. He died shortly after his release from prison, and his father, by now in his eighties, was so overcome by grief that he was unable to attend to the business of state and, ironically given his own earlier request, was asked to abdicate. He died two days later.

Byron's play focuses on the last few days of Doge Foscari's life, and telescopes events for dramatic effect. Having got over the worst of his disgust with the city which had "made" him behave so badly in 1818, Byron is able to appreciate its beauty and mystery once more, having Doge Foscari say to his daughter-in-law Marina,

> *That answer only shows you know not Venice.*
> *Alas! How should you? She knows not herself,*
> *In all her mystery.*

Byron depicts the younger Foscari, Jacopo, as a noble figure who suffers imprisonment and torture at the hands of "demons," the cruel Council of Ten, urged on by the villain of the piece, Loredano, seeking revenge for his father's death for which he holds the Doge responsible. Jacopo prefers a Venetian prison to a comfortable life on the *terraferma*, simply because he loves his city too much to be able to suffer exile from her. The Doge is depicted as a man of great nobility, torn between his desire to be a loving father and his role as figurehead of the state. "I have other duties than a father's," he reminds Marina, "They must then be fulfilled."

The climax of the play comes when Jacopo Foscari dies as he boards the ship that will take him into exile. Now Francesco Foscari emerges as a truly tragic figure,

Inform the signory from me, *the Doge,*
They have no further power upon those ashes.
While he lived, he was theirs, as fits a subject –
Now he is mine – *my broken-hearted boy!*

Twisting the knife, the Council of Ten, at Loredano's insistence, force the Doge to abdicate. A broken man, he hands over his trappings of state and prepares to hobble from the Ducal Palace for the last time, clutching his daughter-in-law's arm. He asks for a glass of water, accepts one from the hand of Loredano and dies. Loredano speaks the play's final words, that the Doge has paid the debt that he owed,

A long and just one: nature's debt and mine.

Byron sent the play to Murray via a friend of the publisher who was Secretary of the Admiralty, an insurance against its being opened en route by papal or Austrian agents. He had every reason to feel pleased with the work, and not just because Murray had offered a thousand guineas for it and *Sardanapalus*. He had used his knowledge of Venice to create a play which, by virtue of being far less angrily allegorical than *Marino Faliero*, managed to be far more successful as a drama, which makes it a pity that the play was not performed until fourteen years after Byron's death, and has rarely been acted since.[72]

Shelley arrived in Ravenna at ten o'clock in the evening of 6th August, and the two friends sat up talking until five the following morning. They began by talking shop, and Byron read extracts from *The Two Foscari* to Shelley, who was (he confided to Mary in a letter) none too impressed with the new direction his fellow-poet was taking. There were also practical matters to discuss: Claire's views on Allegra's upbringing; Byron's situation in Ravenna and his plans for the future; whether Allegra should remain in the convent, where she was settled and content, or face being uprooted again to follow her father. Shelley, who had been so easily shocked by Byron's Venetian lifestyle on their last meeting in 1818, now told Mary that Byron who had "almost destroyed himself in Venice" had completely recovered his health thanks to his relationship with Teresa, "which has reclaimed him from the excesses into which he threw himself from carelessness and pride, rather than taste." Byron had explained that Teresa was at present in Florence, having been "compelled to escape from the Papal territory in great haste, as measures had already been taken to place her in a convent, where she would have been unrelentingly confined for life." Mention of the convent brought to mind Shelley's own recent attachment, which he had no hesitation in mentioning in a letter to his wife. "The oppression of the marriage contract, as existing in the laws and opinions of Italy… is far severer than that of England. I tremble to think of what poor Emilia is destined to."

Although Shelley's main purpose in coming to Ravenna was meant to be a visit to Bagnacavallo in order to allay Claire's fears about Allegra's treatment in the convent, he seemed to be in no hurry to set out. He claimed to Mary that this was due to a pain in his side, so that "I do not feel myself equal to a ride of 24 miles," but his hypochondria did not prevent him from playing the tourist in Ravenna, where he admired the mosaics in the churches of San Vidale and Appolinare, visited the tomb of the Emperor Theodosius and joined his host on his evening rides in the pine forest.

The authorities managed to make use of Shelley's visit to issue another coded reminder to Byron that he was no longer welcome in the city: when Shelley tried to visit the cathedral he was not allowed to enter. Byron immediately wrote to the Papal Legate's secretary. "An English Gentleman & friend of mine has this day been refused admittance to the Duomo by the *Campanaro*[73] in the most insolent manner." Byron made it very clear that he was well-aware of the reasoning behind this action, it was all part of "The readiness of your authorities to inculpate my servants on all occasions," and they must not "suppose that political circumstances have at all diminished my power to make myself properly respected."

The incident was a clear sign that, sooner or later, Byron would have to leave Ravenna, and in their conversations together Shelley encouraged him to settle near to him and Mary in Pisa, rather than travel to Geneva as the Gamba family were planning to do. The two of them remembered 1816, when the inhabitants of Villa Diodati were observed across the lake by telescope, and the rumours of the "league of incest." The last thing Byron wanted was a return to what he called "that persecution," which would now encompass Teresa and be fully reported in the English press and gossiped about in drawing-rooms. He wrote to Teresa to this effect, telling her that "Geneva and all its surroundings are full of English people, even in the winter. You know whether I could live in the same air as that race – Pray therefore abandon that plan – and persuade Ruggero and Pietro to do the same. We can establish ourselves in Tuscany; it will be much better from every point of view." He asked Shelley to write to Teresa in support of this idea, which Shelley did willingly enough, although he could not resist the opportunity to present himself as a martyr to Mary, "an odd thing enough for an utter stranger to write on subjects of the utmost delicacy to his friend's mistress. But it seems destined that I am always to have some active part in every body's affairs whom I approach."

On 14th August, a week after his arrival in Ravenna, Shelley finally made the journey to Bagnocavallo. Although desperate to find evidence of the harsh convent environment of his and Claire's Gothic imagination, he could find little. He found Allegra prettily dressed in a short white muslin dress and knickerbockers, with her hair arranged in curls. She had grown – it was almost two years since Shelley had last seen her – and he had to admit that she was tall for her age, while at the same time doing his best to convince himself that she was pale, "probably from the effect of improper food." Her manners were much improved, so that when given a present of sweets she shared them with her school friends and teachers. However, Shelley found this so unlike "the old Allegra" that he decided it must be the result of "very strict discipline." Strict discipline was not much in evidence, however, when Allegra insisted on Shelley and all the nuns playing a game of hide-and-seek, and rang the convent bell to gather them all together. He had to admit that "nobody scolded her… so I suppose she is well-treated." She showed Shelley her bed, her place at the dinner-table and the little carriage in which she and her friends pulled each other around the garden, and was delighted with a gold necklace he had brought for her. When asked to give a message to her mother, she asked to be sent a beautiful silk dress (Byron had sent part of his peer's state robes to make her a velvet one), leading Shelley to remark that her "love of distinction and vanity" was unaltered. In the end he was forced to admit that, apart from having taught her a considerable number of prayers and "a prodigious list of saints," convent life would "do her no harm."

Shelley was content, therefore, to accept Byron's decision that Allegra should remain at Bagnocavallo when he moved to Pisa. She was settled, happy and well-provided for and Teresa's grandparents, deeply religious people who were delighted that the child was being brought up in the Catholic faith, visited her regularly. He set off back to Pisa, ready to offer Teresa his own and Mary's friendship, begin house-hunting on Byron's behalf and – most difficult of all – try to persuade Claire to accept the new arrangements.

Claire never did, of course, accept them. The following spring, living in Florence (whence the Shelleys had sent her to avoid her creating a nuisance for Byron in Pisa) she hatched a plan straight from a Gothic novel to travel to Bagnocavallo and, after gaining access to the convent by means of a forged letter apparently from Byron, kidnap Allegra. Typically, she was unable to keep the plan a secret and wrote to confide in Shelley. She was angry when he refused to help her and urged her to show patience, be calm and try to benefit from a change of scene. This time, however, Claire's premonitions were proved correct. Allegra died of a fever, probably typhus, on 19th April 1822. Byron was inconsolable. The nuns of Bagnocavallo made a statue and dressed it in Allegra's clothes "to preserve the memory of a most lovable child." Claire, when Byron sent her a miniature portrait and a lock of Allegra's hair as keepsakes, replied with a letter that was allegedly so bitter and cruel that Shelley destroyed it. In her later years Claire came to believe that her child had been spirited away by Byron, and still lived.[74]

In the late summer of 1821 Byron wrote to tell Teresa that there was now "little to keep me here," and expected that they would be together soon. He did not trouble to conceal from her, however, that "I am leaving Ravenna so unwillingly" and even after the Gambas had moved into the Palazzo Lanfranchi in Pisa, which was large enough for Teresa and Byron to keep up a show of propriety by living on separate floors, he still saw no need for haste. One minute, he claimed the delays were caused by Lega Zambelli's slow packing and preparations, the next it was the fault of the carriers of Ravenna, who were demanding too high a price for transporting his furniture. Byron, who had found Ravenna dull and constraining eighteen months earlier, did not now wish to leave the city. He told Teresa that, should her father "be recalled from exile *I shall return that instant* to Ravenna – and… if he is recalled *before my departure* – I shall not leave." He planned to remain in Pisa only for a short time, and was already beginning to think that, since the Italian uprising had failed, perhaps he should go and assist the Greek insurgents.

As he packed up the letters and possessions he had acquired in Italy since 1816, his thoughts took a melancholy turn, with a profound awareness of his mortality. He sent some of his hair to be made into a locket for Ada, "that she may know that she has (or had) a father in the world" along with the request that she study both Italian and music. He wrote to Moore about his future biography, along with the names of various correspondents over the years who might have kept his letters, and gave Murray instructions about giving Moore access to private papers which were in the care of Hobhouse. Writing his biography would, he knew, "require delicacy – but that will not be wanting" as long as

Moore, Hobhouse and Murray outlived him, which was his "very sincere wish. – I am not sure that long life is desirable for one of my temper & constitutional depression of Spirits."

At last, he could find no more reason to delay. He sent his horses (he kept eight at this time) in advance. He ran a critical eye over his menagerie and left those animals which were too frail or ill-tempered to travel – two vicious monkeys, an ancient badger, a crow with half a beak, a lame goat and a small dog – with his banker in Ravenna, Pellegrino Ghighi. Only two dogs, an eagle, a falcon, a monkey and a couple of guinea-fowl accompanied him to Pisa, along with Lega Zambelli, Tita and Fletcher.[75]

On the morning of 30th October 1821, George Gordon, Lord Byron, climbed into his commodious Napoleonic travelling carriage and left Ravenna for the last time, on his way to Pisa, to exile, and to the future.

Chapter Eight

Venice After Byron

... what was good enough for Byron
should be good enough for everyone else.

In September 1826 an excitable twenty-two year-old arrived in Venice, on his first visit to the city. As a teenager he had attended some of John Murray's literary lunches with his father, listening to conversations in which the absent Byron figured so large as to be almost a palpable presence. He had adopted the poet as his hero and role model, and strove to be "Byronic" in his dress. Now, on his first solo trip abroad, he was following his hero across Europe. He came to Venice fresh from interviewing Byron's boatman, Maurice, on Lake Geneva, and was ready to view the city through a Byronic lens. He wrote to his father, who had been Byron's friend: "After a hasty dinner we rushed to the mighty Place of St Mark. It was crowded ... Serenades were constant during the whole night, indeed music is never silent in Venice. I wish I could give you an idea of the moonlight here, but that is impossible. Venice by moonlight is an enchanted city; the floods of silver light upon the moresco[76] architecture, the perfect absence of all harsh sounds of carts and carriages, the never-ceasing music on the waters produced an effect on the mind which cannot be experienced, I am sure, in any other city in the world." He went on, "Sailing down the Grand Canal the palaces of Foscari, Grimani, Barberigo, and other names which make the coldest heart thrill rise rapidly before you...."

This is how the young Benjamin Disraeli recorded his first impressions of Venice. He did not notice that the *palazzi* along the Grand Canal which so delighted him were crumbling into decay, nor that the crowds in the Piazza were poverty-stricken, worn down by years of Austrian rule. He saw the Venice of myth, and was dazzled both by the moonlight and by his Byronic expectations.

Disraeli's reaction was usual among English visitors of the time, whose numbers steadily increased through the 1820s and 1830s.

Their appetite for the city was fed partly by the sheer volume of publications about Venice and Italy which appeared during those two decades, such as Lady Morgan's *Italy*, published in 1821 and praised by Byron. Her ladyship's opinion that the city was more interesting in decay dovetailed nicely with fashionable Romantic sensibilities, which could also feed on works such as the long poem by Byron's friend Sam Rogers, published with engravings by Turner in 1830. Rogers described a fairy-tale city divorced from reality,

...a glorious city in the sea.
The sea is in the broad, the narrow streets,
Ebbing and flowing, and the salt seaweed
Clings to the marble of her palaces.
No track of men, no footsteps to and fro,
Lead to her gates. The path lies o'er the sea,
Invisible; and from the land we went
As to a floating city, steering in,
And gliding up her streets as in a dream.

Rogers' view of the city was adopted by the various annuals, compendiums and companions which were gaining popularity as suitable reading material for the children of the newly-affluent middle-class. These journals filled their pages with descriptions of Venice as "a palace of faery" and "a vision of the Arabian Nights." Such visions fed the growing travel market, as in the post-war period many middle-class families found that they had both the funds and the urge to travel, giving both their sons and daughters the opportunity to see the landmarks of Europe which in the pre-war eighteenth century had been the preserve of the wealthy Grand Tourists.

Venice's popularity with the English was also burnished by the posthumous reputation of the man who had settled there to avoid them. Memoirs and Lives of Byron had been published with indecent haste in 1824 (one was in the bookshops within three weeks of the news of Byron's death reaching England!) and the huge appetite for these books, reminiscent of the spurious works which flooded the market after the death of Diana, Princess of Wales, meant that, when Tom Moore's "official" *Life* was published in two volumes in 1830 and 1831 it became a best-seller, inspiring Benjamin Disraeli to write a book about his hero, a blend of fact, gossip and fiction.

Disraeli's *Venetia* was published in 1837. The author, carefully signalling his subject-matter through his choice of title, hoped for a popular success, as he was sadly in need of cash. In the ten years since his first visit to Venice he had continued to emulate his hero. In 1830 he had re-created Byron's *Childe Harold* journey of 1809, travelling through Spain, Malta and Albania dressed in an array of specially-commissioned "Byronic" costumes, such as "a shirt entirely red with silver studs…green pantaloons with a velvet stripe down the sides, and a silk Albanian shawl with a long fringe of divers colours around his waist, red Turkish slippers and, to complete all, his Spanish jacket covered with embroidery and ribbons." He even managed to acquire his own Byronic souvenir of his travels, as in Malta he found Tita, Byron's former gondolier. After Byron's death Tita had continued to fight for the Greek cause; now he was stranded and poverty-stricken. Disraeli took responsibility for this very palpable reminder of his hero, bringing Tita back to England and settling him comfortably on the family estate in Buckinghamshire.[77]

Returning to England Disraeli was inspired to emulate Byron even further by writing a number of cantos about his travels, *The Revolutionary Epick,* which he would recite, with very little encouragement, at dinner-parties. He struck up an acquaintance with Lady Blessington, whose own celebrity memoir, *Conversations With Lord Byron,* was based on a very brief acquaintance in Genoa in 1823, and was observed flirting with her outrageously, despite the fact that she was fifteen years his senior, married and accompanied everywhere by her lover, the Count D'Orsay, who was himself conveniently married to her stepdaughter.

Disraeli was always in tune with the popular mood, and his novel created a heady mix, combining the widespread interest in Venice and the thirst for any snippet about Byron. Anecdotes from John Murray's Albermarle Street lunches, stories from Tita and juicy morsels of gossip shared with Lady Blessington all found their way into *Venetia,* which is written in the same breathless style which characterised Disraeli's letters from Venice. To make the most of the many facets of Byron's character which he admired, Disraeli shares them between two men in his fiction. The reader first meets Lord Cadurcis, poet, nobleman and heir to Cadurcis Abbey where he lives with his fat, quarrelsome mother. Lord Cadurcis is a model of bodily perfection. "His long dark locks shaded a pale and lofty brow that well became a cast of features delicately moulded yet reserved and haughty, and perhaps even somewhat scornful. His figure had set into a form of remarkable slightness and elegance, and distinguished for its symmetry." Disraeli throws in every Byronic ingredient he can lay his hands on: Cadurcis, on publishing his first collection of verse, wakes "to find himself famous" and has himself painted in Oriental dress. He takes his seat in the House of Lords as a Whig, writes a sonnet to his Newfoundland dog and is infamous for having kept a bear in his rooms at university.

The Cadurcis family are neighbours of Lady Annabel Herbert and her daughter, Venetia. Venetia's mysterious, absent father is never spoken of. One day, taking a key from her mother's dressing-case, Venetia enters a locked room where she finds a portrait of Marmion Herbert, "a being of almost supernatural beauty... Young as he was, command and genius, the pride of noble passions, all the glory of a creative mind, seemed stamped on his brow." Using the characters of Marmion and Annabel Herbert, Disraeli paints a portrait of the Byron marriage, using every bit of gossip at his disposal, including the story, so outrageous that it must be true, that the famous portrait of Byron in Albanian dress was kept under lock and key.[78] Marmion Herbert is alive, well and living at Lake Geneva with a mistress; the reasons for this soon become plain, as Disraeli paints Lady Herbert as a self-centred, manipulative, religious monster.

Cadurcis proposes to Venetia, but is rejected and turns instead to the charms of Lady Monteagle, a portrait of Caroline Lamb which, since she died in 1828, Disraeli does not even take the trouble to disguise. After fighting a duel with the lady's husband, he leaves "his native shores in a blaze of glory, but with the accents of scorn still quivering on his lips," and travels around Italy as, separately, do Venetia and her mother. At an inn in Rovigo, Venetia sees an ageing, desiccated roué and falls upon his bosom crying, "My Father!"

The novel's Venetian scenes draw heavily on Disraeli's recollections of his visit ten years earlier. As Venetia approached the city, "Gliding over the great Lagune, the buildings... rose up before her: the mosque-like Church of St. Marc, the tall *Campanile* red in the sun, the Moresco Palace of the Doges... All was stirring life, yet all was silent; the fantastic architecture, the glowing sky, the flitting gondolas, and the brilliant crowd gliding about with noiseless step, this city without sound, it seemed a dream!"

Annabel and Marmion Herbert are reconciled through the good offices of an Armenian monk at San Lazzaro, and the whole family settle on the Gulf of La Spezia where Cadurcis meets them and is accepted as Venetia's future husband. The novel ends when Herbert and Cadurcis, sailing in the bay of Lerici, are drowned.

For such an over-egged pudding, Venetia is surprisingly enjoyable. On publication it caused something of a stir; enough to warrant an entire chapter in Teresa Guiccioli's *Recollections of Lord Byron* – Teresa summed it up accurately: "truth and error, romance and history are too much intermixed." It also allowed Disraeli to clear his debts and stand for Parliament. In the year of the novel's publication he was elected Tory MP for Maidstone.[79]

Disraeli was not alone in giving the public what they wanted. Through the 1820s and 1830s a number of artists visited Venice and their works, whether hanging in a British middle-class drawing room or engraved as a book illustration, helped develop a sense of familiarity with the city. The best-known artistic interpreter of Venice is of course Turner, who first visited the city in 1819. However many other, now largely forgotten, artists also painted the city. Samuel Prout and George Clarkson Stanfield, prolific artists who specialised in charming scenes of the European towns and villages visited by English middle-class tourists, produced views of the Grand Canal and lagoon peopled with picturesque peasantry. William Etty, whose forte was the nude, painted Venetian windows from which voluptuous ladies leaned. Ironically, these "souvenir of Venice" images, which have their counterparts in the works of the pavement artists whose stalls line the Riva dei Schiavoni today, were more popular with contemporary buyers than the works of Turner.

Turner originally visited Venice for only five days, on his way to Rome. He had been commissioned to produce engravings for a book entitled *A Picturesque Tour of Italy* (he also used the sketches he made on this visit in his 1830 illustrations for Rogers' *Italy*). He did not return to Venice until 1833 and made his final visit in 1840 when he was 65 years old. From these three visits came art which helped encapsulate the idea of Venice.

Some of Turner's images of the city, such as *Juliet and her Nurse*, 1836, which transfers Juliet's Verona balcony to overlook Piazza San Marco, were clearly a response to the public demand for images of the "palace of faery" of the popular consciousness. However, the aspect of the city to which he responded most strongly, from his hurried watercolour sketches of 1819 to the paintings completed after his 1840 stay in the city, was the interplay of the luminous Venetian light upon the water. Turner also had a long-standing interest in loss and decay, exemplified by paintings such as *The Fighting Temeraire*, and much of the crumbling beauty that he saw in Venice struck a chord. This can be clearly seen in paintings made in the last decade of his life, such as *The Campo Santo, Venice*, where the vista across to the cemetery island of San Michele is bathed in golden light, and *The Sun of Venice Going to Sea*, where a fishing-boat sets sail across the lagoon on a pearly Venetian morning. The quotation, from one of his own poems, which he chose for *The Sun of Venice* when it was exhibited at the Royal Academy in 1843 shows that death was on the ageing artist's mind:

Fair shines the morn, and soft the zephyrs blow,
Venezia's fisher spreads his painted sail so gay
Nor heeds the demon that in grim repose
Expects his evening prey.

The constant presence of Venice and Byron in the mid-nineteenth century *zeitgeist* was to have a profound effect on one isolated, indulged boy who went on to write about the city in a way that would encapsulate the English-speaking world's view of it from that time on. John Ruskin, born in 1819 and the adored only child of a late marriage, grew up on a diet of annuals and compendiums such as the very popular *Friendship's Offering* (in which his own first venture into print, a Neapolitan love story, was published in 1836), Rogers' *Italy* – which he remembered being given as a present on his thirteenth birthday – the Bible (which his evangelical mother studied with him every morning) and Byron. He recalled that, when he was in his early teens, his father began reading Byron aloud each evening, although he was not allowed to read the poems unsupervised for several more years. One evening, his father asked young John what he would like to listen to, and he answered "Juan and Haidée." "I recollect that he and my mother looked across the table at each other with something like alarm… My selection was not adopted," and he was given "a bit of *Childe Harold* instead, which I liked at that time nearly as well."

As well as a teenage passion for Byron, the gift of Rogers' *Italy* created Ruskin's other life-long passion, for Turner, whose works he championed when they were regarded as little better than daubs by the art establishment.[80] The book was a gift from his father's business partner, Henry Telford, "and I might, not without some appearance of reason, attribute to the gift the entire direction of my life's energies… Poor Mr. Telford, nonetheless, was always held by papa and mamma primarily responsible for my Turner insanities."

Mr and Mrs Ruskin senior had, through sheer hard work, progressed from poverty to middle-class prosperity. John James Ruskin was a partner in a sherry importing firm who, when his son was small, began to enjoy the fruits of his labours by buying art. At first he bought books of engravings, and later on framed watercolours, by popular artists such as Prout and Stanfield. In 1837, at his son's urging, he became a patron of Turner. Thus the teenage John Ruskin decided to work to emulate his twin heroes,

deciding "that Byron was to be my master in verse, as Turner in colour."
All that remained was for John to see the city about which one hero had written and which the other painted to such perfection. Like many other newly-affluent middle-class families, the Ruskins were not slow in finding out the pleasures of European travel, and in 1833 they made their first European tour, visiting Brussels, Cologne and the Black Forest, then on through Switzerland and into Italy as far as Genoa. On this trip the Ruskins visited the castle of Chillon, and were shown the pillar where Byron had carved his name in1816. Their courier, Salvador, carved John's name into the same pillar, on the opposite side, to the great pleasure of Mr Ruskin senior, whose aim for his son was that he should one day "write poetry as good as Byron's only pious."
In 1835 the Ruskin family finally visited the city of John's Byron and Turner dreams. Fifty years later, Ruskin could still remember his childlike excitement, "the pure childish passion of pleasure in seeing boats float in clear water… and then, all along the canal sides, actual marble walls rising out of the salt sea, with hosts of little brown crabs on them, and Titians inside." At the time, the sixteen year-old John was keeping a diary in verse which, he felt, was in the style of *Don Juan*. In it he recorded his reaction to several "Byronic" locations:

The palaces arise from out the blue waves of the sea
Of marble, marble, wondrous white, they fairylike arise,
The Doge's is upon my right and near the Bridge of Sighs.

………

I've tried St Mark's by midnight moon and in Rialto walked about
A place of terror and of gloom which is very much talked about,
The gondolier has rowed me by the house where Byron took delight
The palace too of Foscari is very nearly opposite.

In emulation of his other master, Turner, John announced to his parents his intention "of making such a drawing of the Ducal Palace as had never been made before," which he proceeded to do by making a few hasty sketches on the spot and "finishing my design elaborately out of my head at Treviso." His method in this, at least, was probably little different from that of many professional artists who painted Venice. Ruskin responded to Venice on his first visit much as did Disraeli ten years earlier: he saw a living version of the fairy city he knew from Rogers and from

Friendship's Offering. He did not see crumbling *palazzi*, but "wondrous white" marble rising "fairylike" out of the Grand Canal. Most of all, he saw the city of Byron. It is easy to share his emotions as, like many others over the years, he gazed open-mouthed at Palazzo Mocenigo with the realisation that Byron had actually lived there.

The Ruskins returned to Venice for a ten-day stay in the spring of 1841, and on this visit John became aware that he was in a real place occupied by breathing people. He opened his eyes and became aware that the city was in a state of decay, "a little of my romance is going. The canals are I think shallower, and I am sure dirtier, than they were of old," 'of old' being, of course, five years previously. However, it was not until 1845, when he made his first visit to Venice without his parents, that he began to look behind his self-created Byron-Turner palimpsest and see the actual city. Much of what he saw did not please him. The Austrians, belatedly realising that the city which had become a pleasure-ground for the aristocrats of their Empire was crumbling before their eyes, had at last begun a modernisation programme. The railway from the mainland was in the process of being extended across the lagoon (the modern Ponte della Liberta rail and road link follows much the same route), both making it easier for visitors to reach the city and removing the centuries-old symbiotic relationship between Venice and the water which surrounded it. Ruskin was shocked to find that, instead of crossing the lagoon and seeing Venice floating on the waters, "behold – the Greenwich railway, only with less arches and more dead wall, entirely cutting off the entire open sea and half the city, which now looks as nearly as possible like Liverpool." Once he set eyes on the new steam-powered *vaporetti* – "omnibus gondolas', he called them – Ruskin felt that the place was on the way to becoming just another seaside resort; he might as well be in Margate.

The railway bridge and station were bad enough, but worse was to come as Ruskin was rowed down the Grand Canal. He arrived in the evening, and in the twilight he saw "*gas lamps!* on each side, in grand new iron posts of the latest Birmingham fashion, and sure enough, they have them all up the narrow canals, and there is a grand one, with more flourishes than usual, just under the bridge of sighs. Imagine the new style of serenades – by gas light."

Bad as the encroaching nineteenth century was, Ruskin was more horrified by what he regarded as the destruction of the past. On the one hand, he finally became aware of neglect and decay, seeing dilapidated *palazzi* mouldering in neglect. One had rents "half a foot wide" and "two turkeys wandering among the weeds." On the other, he found attempts at restoration to be both drastic and insensitive, "they are *scraping* St Mark's clean" he wrote despairingly. So Ruskin began a one-man programme of recording the architecture of Venice, both in his own sketches – although he often found the process soul-destroying, telling his father, "You cannot imagine what an unhappy day I spent yesterday before the Casa d'Oro, vainly attempting to draw it while the workmen were hammering it down before my face" – and by using one modern invention which he actually found to be of value, daguerreotypes. On this first visit he bought a number of images of the *palazzi* along the Grand Canal, later he trained his manservant to take daguerreotypes of the buildings he wished to record.

Ruskin spent a month at this work, becoming almost manic in his urgent need to record as much as possible. "Every hour," he wrote, "is destructive of what I most value. I must do what I can to save a little." Little wonder that on leaving the city he suffered a nervous collapse, and was unwell in Padua. His return to England did nothing to diminish the sense of urgency he felt about recording as much as possible about Venice while there was still time. He had long been interested in architecture; as early as 1837 he had written articles for *the Architectural Magazine*. He now began an in-depth study of architectural styles and periods, especially the Gothic, which he loved best and which he felt had reached its apogee in Venice. The first result of his labours was *The Seven Lamps of Architecture*, published in 1849, where he first set out his belief – developed far more fully in *The Stones of Venice* – that Gothic architecture represented the pinnacle of human achievement, especially when dedicated to the glory of God.

Ruskin was able to pay a brief visit the following year, but the long stay which would be needed for his study of Venice had to be delayed. In 1848 the people of Venice, led by Daniele Manin, rose up against their Austrian rulers and succeeded, for a brief time, in driving them from the city. The ensuing siege and bombardment of Venice caused death, starvation and hardship among the populace and yet more destruction of the buildings. Heavy shelling from the Austrian batteries at Marghera on the mainland damaged such notable buildings as the churches of SS Giovanni e Paolo, San Moise and the Frari, as well as the Scuola Grande di San Rocco (decorated by Tintoretto, the artist at the very top of Ruskin's list of painters, higher even than Turner) and the Accademia, where several paintings were destroyed.

Ruskin returned to commence his great work in November 1849, less than three months after an Austrian army led by Field

Marshal Radetzky had triumphantly re-entered the city. He was accompanied by his wife of eighteen months, Euphemia, known to everyone as Effie.

Effie seemed blissfully unaware that an uprising had occurred at all, save to note somewhat heartlessly that the Venetians left homeless by the bombardment "with no homes at all," were perfectly happy "sleeping under bridges" as autumn turned to winter. She was unable to work out why the populace were so dirty and surly, especially when compared to the Austrian officers. When these exercised outside her hotel on the Riva degli Schiavoni (no doubt to remind the dispossessed and resentful populace that they were the masters once more) Effie found it "very merry and exciting." She threw herself into the Austrian social whirl – her favourite escort was Count Paulizza, who had masterminded an aerial bombardment of Venice by balloon – while John worked tirelessly, making detailed sketches of columns, arches, windows, often taking up a position in the Grand Canal for the best view and cursing his gondolier if he was unable to keep the craft steady whilst his master was at work. He bullied custodians, climbed ladders and was often, he claimed, the first person to see the back of a tomb high up on a church wall for centuries: and he saw the cobwebs to prove it. In despair at the dilapidated state of the Palazzo Ducale, he commissioned casts to be made of the capitals.[81] Everywhere he drew, annotated, read. Invited to a reception for Field Marshal Radetzky, he retired to the library to make sure that the evening was not entirely wasted.

The Ruskins spent five months in Venice, throughout the winter of 1849-50, before returning to London for John to begin writing up his notes and ideas. Volume I of *The Stones of Venice* was published in March 1851, and in August John and Effie set out for another lengthy stay, this time of almost a year. They returned in July 1852, and volumes II and III appeared the following year.

The Stones of Venice is a deeply personal work. Ruskin had a tendency to construct personal mythologies around people or places which meant a great deal to him, and Stones is a prime example. It is by no means a guidebook to Venice. In it, Ruskin used his detailed studies of buildings and architectural styles to construct an elaborate theory which grew out of his love of the Gothic. He links the rise and fall of Venice to her loyalty or otherwise to Gothic architecture. "In the first year of the fourteenth century, the Gothic Ducal Palace of Venice was begun," and for Ruskin Venice's greatness, her domination of both trade and artistic endeavour, is contemporary with this. He is equally definite about the beginning of the city's decline. "I date the commencement of the fall of Venice from the death of [Doge] Carlo Zeno, 8th May 1418." The rot begins when the city abandons the Gothic, initially in favour of Renaissance architecture, which is bad enough. With Palladian classicism comes the city's dotage. Ruskin reserves his particular ire for Palladio, the disciple of "pagan" neo-classicism. This is what he has to say of Palladio's beautiful church of San Giorgio Maggiore, weightlessly floating on the lagoon: "It is impossible to conceive of a design more gross, more barbarous, more childish in conception, more servile in plagiarism, more insipid in result, more contemptible under every point of rational regard." Ruskin was, however, one of the first to truly appreciate the beauties of the Basilica of San Marco. The general view, among both visitors and architects, was still that set down by the Reverend Eustace in his1812 guidebook: the building was gloomy and barbaric, adorned with clumsy mosaics and a monument to bad taste. For Ruskin, as for so many others who enter the Piazza – for the first time or after a long absence – it was as though the other buildings of the square pulled away from the Basilica in worshipful awe before "a vision out of the earth… a treasure-heap, partly of gold, partly of mother-of-pearl" and decorated with statues of angels so that it seems like "Eden, when its gates were angel-guarded long ago."

Never a best-seller (it is too personal and complex for that) *The Stones of Venice* proved hugely influential. Although Ruskin, to his father's lasting disappointment, was not to be another Byron nor – as he himself had long regretfully come to accept – another Turner, his command of prose writing and his detailed sketches of the city that he wanted to "eat all up into my mind – touch by touch" drew public attention to the dangers faced by the city of Byron and Turner. His passion for Turner remained undiminished even after his discovery of the Venetian masters – especially Bellini and Tintoretto – but sadly Ruskin lost his pleasure in Byron. Witness his aside in Stones about the Bridge of Sighs, "a work of no merit, and of late date, owing the interest it possesses chiefly to its pretty name, and to the ignorant sentimentalism of Byron." Perhaps now that he had seen Venice naked, stripped back to her bare bricks, the city was no longer a Romantic vision to him. Perhaps the bitter experience of his marriage left him incapable of viewing anything in a Romantic light for years to come.[82]

As he grew older, Venice increasingly became a source of personal mythology to Ruskin. At times, he was deeply distressed and disturbed by the city, and especially by the increasing number of visitors for which he felt partly responsible. On occasion, however, the old love returned, as in 1877 when the city – liberated from Austrian rule and part of a united Italy since 1866, just as Byron had dreamed of almost fifty years earlier – recognised his work for Venice with membership of its Historical Society. Taking advantage of his new status, he had his favourite painting in the Accademia, Carpaccio's *Dream of St Ursula*, which he had woven into his personal myth of his now-dead love, Rose La Touche, taken from the public galleries and placed in a private room. Here he spent many happy hours copying it.

Meanwhile, the sophisticated visitor was expected to have at least some knowledge of Ruskin. The Bible of the Victorian middle-class traveller, *Baedeker's Handbook*, pointed out that, before arriving in Venice, "it is well to be familiar with Ruskin's 'Stones of Venice,' or at least with the 'Introductory Chapters and Local Indices, printed separately for the use of travellers.'" Ruskin himself wrote two idiosyncratic guidebooks, *St Mark's Rest* which was, he sadly stated, "written for the help of those few travellers who still care about her monuments," and *A Guide to the Principal Pictures in the Academy at Venice*. The young Henry James, arriving for his first visit in 1869 with Ruskin in his hand, was typical of many. The visitors had two expectations: on the one hand all mod cons by way of railway, hotels, and restaurants; on the other a city which appeared unchanged from the one they read about in Byron, Ruskin and popular novels such as Disraeli's Venetia and Fenimore Cooper's *The Bravo*.

Looking back on his life in his memoir, *Præterita*, Ruskin noted "My Venice, like Turner's, has been chiefly created for us by Byron," and Ruskin did his best to ensure that the Byronic Venice he experienced as a young man was preserved for posterity. Yet one of the key events in making sure that all subsequent generations have seen the city through a Byronic lens took place in Ruskin's absence. A meeting was held at the Midland Institute, Birmingham, on 13th November 1879 and chaired by the city's mayor, Joseph Chamberlain. The large audience heard from several speakers, including the distinguished poet and designer William Morris, about plans to restore the west front of the Basilica of San Marco.

Two years earlier, Morris had set up the Society for the Protection of Ancient Buildings, or SPAB, in response to proposals to restore Tewkesbury Abbey. SPAB already had a number of British campaigns under its belt when, in October 1879, Morris learned of the plans for San Marco.

His initial response was a letter, published in The Daily News on 1st November. "I have just received information," Morris wrote, "that the restoration of the west front of St. Mark's in Venice, which has long been vaguely threatened, is to be taken in hand at once." Morris, who had been deeply moved by the beauty of San Marco on his visit to Venice the previous year, was able to give an accurate summation of the present state of the Basilica which, he felt, could be made "as sound as any building of its age can be" by a "very moderate exercise of engineering skill." He expressed his concern that the restoration would be carried out by someone who would "prefer gilding, glitter and blankness, to the solemnity of tone, and the incident that hundreds of years of wind and weather have given to the marble, always beautiful, but from the first meant to grow more beautiful by the lapse of time," before calling on all who shared his love – not only of the Basilica but of all beautiful and ancient things – "to join earnestly in any attempt that may be made to save us from an irreparable loss."

The immediate result of this letter was the meeting at Birmingham two weeks later. In his address Morris, who in his role as secretary of SPAB always insisted on first-hand observation of a building, drew on his own visit to Venice to re-inforce his message. First of all he described to his audience Gentile Bellini's painting *Procession in Piazza San Marco,* which shows the Basilica as it was in 1496, and which Morris had seen in the Accademia. He contrasted this almost photographic depiction with the building he had seen, little-changed apart from the replacement of some of the west front mosaics in the seventeenth century, which Morris regretted, "even though no less a man that Titian was concerned in the alteration."

Two days later a similar meeting was held at the Sheldonian Theatre in Oxford. Morris again spoke, and was this time supported by a host of architectural and intellectual luminaries including G. E. Street, whose pupil Morris had been, and Henry Liddell, Dean of Christ Church, who chaired the meeting. Morris had urged Ruskin to be present, but he felt too frail to attend.[83] His absence from any symposium on the future of Venice was so remarkable that Dean Liddell felt obliged to comment on it in his opening remarks. After – inevitably – quoting Byron and referring to the illustrious place Venice held in the British imagination thanks to Shakespeare, Byron and Turner, he was applauded when he referred to the writings of "one whose name in this place was a household word – Ruskin." Ruskin cast a powerful aura even in his absence, and the meeting resulted in the presentation to the Italian government of a SPAB memorandum against restoration, signed by a host of luminaries including Disraeli.

Initially, the Italian, and particularly the Venetian, authorities were annoyed as what they saw as British "interference."

Having recently thrown off the yoke of one imperial power, the Venetians were in no mood to take instructions from another. In Venice, the restoration was seen as just one part of a much larger programme of public works intended to improve and beautify the city, including the widening particularly narrow *calli* and filling in some canals to create modern pedestrian thoroughfares such as the Strada Nova, linking the railway station to the Rialto. Morris made an attempt to pacify Venetian grumbling about "newly-acquired' British "tenderness for their glorious monument" in a second letter to the Daily News, where he also called on Italian lovers of art to add their voices to the campaign "to induce the authorities to forbid for the future all meddling with the matchless mosaics."
In the spring of 1880 Morris received the news he had hoped for: the planned restoration had been cancelled. SPAB was able to claim much credit for this at home, although it is likely that campaigns by Italians, such as Ruskin's protégé Alvise Zorzi, were ultimately more effective. The end result was the same. For good or ill, the city had now become, and still remains, *Venice Preserv'd*.

Before St. Mark still glow his steeds of brass,
Their gilded collars glittering in the sun.

Venetian Postscript

When the kissing had to stop

As for Venice and her people, merely born to bloom and drop,
Here on earth they bore their fruitage, mirth and folly were the crop:
What of soul was left, I wonder, when the kissing had to stop?

Almost two hundred years have gone by since Byron's time in Venice. Should his shade venture out into the city from Palazzo Mocenigo today, what would he find?

At first sight, things would appear to have changed very little. It is, after all, still possible to find one's way using Jacopo di Barbari's map first published in 1500, and to see the sights using Reverend Eustace's guidebook of 1812 or an edition of Baedeker from the early twentieth century. However, should Byron return to is former lodgings on the Frezzeria he would find that the modern equivalent of Pietro Segati's draper's shop now provides passing tourists with keyrings shaped like gondolas and *carnevale* masks made in Taiwan. Although a man notoriously attached to a "lowering diet" might not notice, housekeepers and his valet Fletcher would find great difficulty in buying everyday provisions. There has been a sharp decline in the number of butcher's shops, for example, their place taken by bars and fast food outlets. By some strange serendipity, however, there is still a shop selling cheese in the Calle de la Mandola, where William Dean Howells found that "fat sinner" who may have been Margarita Cogni, dealing in butter, cheese and reminiscences of Byron.

On a trip along the Grand Canal in his gondola, Byron would quickly notice and appreciate the work to preserve and restore the city which he last saw crumbling into disrepair through a combination of patrician poverty and Austrian taxation. He would no doubt be greatly diverted to find that many people believe that his connection with the city lies at the heart of this restoration. "My Venice," Ruskin wrote, "like Turner's, has been chiefly created for us by Byron," and one of Byron's finest biographers, Michael Foot, goes further, "Byron changed the way the whole world would view his adopted city."

Once the ghostly gondola approached the Piazzetta of San Marco, Byron would have to give a wry smile at the huge number of tourists. The dearth of visitors, and particularly the English who were his aversion, had been one of Venice's chief attractions for him, as he told John Murray, "Venice is not a place where the English are gregarious… and to tell you the truth, this was one reason why I stayed here."
The wry smile would turn to uproarious laughter as the gondola drew near to the human log-jam on the Ponte della Paglia and the realisation dawned that this constant parade of tourists photographing and being photographed at the Bridge of Sighs were drawn there not by an interest in crime and punishment during the Venetian Republic, but by a half-remembered, half-understood memory of two lines of poetry out of the thousands he wrote, quoted by practically every guidebook:

I stood in Venice on the Bridge of Sighs,
A palace and a prison at each hand.

Turning back to walk in "St Mark's by moonlight," Byron would find the Piazza still lively and bustling, the porticoes crowded with strollers and passers-by, Florian and Quadri keeping up their centuries-old rivalry from opposite sides of the square. All of this: so long as he visited before midnight. Later, and he would find the Piazza almost empty and Venice once more a place of "marine melancholy" as waiters, cooks and bar staff headed off in a rush for the last buses back to the mainland. In the small hours, once so popular for *passeggiata* and assignations, he would find the city practically deserted. The city's population is now even lower than the 100,000 which Hobhouse had found so shocking in 1816. After a steady improvement in the twentieth century, peaking at 170,000 after World War II, the permanent population of Venice stands at less than 60,000. Twenty-one million tourists visit the city each year.
Perhaps he has seen enough: the ghost of a smile, the fading scent of gentleman's pomade; the Piazza is empty.

* * *

For good or ill, over the past 200 years Venice has become fixed in Byronic aspic. Modern visitors expect, on the one hand, to see traditionally-dressed gondoliers and hear Vivaldi, to enjoy *carnevale* with the participants dressed in eighteenth-century costume; and on the other to step out of the elevator in their air-conditioned hotel and walk right into the Hard Rock Café or Disney

Store. The twentieth century saw a process of tidying industry away from Venice and into the new port and town of Marghera and Mestre on the mainland. Workers followed, settling into characterless but dry and cosy modern homes. Many who care about the city are concerned that the Byronic aspic is brown and cracking, that Venice is in danger of becoming little better than Disneyland, the remaining population whittled away by the attrition of old age and low birth-rate, young people unwilling to replace them because of the hazards of inadequate shops, aqua alta, crowds and lack of green spaces. Others are more sanguine: Venice has existed for more than 1500 years due to a constant ability to adapt and survive: in the middle ages people flocked here for trade; then Venice transformed herself into a city of hedonistic pleasures; today she attracts tourists; tomorrow… who can say?

In November 1816 Byron came to what seemed to be a dying city, with crumbling *palazzi* and an oppressed populace. Ruskin, in turn, was convinced that Venice was being destroyed before his eyes and it would end like the city of Tyre, remembered by historians and as a few fragments of marble in museums. Were they right? Will the city fall beneath the waves, the victim of rising sea-levels, as Byron predicted, her "marble walls… level with the waters"? Or will the much-trumpeted, long planned MOSE barrier act as her saviour? Or will she simply crumble into dust, eroded by a constant stream of tourist feet and pigeon excrement? Let us hope that generations as far from our time as we are from Byron will still be able to visit, appreciate and fall in love with this impossible city, and say of her,

My beautiful, my own,
My only Venice.

Notes

1. The original carriage had been captured by British soldiers after Waterloo, brought to London as a gift for the Prince Regent and put on public display.
2. Drury Lane was considered to be the London theatre of the Whig interest, in contrast to Tory Covent Garden.
3. The great Doris Langley Moore, writing about Col Stanhope, who knew Byron in Greece. However, the words apply equally well to Polidori.
4. Byron continued to show a dilettante interest in galvanism. He referred to it two years later, in Canto I of *Don Juan*: "galvanism had set some corpses grinning" (*Don Juan* Canto I, CXXX, 1818)
5. Like Mrs Radcliffe, Schiller wrote his novel without ever visiting Venice. However, his friend Goethe stayed in the city in 1786, and would have been able to provide details of the local colour – the chants of the gondoliers, the passegiata, carnevale – which find their way into the pages of *The Ghost Seer*.
6. Although some of the works of art which the French had looted from Italy were returned after the fall of Napoleon, Veronese's epic work remains in the Louvre. However, the modern visitor to San Giorgio Maggiore is more fortunate than Byron, as computer technology allowed an exact replica to be installed in the refectory in 2007. Reproduced on a huge Irish linen canvas, it is so detailed that the cuts made in the French removal are clearly visible.
7. In fact, the position of the Jews in Venice was rather better than the picture painted by Shakespeare: despite the locked gates they were necessary members of society, valued as moneylenders and as doctors. Unlike their counterparts in other parts of Europe, especially Spain, Venetian Jews were never persecuted or forced to convert to Christianity. The Patriarch of Venice once received a letter from the Inquisition in Rome asking why he had not burned any Jews as heretics. He replied that it was impossible for them to be heretics as they weren't Christians.
8. The most famous condottiere was Bartolomeo Colleoni, whose statue can be seen in Campo San Giovanni e Paolo. A key scene of one of Byron's Venetian plays, *Marino Faliero,* takes place in front of this statue.
9. Twelve radicals who had demanded that all men should have the right to vote had been put on trial in 1794 accused of plotting against the King.
10. He had been following his "lowering" diet at Villa Diodati. Mary Shelley told Moore that he survived on "a thin slice of

bread, with tea, at breakfast – a light, vegetable dinner, with a bottle or two of seltzer water, tinged with vin de Grave, and in the evening, a cup of green tea without milk or sugar."

11. The island of Corsica, Napoleon's birthplace, had been ruled by Genoa until 1768, the year before he was born, when it was handed over to France. It was still widely regarded as part of Italy.
12. Napoleon was notorious for the amount of paintings, manuscripts and statuary which had been carted across the Alps on his orders. Some of the loot eventually found its way back to Italy, but a great deal is still in the Louvre.
13. Hobhouse's book ,*The Substance of Some Letters, Written by an Englishman Resident at Paris During the Last Reign of the Emperor Napoleon*, had been published in 1816.
14. Hobhouse soon began to find Foscolo, who was perpetually in debt and always trying to borrow money from him, something of a nuisance. Their acquaintance came to an abrupt end in 1824 when, in what Hobhouse called "a pretty piece of impudence" the 46 year-old Foscolo proposed marriage to Hobhouse's half-sister, aged 23. (See E. R. Vincent, *Ugo Foscolo*, p. 85).
15. Entertainments like this were very popular with all classes. In the interval of the premiere of Beethoven's Violin Concerto in Vienna in 1806, the audience was entertained by a man playing a violin held upside-down.
16. Indeed, Doctor Bowdler was working on his famous Family Shakespeare at this exact time: it would be published in1818.
17. In 1812, at the height of his affair with Lady Oxford, Byron compared her home, Eywood, to "the bowers of Armida." *Letters & Journals* Vol II p. 238.
18. Today there is greater understanding of the link between the seasons and mental health. Byron, in an age before central heating and artificial lighting, was only too aware that the time of year had a considerable impact on his mental state. In 1820 he wrote to Teresa Guiccoli: "As to my sadness – you know it is in my character – particularly in certain seasons." *Letters & Journals* Vol 7, p. 186.
19. Byron refers to the German ("Suabian") Holy Roman Emperor Frederick Barbarossa, who knelt before Pope Alexander III in a peace-making ritual brokered by the Venetians and recalled in a memorial stone in the vestibule of San Marco, where the ceremony took place in 1177.
20. The hotel was in Palazzo Farsetti on Riva del Carbon, just a few hundred yards from the Rialto Bridge.
21. Pius VII, elected Pope in Venice, presided over Napoleon's

coronation in the cathedral of Notre Dame. However, he did not crown the Emperor: Napoleon did that with his own hand.

22. In return, the Venetians were given a brand-new fresco – allegorical if not accurate – showing the victorious Napoleon accepting a crown from Venice as rejoicing citizens look on. The fresco, by Giovanni Carlo Bevilacqua, was commissioned by General Baranguay d'Illiers, the new French governor, for his residence in Palazzo Loredan in Campo San Stefano, where it was rediscovered during recent restoration work.
23. As late as 1879 this was still a widely-held view; the newly-united Kingdom of Italy made plans to "restore" the Basilica, this would have included the removal of some of the mosaics and their replacement with something more in tune with late nineteenth century taste.
24. When Byron and Hobhouse first visited San Marco on the day after their arrival in Venice, Hobhouse – who, with Byron, had visited Constantinople in 1810 – sniffily noted in his diary that the inscription did not record their original removal from that city "by hostile cupidity" of the Venetians during the Fourth Crusade. See Hobhouse, J. C. Diary, November 11th 1816.
25. Hobhouse's Latin term for the Imperial committees.
26. Hobhouse, a political radical, was being neither snobbish nor anti-Semitic, simply pointing out the new realities of the world after Napoleon.
27. Examples include: Byron was a leading Freemason; he was about to be visited by a close friend who had tried to shoot the Duke of Wellington; he was leaving Ravenna to stay with his close friend the Princess of Wales in the Borromean Islands, in the middle of Lake Maggiore. (Origo, *The Last Attachment*, pp. 125-126).
28. The felze gradually began to disappear from gondolas at the end of the 19th century. A rare example of a gondola with felze can be seen in the Museum of Eighteenth Century Venetian Life at Ca' Rezzonico.
29. Byron lodged with the Segati family at number 1673. Thousands of tourists have inadvertently slept in Byron's lodgings, as they now form part of the Locanda Antica Venezia hotel.
30. The statement, first made by Madame Albrizzi who should have known better, but since repeated so often that it has gained the status of fact, that Byron avoided walking across the Piazza because of his limp, is simply untrue. In the statement quoted above, Byron was writing to his publisher about Schiller's Gothic novel *The Ghost Seer*, stating clearly "I never

walked down St Mark's by moonlight without thinking of it." Both Schiller's characters and Byron were strolling in Piazza San Marco.

31. When Byron's grandson the Earl of Lovelace published a selection of family correspondence intended to support his belief that Byron's relationship with Augusta had been incestuous, he called the book *Astarte*.
32. The ground floor of the villa is now retail premises. The plaque stating Lord Byron abito 1817 is sandwiched between a travel agent and an Irish pub.
33. The author was John Hookham Frere, a former M.P. and diplomat. Byron knew of him, and soon guessed that the poem was by Frere.
34. The story of Beppo has close similarities with the libretto of *Così fan tutte*, written by the Venetian Lorenzo da Ponte. In the opera, the male protagonists disguise themselves as Albanians to test their lovers' constancy. Beppo returns disguised as a Turk. It is easy to see how stories like this could develop in a maritime city from which sailors could be absent for years, cargoes feared lost would unexpectedly arrive in port and which had an ever- shifting population of foreign merchants, traders and visitors.
35. This particular Palazzo Gritti is near to the modern Casino and Railway Station; it is not the building facing Santa Maria della Salute which is now the prestigious Gritti Palace Hotel.
36. The Palazzo Mocenigo is a complex made up of four adjoining palazzi. Byron's apartments are now marked with a plaque: qui abito Lord Byron dal 1818 al 1819.
37. ie; not even as far as the nearest terraferma towns, a short gondola ride from Venice across the lagoon. Although Venice is now linked to the terraferma by a road and rail bridge, this attitude is still common today, especially amongst the older generation. My Venetian neighbour, preparing for a visit from her niece, comments, "she lives a long way away, in Mestre."
38. An Italian military base occupies the same site today.
39. The fort, almost swallowed by encroaching vegetation, is still surrounded by gardens and allotments.
40. The canal and church of Santa Chiara can be found near Piazzale Roma, Venice's bus-station and car park. The canal is near to the Ponte della Libertà, the modern road-bridge to the mainland.
41. There are three possible locations for Byron's casino, on one of three rii running from the Grand Canal towards the Giglio. They are Rio de San Maurizio/Rio Malatin and the two waterways leading to the water entrance of La Fenice, Rio di

S Maria Zobenigo (behind the church) and Rio dell'Allbero.

42. The libretto of Gazzaniga's opera, written by Giovanni Bertati and using Moliere, Goldoni and the commedia dell'arte as its sources, was known to Lorenzo Da Ponte, Mozart's Venetian librettist. In fact the plots and characters of the two operas are very similar, except that Gazzaniga / Bertati's Pasquiarello becomes Leporello for Da Ponte. The difference lies in the music. Gazzaniga wrote a pleasant, light-hearted opera; Mozart created a work of genius.
43. The full list is given as the epigraph to this chapter.
44. Byron wrote to his friend the British consul to make sure that no passport was granted to Tiretta. William Fletcher was married three times. After the death of his second wife, Susan Boyce, the mother of his two sons, he had married Anne Rood, Lady Byron's maid. Lady Byron had dismissed her because she gave a legal statement at the time of the Separation supporting Byron's belief that he had not been a cruel or violent husband. Fletcher regularly sent his wife money while he was abroad with Byron since, in a particularly spiteful piece of behaviour, Lady Byron had refused to give her a reference for another position. (Thanks to Ralph Lloyd-Jones).
45. Byron often referred to his wife as Clytemnestra, after the mythical queen who gloried in the destruction of her husband Agamemnon.
46. The island of San Servolo continued to house Venice's mental hospital until 1978. It now houses a university campus as well as a museum of madness and mental health which contains some disturbing exhibits.
47. Although many Venetian churches are used for concerts, these tend to be either purely secular (all Venetian musicians must be able to play *Quattro Stagioni* in their sleep) or performed by visiting choirs. The church of Santa Maria della Salute, where organ vespers take place regularly, is a rare example of a Venetian church resurrecting the city's tradition of religious music.
48. Byron is referring to the character in Shakespeare's *Much Ado About Nothing*, part of the unlikely married couple Beatrice and Benedict.
49. The two Emperors were Napoleon, who had visited Venice in 1807 and the Austrian Emperor Francis I, who came in 1816.
50. He was unable to express this belief in any of the operas he wrote for the Italian stage, since the censors would not have allowed them to be performed. However, *Guilliame Tell*, premiered in Paris in 1829, had as its theme freedom from Austrian tyranny.
51. The proprietor, John Hunt, was the brother of Leigh Hunt,

whom Byron had invited out to Pisa at Shelley's suggestion. He and his family had lived there at Byron's expense whilst storing up petty grievances. After Byron's death Leigh Hunt wrote a memoir which was very critical of the poet.

52. The dedication was not published until 1833: after Byron's death but in Southey's lifetime.
53. Ravenna was in the territory of Emilia-Romagna. "Romagnuola" means "from the Romagna."
54. Byron and Hobhouse referred to Polidori as "Polly-Dolly".
55. Coincidentally, the first English translation of Goethe's poem was also published in 1819.
56. His "lady-friend", ie: Teresa.
57. O'Connell, a campaigner for Irish Home Rule, was the first Irish Catholic to sit in the House of Commons. O'Connell's struggle to become an MP was one of the triggers for the Catholic Relief Act of 1829, which removed many of the barriers which prevented Catholics joining the civil service or sitting in Parliament.
58. Byron is also rumoured to have entrusted documents about his life in Venice and his thoughts on the Carbonari to Angelo Mengaldo, who allegedly burned them on Lido – where Byron had hoped to be buried – when he learned of his friend's death at Missolonghi. There are times when the biographer of Byron feels that the fates conspire against them.
59. A visit to the salone in the Museum of Eighteenth Century Life in the Ca'Rezzonico brings a Venetian conversazione to life.
60. "Countess" was an Austrian title. Before the fall of the Republic Venetian patricians had not used titles, but the Austrians had handed them out as a kind of compensation for becoming subjects of the Empire.
61. Shortly after Byron left Venice, Countess Benzoni and Count Rangone, both widowed, decided to marry. "Beppe" Rangone was over seventy and the Countess past sixty. He had been her cavaliere servente for over thirty years. They enjoyed eleven years of married happiness in their old age.
62. Byron was not following his lowering diet at this time. As a result he had put on weight and was not in good mental or physical shape.
63. Teresa's mother had died giving birth to the youngest child.
64. Freemasonry was illegal in the Papal States. Freemasons were regarded with great suspicion since their secrecy was regarded as a front for other nefarious activities such as plotting against the State. The initiation rituals of the Carbonari owed much to Freemasonry, and it is likely that a number of Carbonari were also Masons.

65. This suggestion was made by the Italian author Giovanna Foa in 1934. She had examined the surviving files of the Austrian, Vatican and Tuscan secret police, which were collected together after Italy was united.
66. Byron kept a draft of the letter, which was found in his papers after his death.
67. Hoppner had met both Claire and Shelley, who had stayed at his home when they came to Venice to see Allegra in 1818. Allegra had also spent some time in the Hoppners' nursery after her nursemaid Elise had proved to be less than ideal. Since he knew both the child and her mother, Byron confided his plans for Allegra more closely in Hoppner than in any of his male London friends, who would doubtless have found it strange to spend so much thought and concern over a child, especially an illegitimate female.
68. Byron is referring to a foundling hospital, such as Coram's Hospital in London.
69. Teresa revoked her ban when they were settled in Pisa. Byron went on to produce eleven more cantos and had just begun Canto XVII when he sailed for Greece.
70. It was performed at Byron's old stamping-ground, Drury Lane, in April 1821.
71. Modern visitors to Venice can see Doge Foscari kneeling before the Lion of St Mark above the Porta della Carta entrance to the Ducal Palace. However, this sculpture did not provide inspiration for Byron's play, as it was destroyed by the French in 1797 and only the head of the original survives: the Doge we see today is a nineteenth-century copy.
72. The play was, however, the inspiration for Verdi's opera *I due Foscari*, which was premiered in 1844 and has maintained its place in the operatic repertoire.
73. The bell-ringer.
74. At Byron's request Allegra's body was sent to England for burial at Harrow church, which he had attended as a schoolboy. An over-zealous Evangelical vicar refused to bury an illegitimate child inside the church and insisted that she be buried in an unmarked grave.
75. These three men were so loyal that they stayed with Byron until his death, travelling to Greece with him along with Pietro Gamba.
76. "Moorish."
77. Tita ended his days as a respectable gentleman. He married the D'Israeli family housekeeper and when Disraeli was in office Tita was given sinecures, first as messenger at the Board of Control and later at the India Office. When Tita

died in 1874 Disraeli personally obtained a royal pension of ?50 a year for his widow.

78. This was one of the conditions in the will of Annabella Byron's mother, Lady Noel, who had died in 1822. "I give and bequeath the portrait of my Son in Law the Right Honourable George Gordon Lord Byron which is now enclosed in a case at Kirkby Mallory"...to her trustees "to keep... safely inclosed and shut up in the said case... until my Grand Daughter the Honourable Ada Augusta Byron shall attain her age of twenty-one years." Should Lady Byron still be living at that date, "the said portrait shall remain inclosed and shut up... unless she shall wish the same to be previously delivered to my said Grand Daughter." See Malcolm Elwin, *Lord Byron's Family*, pp227-228.
79. Disraeli's time as a Byronic young man was not wasted. His Childe Harold journey of 1830 was not simply an exercise in narcissism. He digested and ruminated on his hands-on experiences of Turkey, Syria and Palestine so that when he entered politics he was far more at ease than his rival, Gladstone, when Middle –Eastern issues crept up (as they periodically continue to do) to trouble British politics.
80. Ruskin wrote one of his most influential works, *Modern Painters* (1843-1860), in order to champion Turner's works. He knew the artist quite well and was appointed executor in Turner's will: we owe the Turner bequest in the Tate Gallery to Ruskin's hard work and determination.
81. These can still be seen, in the Sculpture Room of the Victoria & Albert Museum.
82. The Ruskin marriage ended in 1854 after Effie fell in love with John's protégée, the artist John Everett Millais. The marriage was annulled on the grounds of non-consummation, but any sympathetic observer would have seen that the two were totally incompatible. Despite marriage to Millais and motherhood (to eight children) Effie was never able to forgive Ruskin. In later years she conducted a whispering campaign worthy of Lady Byron in order to prevent his marriage to his late love, Rose La Touche.
83. He was recovering from a period of madness and still felt bruised at the outcome of the libel action brought against him by Whistler. In a review of an exhibition of Whistler's work Ruskin had accused him of being a con-artist rather than a serious artist, "throwing a pot of paint in the public's face." Although Whistler successfully sued Ruskin, the judge showed his opinion of the matter by awarding him the derisory sum of a farthing in damages.

Gazetteer
Looking for Byron

A visitor to Venice can still see many sites associated with Byron, most of them little changed in 200 years.

Canal of Santa Chiara: near the modern Piazzale Roma bus station, where Byron emerged from the water after his swim from Lido up the Grand Canal on 25th June 1818.

Ca' Benzon: home of the celebrated hostess Countess Marina Benzoni. Byron enjoyed many comfortable and gossipy *conversazioni* here. The palazzo is on the Grand Canal between the Rialto and Sant' Angelo *vaporetto* stops. During the Biennale it is often used as an exhibition space, giving the chance of a glimpse inside.

Frezzeria: Byron's first Venetian lodging, over Pietro Segati's draper's shop at Piscina de Frezzeria number 1672, is now part of the *Locanda Antica Venezia*. A combination of local gossip and folk-memory suggests that Byron's first floor rooms can still be seen above the modern chemist's shop (which, ironically, specialises in orthopaedic footwear) on the main Frezzeria.

Gran Teatro La Fenice: Venice's finest theatre, both in terms of performances and social cachet, both then and now. Byron rented a box here. Modern visitors are able to take an audio tour of this opulent and beautiful building.

Hotel Gran Bretagna/Palazzo Farsetti: Byron and Hobhouse stayed here on their arrival in Venice on 10th November 1817, and Byron later recommended it to his lawyer John Hanson. Palazzo Farsetti was leased out as a hotel by its owners, a Venetian patrician family who had fallen on hard times due to Napoleonic taxes, from 1808. When Venice became part of a free and united Italy it was brought by the Municipality, and still houses local government offices.

Lido: Byron kept his horses here and enjoyed a daily gallop along the island throughout 1818. The best places to find an impression of Lido as Byron knew it are on the sand-dunes at the northernmost tip of the island, around the village of Malamocco in the south, or near the ruins of the Austrian fort where he wished to be buried. Both the fort and Malamocco can easily be reached on bus 11. The fort is just off Via Malamocco in a quiet residential area. Simply walk along Via G. B. Costa and then south along the sea-wall. Byron's Lido is all around you.

Palazzo Albrizzi: on Campiello Albrizzi near Campo San Polo. Byron was a regular visitor to Madame Albrizzi's famous *conversazioni* during his first year in Venice, and was first introduced to Teresa Guiccioli here.

Palazzo Barzizza: on the Grand Canal adjacent to the San Silvestro *vaporetto* stop (although the best view is from the opposite bank of the Grand Canal, in front of Palazzo Farsetti). This was the home of Angelo Mengaldo, who challenged Byron to his famous exploit of swimming along the Grand Canal from Lido. Mengaldo remained in Venice for many years after Byron's departure, and was a trusted lieutenant of Daniele Manin during the Venetian uprising of 1848-9.

Palazzo Mocenigo: Byron leased apartments here in July 1818, and made them home to his menagerie, his daughter Allegra and, briefly, his fiery mistress Margarita Cogni. Byron lived in the middle "new" palazzo, marked with a plaque and best seen from the San Toma *vaporetto* stop across the Grand Canal.

Palazzo Giustinian: on Calle Giustinian near Campo San Stefano, now the home of the Fondazione Ugo e Olga Levi. Doctor Aglietti, the only doctor in Venice for whom Byron had any respect, lived here, a short gondola-ride from Palazzo Mocenigo. He treated Allegra Biron and Teresa Guiccioli, but was too late to save Mary Shelley's baby Clara.

Piazza San Marco: in common with his Venetian hosts, Byron enjoyed the *passeggiata* "down St Mark's by moonlight," strolling along the arcades of the procuratie and calling at Caffé Florian, where he shared hot punch with Tom Moore on a memorable evening.

San Lazzaro degli Armeni: to take the tour of the island housing a community of Armenian monks and see the book-lined study where Byron learned Armenian, catch *vaporetto* number 20 from San Zaccharia. The tours take place at 2.30pm daily.

Teatro San Benedetto: The remains of this once-thriving theatre, where Byron saw Rossini conduct the premiere of his opera *Eduardo e Cristina*, are now incorporated into the new Punto Simply supermarket and Cinema Rossini, on Rio di San Luca.

Glossary

Acqua Alta: "High water," usually in spring and autumn, caused by a combination of seasonal high tides and a wind from the south blowing up the lagoon.

Bacino: The expanse of water in front of the Palazzo Ducale where the Grand Canal widens into the lagoon.

Barcarole: Gondoliers' song or chant to help keep time with the rhythm of the oar and the waves.

Campanile: Bell-tower, usually built a short distance from the church which it serves.

Carnevale: "Farewell to meat," a time of festivity and enjoyment before fasting during Lent.

Casino: "Little house" kept for informal evenings with friends or sexual assignations.

Cavaliere Servente: Gentleman attendant whose function is to act as gossip and walker. By the early 19th century the term often indicated that the gentleman was also his lady's lover.

Cicisbeo: "Whisperer". Alternative name for a cavaliere servente.

Conversazione: A Venetian social or literary gathering.

Felze: The canopy which made a gondola a private and comfortable space – whatever one's purpose.

Fondamenta: Street abutting the canal.

Liston: The *passeggiata* or evening stroll the purpose of which is to see and be seen.

Palazzo: A large house belonging to a Venetian noble family, often fronting the Grand Canal.

Putti: Baby-faced, chubby cherubs, a feature of eighteenth century art and architecture.

Rio: Any one of the numerous small waterways of Venice: the city has only three canals: the Grand Canal, the Guidecca Canal and the Cannaregio Canal. The rest are all *rii*.

Scuola: Charitable organisation with a religious impulse. The members did not belong to a religious order. *Scuole* were democratically organised and were responsible for caring for many of the less fortunate in Venetian society. Many scuole had fine meeting-houses. Closed by Napoleon in 1810.

Terraferma: "Dry Land;" the provinces of the Venetian Republic on the Italian mainland, including the cities of Treviso, Padua, Vicenza and Verona.

Traghetto: A gondola-ferry which plies a shuttle service at designated points across the Grand Canal.

Villeggiatura: Summer or autumn stay at one's villa on the terraferma, usually on the Brenta Canal.

Acknowledgments

When we first moved to Venice it didn't take me long to discover that Lord Byron had been a near neighbour, living just around the corner. Being the sort of person I am, I decided that I needed to read a book about Byron's time in the city. When it became clear that none was available, I decided to write my own, and it soon grew to include glimpses of Venice herself during Byron's time, which in turn meant that it also had to deal with the contemporary political situation in Europe. If nothing else, I have learned a great deal whilst writing it.

A number of people have helped me, and I would like to particularly thank:

Taranvir Singh Assi for his help in understanding chemical compounds and their uses.

Graeme Clark of the Samuel Johnson Birthplace Museum, Lichfield, for enabling me to consult Mrs Piozzi's Glimpses of Italian Society in the Eighteenth Century.

Gilly French of Bampton Classical Opera for help with the libretto of Gazzaniga's *Don Giovanni.*

Ralph Lloyd-Jones, author of the Dictionary of National Biography article on William Fletcher, Byron's valet, for information about Fletcher's complex personal life.

The Archives of Teatro La Fenice, Venice, on-line.

Peter Cochran, whose excellent website (petercochran.wordpress.com) has made the diaries of John Cam Hobhouse easily accessible to scholars.

The Marxist Internet Archive, who are steadily and carefully making the entire works of my hero William Morris freely available to all.

The contributors to the Slow Travel: Italy internet forum who helped me calculate the exact distance of Byron's Venetian swim.

The staff of the Codsall branch of Staffordshire Library Services for their unfailing assistance and good humour in the face of some bizarre requests. At a time when libraries are under threat by Governments and Local Authorities of all political persuasions, we would do well to remember that face-to-face human contact and assistance can never be replaced by the internet.

The late Nigel Rainbow, in whose vast collection of recorded music I found Gazzaniga's *Don Giovanni*, Pergolesi's La Serva Padrona and Rossini's La cambiale di matrimonio.

Conversations with Cristiano Brussa, Giampaolo Fiorese, Umberto Simeoni, Alberto Turchetto, Ugo Ugolani: my thanks to them for sharing their knowledge of Venice – any mistakes are entirely my own!

John Francis Phillimore for his careful reading of the manuscript and his perceptive comments.

My friend Peter Green and my dear comrade Jack Potts for help, support and encouragement.

My partner Michael for his good humour and patience over the long period in which this book was being researched and written. In particular for his encyclopaedic knowledge of early nineteenth century British and European history and music: he was able to help me find answers for a number of difficult questions relating to Napoleon, Castlereagh and the Italian Risorgimento, and without his help I would never have been able to track down the opera based on Livy which Byron saw at La Fenice.

Derek Jacobi, whose fault the whole book is: my interest in Byron can be dated from seeing him perform "Mad, Bad & Dangerous to Know" at the Swan Theatre, Stratford, in 1984.

A note on sources

My aim has been to use original materials as far as possible, so that Byron, Hobhouse and their contemporaries can speak.

My main source for Byron's thoughts, opinions, movements during the period covered by this book had been Leslie A. Marchand's magisterial edition of Byron's Letters and Journals, particularly Vol V, So Late Into the Night, and Vol VI, The Flesh is Frail. I would like to put on record the fact that between March and October 2012 I made three separate attempts to contact John Murray Ltd for permission to quote from Prof. Marchand's works. Unfortunately I have not, at the time of writing, received any reply.

All quotations from Hobhouse's diaries come from the online version edited by Peter Cochrane, and quotations from his letters are from Peter W. Graham's collection Byron's Bulldog: Letters of John Cam Hobhouse to Lord Byron, published by Ohio State University Press.

A huge number of books about Byron, covering the spectrum from scholarly to sensational, have been published over the past 200 years, and I have consulted a wide selection whilst writing this book. There are two authors to whom I owe a great debt, however. Byron's first biographer, Tom Moore, may be sometimes sycophantic and sometimes prudish, but he is often very funny and always hugely readable and was, of course, writing at first-hand. Doris Langley Moore's two books about Byron, Accounts Rendered and The Late Lord Byron, are to me a perfect example of biographical writing: primary sources and careful analysis combined in such a way as to make their subject leap from the page. She has been my role-model during my writing and research, and an image from Accounts Rendered, of a laundry-list written by William Fletcher, seems a perfect symbol of the way I have rummaged around in the minutiae of Byron's life.

Similar principles were adopted in researching Venice: original voices wherever possible, from Goldoni to Mrs Thrale, from Casanova to John Ruskin. I have also used a lot of shoe-leather walking the city, visiting theatres, *palazzi,* scuole, museums, clutching my copy of *Calli, Campielli e Canali* (the Venetian A-Z). In short, if a location is mentioned in the text, I've done my best to visit it: my partner once remarked that if Byron were alive today he would take out a restraining order on me.

Since too many footnotes can be tedious for the reader I have chosen to keep them to a minimum for this edition; I hope that a fully-referenced version can be published one day, but for now the main sources for each chapter can be found below.

Anne Amison
Venice, 2014

Marchand, Letters and Journals, and Moore, The Letters & Journals of Lord Byron, are the key sources for every chapter. A full list of books consulted can be found in the Bibliography.

Prologue.
Epigraph: *Don Juan,* Canto I, i.

Chapter 1, *Fare Thee Well.*
Epigraph: *Childe Harold's Pilgrimage*, Canto III, xvi.
Main sources:
Elwin, *Lord Byron's Wife*
Glynn Grylls, *Claire Clairmont*
Polidori, *Diary*
Seymour, *Mary Shelley*
Stommel & Stommel, *Volcano Weather.*

First Venetian Interlude: I loved her from my boyhood…
Title: *Childe Harold's Pilgrimage,* Canto IV, xviii.
Main sources:
Radcliffe, *The Mysteries of Udolpho*
Otway, *Venice Preserv'd*
Schiller, *The Ghost-Seer*

Chapter 2: Thus Far on my Way to Venice.
Epigraph: Hobhouse, *Diary,* 25th October 1816.
Main sources:
Elwin, *Lord Byron's Family*
Hobhouse, *Diaries*
Hurd, Peel, *A Biography.*
Langley Moore, *Lord Byron, Accounts Rendered*
Polidori, *Diary*
Vincent, *Ugo Foscolo*

Second Venetian Interlude: In Venice Tasso's echoes are no more…
Title: *Childe Harold's Pilgrimage,* Canto IV, iii.
Main sources:
Goldoni, *Memoirs*
Nicholson, (ed) *Lord Byron: The Complete Miscellaneous Prose*
Piozzi, *Glimpses of Italian Society in the Eighteenth Century*

Chapter 3: The Most Oppressed People in Europe.
Epigraph: *Childe Harold's Pilgrimage,* Canto IV, xii.
Main Sources:
Eustace, *Classical Italy from Venice to Rome*
Hobhouse, *Diaries*
Laven, *Venice & Venetia under the Habsburgs, 1815-1835*
Rhys, (ed) *Essays & Letters by P. B. Shelley*
Zorzi, *Venezia Austriaca*

Third Venetian Interlude: ...and silent rows the songless gondolier
Title: *Childe Harold's Pilgrimage,* Canto IV, iii.
Main sources:
Goethe: *Italian Journey*
Holme, *Gondola, Gondolier*
Lamberti, *La Biondina in Gondoleta,* (translation: Laura Sarti)
Lutyens, *Effie in Venice*

Chapter 4: Marianna.
Epigraph: *Beppo,* XLI.
Main sources:
Glynn Grylls, *Claire Clairmont*
Hobhouse, *Diaries*
Langley Moore, *Lord Byron: Accounts Rendered*
McGann, *Don Juan in Context*
Murray, (ed) *Lord Byron's Correspondence Vol 2*
Nicholson, (ed) *Lord Byron: The Complete Miscellaneous Prose*
Rowdon, *The Fall of Venice*

Fourth Venetian Interlude: ... while this play is presenting with much applause...
Title: Byron, *Letter to Douglas Kinnaird,* 3rd Feb 1817.
Main sources:
Goethe: *Italian Journey*
Goldoni, *Memoirs*
Howard, D. *The Architectural History of Venice*
Piozzi, *Glimpses of Italian Society in the Eighteenth Century*

Chapter 5: Don Juan.
Epigraph: Byron, *Letter to John Cam Hobhouse & Douglas Kinnaird,* 19th January 1819.
Main sources:
Di Robilant, *Lucia in the Age of Napoleon*
Gottardi, M, *Angelo Mengaldo* (website of the Comune of Cimadolmo)
Kelly, *Casanova*
Murray, (ed) *Lord Byron's Correspondence* Vol 2
Rhys,(ed) *Essays & Letters by P. B. Shelley*
Seymour, *Mary Shelley*

Fifth Venetian Interlude: Oh! the long evenings of duets and trios!
Title: *Don Juan*, Canto XVI, xlv.
Main sources:
Goethe: *Italian Journey*
Gossett, Philip, *programme notes to An Evening of Rossini* (WNO at Hippodrome Theatre, Birmingham 18 June 2008)
Kendall, *Gioacchino Rossini*

Chapter 6: Teresa.
Epigraph: *Stanzas,* 1819.
Main sources:
Fleming, *Bright Darkness*
Graham, (ed) *Byron's Bulldog: Letters of John Cam Hobhouse to Lord Byron*
Kelly, *Ireland's Minstrel, A Life of Tom Moore*
Origo, *The Last Attachment*
Polidori,*The Vampyre*
Ruddick, *Byron & England,* in Trueblood, (ed) *Byron's Political & Cultural Influence in Nineteenth Century Europe*

Sixth Venetian Interlude: ...there are one or two *Conversazioni*...
Title: *Byron, Letter to Samuel Rogers,* 3rd March 1818.
Main sources:
Elwin, *Lord Byron's Family*
Origo, *The Last Attachment*

Chapter 7: Byron After Venice.
Epigraph: Claire Clairmont, *Letter to Lord Byron,* 15th May 1819.
Main sources:
Foa, *Lord Byron, Poeta e Carbonaro*
Graham, (ed) *Byron's Bulldog: Letters of John Cam Hobhouse to Lord Byron*
Origo, *The Last Attachment*
Paston & Quennell, *To Lord Byron*
Rhys,(ed) *Essays & Letters by P. B. Shelley*

Chapter Eight: Venice After Byron.
Epigraph: Michael Foot, *My Only Venice* (1988) in Foot, *The Uncollected Michael Foot: Essays Old & New 1953-2003.*
Main sources:
Bradley, *Ruskin's Letters from Venice, 1851-1852*
Clegg, *Ruskin & Venice*
Hibbert, C. *Disraeli: A Personal History*
Pinkney, T. *William Morris in Oxford, the Campaigning Years 1879-1895*
Ruskin, *Præterita*
– *St Mark's Rest*
– *The Stones of Venice*
Shapiro, (ed) *Ruskin in Italy; Letters to his Parents, 1845*
Stainton, *Turner's Venice*

Venetian Postscript: When the Kissing had to Stop.
Epigraph: Robert Browning, *A Toccata of Galuppi's,* 1855.
Main sources:
Foot, *My Only Venice*
Ruskin, *Præterita.*

Bibliography

Byron

George Gordon, Lord Byron,
– *Poems*, Vols I, II & III, Everyman's Library (Dent & Dutton) London, 1948.
– Letters & Journals Vol 4, *Wedlock's The Devil*, ed Leslie A. Marchand, John Murray, London, 1975.
– Letters & Journals Vol 5, *So Late Into The Night*, ed Leslie A. Marchand, The Belknap Press, Cambridge, Massachusetts, 1976.
– Letters & Journals Vol 6, *The Flesh is Frail*, ed Leslie A. Marchand, The Belknap Press, Cambridge, Massachusetts, 1976.
– Letters & Journals Vol 7, *Between Two Worlds*, ed Leslie A. Marchand, John Murray, London, 1977.
– Letters & Journals, Vol 8, *Born For Opposition*, ed Leslie A. Marchand, The Belknap Press, Cambridge, Massachusetts, 1978.
– *The Complete Miscellaneous Prose*, ed Andrew Nicholson, Clarendon Press, Oxford, 1991.
– *Lord Byron's Correspondence Vol II*, ed John Murray, John Murray, London,1922.

Burdett, T. A. J, *The Rise & Fall of a Regency Dandy; The Life & Times of Scrope Berdmore Davies*, OUP, Oxford, 1983.

Butler, E. M. *Byron & Goethe*, Bowes & Bowes, London, 1965.

Chew, Samuel, *Byron in England:* His Fame & After-Fame, John Murray, London, 1924.

Calder, Angus, (ed) *Byron & Scotland: Radical or Dandy?* Edinburgh University Press, Edinburgh, 1989.

Colbourn Mayne, Ethel, T*he Life of Anne Isabella, Lady Noel Byron*, Constable, London, 1929.

Elwin, Malcolm,
– *Lord Byron's Wife*, Macdonald, London, 1962.
– *Lord Byron's Family: Annabella, Ada & Augusta*, 1816-1824, John Murray, London, 1975.

Fleming, Anne,
– *Bright Darkess*, Nottingham Court Press, London, 1983.
– *Byron the Maker, Vol I: Byron in England*, Book Guild Publishing, Lewes, 2006.

Foa, Giovanna, *Lord Byron, Poeta e Carbonaro*, Nuova Italia editrice, Firenze, 1934.

Gilmour, Ian, *The Making of the Poets: Byron & Shelley in Their Time*, Chatto & Windus, London, 2002.

Gleckner, Robert, & Beatty, Bernard, (ed) *The Plays of Lord Byron: Critical Essays*, Liverpool University Press, Liverpool, 1997.

Graham, Peter W. (ed), *Byron's Bulldog: Letters of John Cam Hobhouse to Lord Byron*, Ohio State University Press, Columbus, 1984.

Guiccioli, Teresa, *Recollections of Lord Byron*, Richard Bentley, London, 1868.

Hobhouse, John Cam, *Diaries*, (From the website of Peter Cochrane)

Kelsall, Malcolm, *Byron's Politics*, The Harvester Press, Sussex, 1987.

Marchand, Leslie A, *Byron, A Portrait*, Hutchinson, London, 1987.

McGann, Jerome
– *Fiery Dust: Byron's Poetic Development*, University of Chicago Press,

Chicago, 1968.
– *Don Juan in Context,* John Murray, London, 1976.
Medwin, Thomas, *Conversations of Lord Byron: noted during a residence with His Lordship in Pisa, in the years 1821 & 1822,* Henry Colburn, London, 1824.
Moore, Thomas, *The Letters & Journals of Lord Byron,* Chatto & Windus, London, 1900.
Langley Moore, Doris
– *The Late Lord Byron,* John Murray, London, 1961.
– *Lord Byron: Accounts Rendered,* John Murray, London, 1974.
Origo, Iris
– *Allegra, La Figlia Di Byron,* Mondadori, Milano, 1992.
– *The Last Attachment,* Fontana, London, 1962.
Paston, George & Quennell, Peter, *To Lord Byron,* John Murray, London, 1939.
Polidori, John William, *The Diary of Dr John William Polidori* in Polidori, J, *The Vampyre & other writings,* ed Franklin Charles Bishop, Fyfield Books, Manchester, 2005.
Shelley, Percy Bysshe, *Essays & Letters*, ed Ernest Rhys, Walter Scott Ltd, London, no date.
Trueblood, Paul (ed), *Byron's Political & Cultural Influence in Nineteenth Century Europe,* Humanities Press, Atlantic Highlands, New Jersey, 1981.
Zegger, Robert E., *Hobhouse: A Political Life 1819-1852,* University of Missouri Press, Columbia, 1973.

England

Hilton, Boyd, *A Mad, Bad & Dangerous People? England 1783-1846,* Clarendon Press, Oxford, 2006.
Hunt, J. W. *Reaction & Reform 1815-1841,* Collins, London, 1972.
Peacock, H. L. *A History of Modern Britain, 1815-1968,* Heinemann, London, 1968.
Thompson, E. P. *The Making of the English Working Class*, Victor Gollancz, London, 1963.
White, R. J. *Waterloo to Peterloo*, Penguin, Harmondsworth, 1968.

Venice

Berendt, John, *The City of Falling Angels*, Hodder & Stoughton, London, 2005.
Bradley, John Lewis, *Ruskin's Letters from Venice, 1851-1852,* Yale University Press, New Haven, 1955.
Casanova, Giacomo (ed. Frances Wilson), *Episodes from the History of my Life,* Folio Society, London, 2007.
Clegg, Jeanne, *Ruskin & Venice,* Junction Books, London, 1981.
Di Robilant, Andrea, *Lucia in the Age of Napoleon*, Faber & Faber, London, 2007.
Douglas, Hugh A. *Venice on Foot*, Scribner, New York, 1907.
Dowling, Gregory, *In Venice and in the Veneto with Lord Byron,* Supernova, Venezia, 2008.
Eustace, Rev. John Chetwode, Classical Italy from Venice to Rome, Ward Lock & Co, London, 1812.
Fenlon, Iain, *Piazza San Marco,* Profile Books, London, 2009.
Freeley, John, *Strolling Through Venice*, Penguin, London, 1984.

Goethe, Johann Wolfgang von (trans W. H Auden & Elizabeth Mayer), *Italian Journey,* Penguin Books, London, 1970.
Goldoni, Carlo, (trans John Black) *Memoirs*, Alfred A. Knopf, N. York, 1926.
Hewison, Robert, *Ruskin's Venice,* Pilkington Press, London, 2000.
Hibbert, Christopher, *Venice: The Biography of a City,* W. W. Norton & Co, New York, 1989.
Holme, Timothy, *Gondola, Gondolier,* Gentry Books, London, 1971.
Howard, Deborah, *The Architectural History of Venice,* Yale University Press, New Haven, 2002.
Howells, W. D. *Venetian Life,* Northwestern University Press, Illinois, 2001.
Kelly, Ian, *Casanova: Philosopher, Gambler, Lover, Priest,* Hodder & Stoughton, London, 2008.
James, Henry, *Letters From the Palazzo Barbaro* Pushkin Press, London, 1998.
Keates, Jonathan, *The Siege of Venice,* Random House, London.
Laven, David, *Venice & Venetia Under the Habsburgs, 1815-1835*, Oxford University Press, Oxford, 2002.
Laven, Mary, *Virgins of Venice,* Viking Penguin, London, 2002.
Lucas, E. V. *A Wanderer in Venice,* Methuen, London, 1923.
Lutyens, Mary, ed, *Effie in Venice,* Pallas Editions, London, 1999.
Morris, James, *Venice,* Faber & Faber, London, 1960.
Norwich, John Julius,
– *A History of Venice,* Penguin, London, 1983.
– *Paradise of Cities: Venice & Its Nineteenth Century Visitors,* Viking Penguin, London, 2003.
Piozzi, Mrs Hester, *Glimpses of Italian Society in the Eighteenth Century,* Seeley & Co. Ltd., London, 1892.
Plant, Margaret, *Venice, Fragile City*, Yale University Press, New Haven, 2002.
Rowdon, Maurice, *The Fall of Venice*, Weidenfeld & Nicolson, London, 1970.
Ruskin, John, *The Stones of Venice*
– *Volume I: The Foundations,*
– *Volume II: The Sea-Stories,*
– *Volume III: The Fall.*
Waverley Book Company, London, no date.
Shapiro, Harold, *Ruskin In Italy: Letters to his Parents 1845,* Clarendon Press, Oxford, 1972.
Stainton, Lindsay, *Turner's Venice,* British Museum Publications, London, 1985.
Tanner, Tony, *Venice Desired,* Harvard University Press, Cambridge Mass, 1992.
Zorzi, Alvise,
– *Venice: a City, A Republic, An Empire,* The Overlook Press, New York, 1999.
– *Venezia Austriaca,* Libereria Editrice Goriziana, Gorizia, 2000.

The Shelleys/Claire Clairmont:

Glynn Grylls, Rosalie (Lady Mander), *Claire Clairmont: Mother of Byron's Allegra,* John Murray, London, 1939.
Holmes, Richard, *Shelley; The Pursuit*, Weidenfeld & Nicolson, London, 1974.
Seymour, Miranda, *Mary Shelley,* John Murray, London, 2000.
Todd, Janet, *Death & the Maidens:* Fanny Wollstonecraft & the Shelley Circle, Profile Books, London, 2007.

General

Abse, Joan, John Ruskin, *The Passionate Moralist,* Quartet Books, London, 1980.

Asprey, Robert, *The Rise & Fall of Napoleon Bonaparte, Vol I: The Rise,* Little, Brown & Co., London, 2000.

Cecil, David, *The Young Melbourne & Lord M,* Phoenix Press, London, 2001.

Droz, Jacques, *Europe Between Revolutions, 1815-1848,* Fontana, London, 1967.

Duggan, Christopher, *The Force of Destiny: A History of Italy Since 1796,* Allen Lane, London, 2007.

Hales, E. E. Y., *Mazzini & the Secret Societies,* Eyre & Spottiswoode, London, 1956.

Hibbert, Christopher, *Disraeli: A Personal History,* HarperCollins, London, 2004.

Hurd, Douglas, *Peel: A Biography,* Weidenfeld & Nicolson, London, 2007.

Jamison, Kay Redfield, *Touched With Fire: Manic Depressive Illness & the Creative Temprament,* Simon & Schuster, New York, 1993.

Kelly, Ian, *Beau Brummell: the Ultimate Dandy,* Hodder & Stoughton, London, 2005.

Kelly, Linda, *Ireland's Minstrel, A Life of Tom Moore: Poet, Patriot & Byron's Friend,* I. B. Tauris & Co, London, 2006.

Kendall, Alan, *Gioacchino Rossini: The Reluctant Hero,* Victor Gollancz, London, 1992.

Moneypenny, William F. & Buckle, George E, T*he Life of Benjamin Disraeli, Earl of Beaconsfield, Vol I: 1804-1859,* John Murray, London, 1929.

Pinkney, Tony, *William Morris in Oxford, the Campaigning Years 1879-1895,* Illuminati Books, Grosmont, 2007.

Porter, Roy, *Mind Forg'd Manacles: A History of Madness in England from the Restoration to the Regency,* The Athlone Press, London, 1987.

Ruskin, John, *Præterita,* Oxford Uiversity Press, Oxford, 1978.

Schenk, H. G. *The Mind of the European Romantics,* Constable, London, 1966.

Stommel, Henry & Stommel, Elizabeth, *Volcano Weather: The Story of 1816, The Year Without a Summer,* Seven Seas Press, Newport, Rhode Island, 1983.

Vincent, E. R. *Ugo Foscolo, An Italian in Regency England,* Cambridge University Press, Cambridge, 1953.

Ward, Maisie, *The Tragi-Comedy of Pen Browning,* Sheed & Ward, New York, 1972.

Fiction

Disraeli, Benjamin, *Venetia,* Peter Davies, London, 1927 (first published 1837)

Goethe, Johann Wolfgang von (trans Bayard Taylor), *Faust, Parts I & II,* Sphere Books, London, 1969.

Lamb, Lady Caroline, *Glenarvon,* J. M. Dent, London, 1995.

Otway, Thomas, *Venice Preserv'd,* Edward Arnold, London, 1969.

Polidori, John, *The Vampyre & other writings,* ed Franklin Charles Bishop, Fyfield Books, Manchester, 2005.

Radcliffe, Mrs Ann, *The Mysteries of Udolpho,* Oxford World Classics, 1998 (first published 1794).

Schiller, Friedrich von (trans. Andrew Brown), *The Ghost-Seer,* Hesperus Press, London, 2003.